Self-Reliance Versus Power Politics
The American and Indian Experiences in Building Nation States

THE POLITICAL ECONOMY OF INTERNATIONAL CHANGE
John Gerard Ruggie, General Editor

THE POLITICAL ECONOMY OF INTERNATIONAL CHANGE
John Gerard Ruggie, General Editor

SELF-RELIANCE
versus
POWER POLITICS

*The American and Indian
Experiences in
Building Nation States*

J. ANN TICKNER

New York COLUMBIA UNIVERSITY PRESS *1987*

Library of Congress Cataloging-in-Publication Data

Tickner, J. Ann.
Self-reliance versus power politics.

(The Political economy of international change)
Bibliography: p.
Includes index.
1. Autarchy. 2. Autonomy. 3. United States—
Economic policy—To 1933. 4. United States—Politics
and government—Revolution, 1775–1783. 5. United
States—Politics and government—1783–1865. 6. India—
Economic policy—1947-   7. India—Politics and
government—1947-   Title. II. Series.
HD78.T53 1986   338.973   86-12989
ISBN 0-231-06272-9

Columbia University Press
New York   Guildford, Surrey
Copyright © 1987 Columbia University Press
All rights reserved

Printed in the United States of America

This book is Smyth-sewn.

For
Hayward, Joan, Heather, and Wendy

CONTENTS

Part 5   Conclusions

            Development in the Contemporary Third World   *209*

            Notes   *231*

            Index   *269*

PREFACE

THE THEME of this book, reflected in its title, came to me rather
slowly. Let me explain why. First, I am British by birth and school-
ing. As a person of English background I was disposed to dismiss
those who had rebelled against the British Empire. Every English
student knows Winston Churchill's caricature of Gandhi as "a fakir
in a loincloth." An Englishman visiting the United States around
1800 expressed similar views:

> Though naught but woods and Jefferson they see
> Where streets should run and sages ought to be.

It took me a while to revise such attitudes. I now think that a
deeper interpretation of both the American and Indian revolutionary struggles would be to see them as confrontations between
weaker advocates of self-reliance development and stronger, more
central players in the game of global power politics. This question,
as to how new nations should be built in a world of more powerful
states, merits serious consideration. The contemptuous attitudes,
so common among citizens of more developed nations, only serve
to obscure its importance.

On the other hand revolutionary anticolonialists have sometimes
been accused of moral arrogance. Often their idealism cannot be
fully sustained when charting the realistic possibilities of national
development in such a world. A balanced assessment is called for
that is both sympathetic to the noble ideals invoked by advocates of
a new order and sobered by the experience of frequent failures by
older advocates of a better world.

It was fifteen years after doing graduate work at a leading American university that I first heard a serious scholarly advocacy of self-
reliance as a preferred strategy of development for the Third

World today. This occurred during Johan Galtung's lectures at the
Institute for Development Studies in Geneva. Conventional liberal
strategies of development, fashionable in American universities
during the 1960s, ignored this type of development. The emphasis
on global interdependence in the early 1970s moved the field even
further away from any consideration of self-reliance. I now find it
ironic that so many international relations scholars in my new home
are unaware of their own national post-independence debates
which were centered on alternate versions of self-reliance development.

The profoundest revelation that has come to me in my comparative study of the theoreticians and practitioners of American
and Indian post-colonial development is the deep communality of
the problems they faced. Their hopes and aspirations were remarkably similar and their strategies for resolving developmental dilemmas contain many parallels. It is not common today—in England,
the United States or any other Western country—to recognize this
communality of experience and aspiration between the North and
the South, the old and the new.

Finally, as a woman in a world in which most of the dominant
powers are male, I have been fortunate to have had parents, a
husband and teachers who have encouraged my own self-reliant
development as an individual and a scholar. Learning to overcome
the dependencies of these relationships has been a more personal
dimension of the odyssey that this book represents.

Learning to distinguish intellectual self-reliance from academic
autarky and disciplinary isolation has been an important part of
this process. My book has benefited immeasurably from the helpful
advice of teachers, colleagues, and friends. In its early stages insights and encouragement were received from Mary Anderson,
Karl Deutsch, Paul Streeten, and Dov Ronen. For their invaluable
help in shaping the project into its present form and reading and
rereading the entire manuscript, I am particularly indebted to
Robert Keohane, Thomas Biersteker, and Susan Okin. Since each
chapter delves into a different literature, I am most grateful for the
comments and advice of experts in each of these fields: Dieter
Senghaas and Raimo Vayrynen on Friedrich List, Harvey Mansfield Jr. on Thomas Jefferson, and Walter Dean Burnham on the
early development of the United States. My understanding of the

ideas of Mohandas Gandhi was deeply enriched by discussions with Gene Sharp and Lakshmi and Devaki Jain. Comments on the Indian chapter were gratefully received from John Field, Mary Katzenstein, and Myron Weiner. I am also indebted to the Center for International Affairs at Harvard University which provided the supportive atmosphere in which the final draft of the book was written. Finally my thanks go to Hayward Alker, who not only offered his thoughts on the manuscript but also provided the help with home and family necessary for such an undertaking. For any shortcomings I am solely responsible.

INTRODUCTION

SELF-RELIANCE as an expression of the individual's desire for autonomy and self-determination has captured the imagination of political writers over centuries and has provided a unifying theme across various ideological perspectives. In the liberal tradition of Western political theory, originating with English contract theorists such as Thomas Hobbes and John Locke, self-reliance was consistent with the minimal role assigned to the state, a role limited to that of assuring individual rights and the protection necessary for the pursuit of individual private interests. Also in the name of self-reliance, Fabian socialists advocated voluntarist, functionalist associations which would foster self-government among individuals and thus decrease their reliance on state institutions.[1]

The contemporary conservative backlash in the West, which is critical of the modern state's increasing penetration into the daily lives of individuals and which looks back with nostalgia to this earlier liberal tradition, is articulated in terms that suggest that the ethic of self-reliance is far from dead.[2] More radical proponents of "autogestion" or workplace democracy are also searching for a framework in which individual autonomy can be preserved in a world in which dependence and powerlessness extend beyond the realm of political and bureaucratic arrangements. Concerned with the individual's sense of anonymity in a web of impersonal large-scale economic institutions, epitomized by the modern corporation, they are expressing dissatisfaction with materialism, technological dependence and lack of individual control over economic and political decision making, which they see as characteristic of advanced industrial societies.[3]

If contemporary advocates of self-reliance in the West, conservatives and radicals alike, are expressing frustration with the sense of powerlessness and anonymity felt by the individual in post industrial society, self-reliance is a theme which is also growing in importance in a quite different context, that of Third World development debates, where the crucial issues are not those of overdevelopment but of underdevelopment and poverty. In its Third World manifestation, self-reliance is more collectivist in orientation; it is associated with political and social movements ranging from the development practices of Maoist China to New International Economic Order (NIEO) attempts to pressure the advanced countries into a redistribution of global resources.[4]

More generally, self-reliance in its Third World context is an expression of frustration with liberal capitalist models of development, prominent in the West during the era of American hegemony, which assume that linkage to the international system accelerates economic growth and promotes world welfare. The failure of such models for many less developed countries, demonstrated by an increase in the gap between the rich and the poor, has led to calls for "a temporary detachment from the present economic system" and a reorientation of development planning away from export or industrially led growth strategies toward a greater emphasis on agriculture, employment and the indigenous production of basic needs.[5] For the Third World, self-reliance has become a catchword both for this reassessment of development planning and for the demands which it is placing on the North for global redistribution. Although its use in such a wide variety of contexts has led to a certain imprecision in meaning, self-reliance is as popular a symbol in contemporary Third World rhetoric as interdependence was in the West during the 1970s.

In spite of the popularity of self-reliance as a rhetorical force for Third World solidarity, it is rarely defined adequately or examined systematically. While self-reliance rhetoric has been useful for the Third World as a basis for organizing responses to what is perceived as First World domination, the scholarly literature on self-reliance development is extremely sparse and the status of self-reliance as a theoretical concept has not been advanced as has been the case with interdependence.[6] Moreover, in spite of the assault on interdependence manifested in the current crisis in the world economy, the growth of protectionist sentiment in the advanced countries, and an increase in East-West tensions, self-reliance in its

Third World context is still dismissed by the West as ideological jargon, a concept which, with its Maoist connotations and reactive stance against conventional development strategies, is seen as alien and anachronistic in the modern world. Self-reliance development has been attempted in relatively few countries, which seems to strengthen the argument for its dismissal.[7]

Recent trends in the world economy suggest, however, that self-reliance may become even more prominent in Third World development debates in the future. Global recession, debt crises and the increasing intransigence of the North toward southern demands for redistribution may force scholars and policymakers alike to look more closely at self-reliance, not just for its ability to organize rhetorical responses, but also as a serious alternative development strategy. As a contribution to this reevaluation, this book is an attempt to go beyond the discussion of self-reliance as rhetoric and examine whether it might have any viability as a coherent, realistic or successful strategy of development. The concept of self-reliance will be examined broadly and critically in order to define the kinds of policy choices that such a strategy might involve including the degree of restructuring of both internal and international relations that might be required.

I shall address these questions by examining the writings of four theorists of self-reliance whose works lie outside NIEO rhetoric, and two cases, far removed from Maoist development practice, in order to see whether self-reliance has any wider meaning than that with which it is usually associated. Chosen from different political traditions, time frames and national settings, the works of Jean-Jacques Rousseau, Friedrich List, Thomas Jefferson and Mohandas Gandhi will be examined for evidence of comparative or contrasting themes of self-reliance. Paralleling the discussion of these theorists, the development of the United States and India as newly independent nations will be analyzed to see whether self-reliance strategies were ever considered in policy debates or implemented in practice. Although two of the theorists to be discussed, List and Gandhi, are cited in the contemporary self-reliance literature, the other two are not. If, however, there is evidence that these European, American and Asian theorists were concerned with self-reliant conceptions of development, then efforts to downplay self-reliance as parochial, dependency fixated, or mere rhetoric must be seriously undermined.

American and Indian thought and practice during the post-independence eras are not typical cases for an analysis of self-reliance. These two cases, the United States from 1776–1829 and India from 1947–1980, were chosen because they are not normally considered examples of self-reliance development and therefore present a hard test. Both, however, are large geographical entities with predominant continental positions, which makes the potential for self-reliance more feasible. While I realize that examining different time periods makes comparison more problematic, I have chosen a case from an earlier period in order to see whether self-reliance as a development strategy was an issue two hundred years ago when a new nation was trying to protect its autonomy vis-à-vis a more powerful international system. If it is possible to discover an articulated, coherent self-reliance problematique in the writings of policy leaders of the early United States and postindependence India, then we might expect that it could also be found in many other development situations faced with the same dominant and superior international political and economic system. If we find that self-reliance was rejected in the case of the United States or India, it may help us to understand some of the contemporary problems and possibilities inherent in such strategies of development.

The choice of a historical case and a contemporary one is also justified by what I believe is an important and significant trend in current development literature which is seeking to reinterpret Western history in the light of contemporary development problems. As mentioned earlier, self-reliance is a reaction against conventional liberal models of development which were implicitly assumed by liberal theorists to approximate the development path taken by the West.[8] By looking at the experience of the United States as a new nation, I shall demonstrate that the belief that liberal interdependence was universally perceived at that time to be the correct strategy for development is questionable.

The existing literature on self-reliance development in the Third World has generally focused on what are considered to be more typical cases, such as Mao's China, Nyerere's Tanzania or Kim Il Sung's North Korea, all of which are socialist. By choosing the early United States and India, neither of which followed a socialist pattern of development, I hope to enrich the contemporary discussion of self-reliance by extending it to cases of capitalist development and thereby giving those who look at socialist states a wider scope for their interpretations. The choice of theorists and cases from both the First and Third Worlds is an attempt to bridge the gap between Western and Third World attitudes toward self-reliance. I will show that the contemporary Third World concern with self-reliance, often dismissed as mere rhetoric in the West, actually parallels earlier Western development theory and practice in many important respects.

Having developed a common analytical framework in part 1, I shall introduce the theoretical discussion in part 2 with an examination of the works of Jean-Jacques Rousseau and Friedrich List. While both of these writers were concerned with self-reliance, the meanings which they gave to this concept were strikingly different. Rousseau, a leading political theorist of the eighteenth century, was deeply involved with issues involving individuals' autonomy and dependence and he was also engaged in devising schemes for building self-reliant nation-states which would be insulated from the corrupting realities of international politics. His reaction against modernity and scientific progress, epitomized by the French Enlightenment, and his preference for small agrarian communities are surprisingly similar to the reactions of some contemporary self-reliance theorists such as Gandhi and Mao against Western-imposed "modernization" strategies.

The writings of List, a nineteenth-century German economist frequently cited by contemporary proponents of self-reliance, stand in strong contrast to Rousseau's. Concerned primarily with achieving economic power for his native Germany, List constructed a development strategy which he believed would assure autonomy and self-reliance vis-à-vis the international system but which would also allow eventual participation in that system on better terms. Drawing on his experiences in the United States during the 1820s as a member of a Pennsylvania protariff circle, List advocated industrialization and national economic self-sufficiency as bases for building national power.

In part 3, self-reliance as it relates to the political and economic development of the early United States will be discussed. In conjunction with the American case, I shall analyze the writings of

Thomas Jefferson. As the principal author of the Declaration of Independence, Jefferson was crucially concerned both with nation building and with constructing the kind of society most fitting for the political participation and self-reliance of every individual. Yet Jefferson's long feud with Hamiltonian Federalists suggests that there may be tensions between these two goals. As President, Jefferson's preference, which he shared with Rousseau, for small agrarian communities proved to be incompatible with his concern for building national power and autonomy with respect to the international system.

The Indian case, to be discussed in part 4, will be accompanied by an analysis of the writings of Mohandas Gandhi. Gandhi's preoccupation with creating the kind of social structure for postindependence India in which every individual could realize dignity and autonomy fits quite closely with the concerns of Rousseau and the early Jefferson. Gandhi was also engaged in nation building and his views on national development will be compared and contrasted with those of subsequent Indian policymakers and the path Indian development has actually taken since 1947. I will show that Gandhi's preference for rural decentralized development was discarded in favor of a model that is much closer to the type of development strategy advocated by List.

Part 5 will draw comparisons and contrasts across theorists and cases in order to see whether self-reliance was considered by these theorists and in these cases to be a coherent, viable or realistic strategy of development. The implications of these conclusions will be evaluated in the broader context of the problems and possibilities for self-reliance development in the contemporary Third World.

My analysis of these theorists and cases will be fundamentally interpretive[9] and will, I hope, raise some new and important issues in the debate on self-reliance development. A number of the claims to be made will be validated in terms of their coherence and importance as thematics in the writings of the theorists under consideration. Relying on interpretation, I shall attempt to contribute to the normative tradition of political theory through an evaluation of the relative merits of various self-reliance strategies in terms of their implications for individual autonomy, national development and international cooperation.

PART ONE
SELF-RELIANCE AS A MULTILEVEL STRATEGY FOR DEVELOPMENT

CHAPTER ONE

SELF-RELIANCE IN THE CONTEMPORARY DEVELOPMENT DEBATE: DEVELOPING A FRAMEWORK FOR ANALYSIS

Self-Reliance in the Third World: A Survey of the Literature

WHILE MOST of the existing literature on the subject agrees that self-reliance is a strategy rather than a goal, clearly there are certain normative goals which proponents of self-reliance associate with such a strategy, although there is no consensus about their order of importance. The pursuit of different goals tends to lead authors to emphasize different characteristics of self-reliance according to their ideological orientations. For the sake of clarity in synthesizing a very diverse literature, I have divided the authors into three groups, which I have labeled communitarians, statists and stage theorists. I am aware that there is a great deal of overlap between each of these groups and that any attempt to categorize such a wide body of literature is problematic: nevertheless I feel that such an attempt can be of value for heuristic purposes, even if it involves oversimplification. Although quite different in their orientation, communitarians and statists both reject the liberal model of political and economic development. Like liberals, communitarians emphasize the primacy of the individual and reject the dehumanizing tendencies of large-scale institutions, but they are critical of the excessive individualism associated with liberalism. Statists, on the other hand, reject liberalism because it does not allow a sufficiently interventionist role for the state in building a national economy.

For communitarians, the effect that development has on the self-respect and material well-being of every individual is of crucial concern.[1] Communitarians tend to define self-reliance broadly, as a "philosophy of life,"[2] the practical realization of which requires a radical reorientation of both the strategies and goals of development. In this context self-reliance, in a similar vein to "small is beautiful,"[3] calls for the use of local resources and indigenous technology wherever possible, if necessary at the expense of growth, and a decreased reliance on foreign aid and investment.[4] The production of consumer goods should be limited to those that can be consumed by most of the population; luxury goods should not be manufactured or imported. There is a strong emphasis on the domestic production of basic material needs, particularly food, up to the level necessary for the needs satisfaction of every individual.[5] While the indigenous production of basic needs is a component of almost all self-reliance strategies, communitarians stress that, where possible, they should be produced locally rather than traded through internal markets. Self-reliance then should be built upwards, beginning at the local level, through a kind of "trickle-up" strategy which relies on distant markets only when necessary items and resources cannot be obtained locally.[6]

Unlike trickle-down strategies, more typical of conventional models of development, which rely on industrialization using foreign capital and technology where necessary to pull up the agricultural sector and provide increased employment opportunities, this type of locally based self-reliance development is essentially rural and agrarian. Low-level technology, together with a direct focus on rural development, is thought to be a more appropriate solution for societies with severe unemployment problems.[7] Moreover, there is a strong antiwelfare component to this kind of strategy; the importance of employment is stressed, not only in order to increase productivity and provide income, but also to provide the kind of occupations that enhance the self-respect of the individual.[8] Production techniques that require a highly differentiated division of labor, characteristic of industrial societies, are not deemed appropriate. There is also a concern with devising the kind of development that utilizes alternative energy resources and intermediate technologies in order to inflict minimum damage on the environment.[9]

Communitarians are also concerned that political participation in the development process be as widespread as possible. Political institutions should be decentralized, democratic and responsive to the needs of individuals. The satisfaction of the individual's needs for autonomy and self-respect is deemed as important as the satisfaction of his or her material needs. The individual then becomes the key element in devising an appropriate development path, and a social structure most conducive to furthering the self-reliance of the individual is considered crucial. "Development is fundamentally about human beings and they must participate in the decisions that affect them."[10]

Most of the authors in this group express strong reservations about whether the nation-state is the best instrument for implementing the type of development strategy most suited to the realization of individual self-reliance.[11] Arguments are often similar to those made by the liberal and radical proponents of self-reliance in the West who were mentioned earlier; large institutions are impersonal and contribute to the alienation of the individual, a process that is antithetical to self-reliance.[12] Moreover, the administration of a locally oriented development strategy can become cumbersome and unresponsive when undertaken by large national bureaucracies. Prescriptions often take the form of the reordering of society into small units;[13] the Greek city-state is frequently mentioned as the optimal size for the effective political participation of individuals. Some authors call for a new world order which would deemphasize the primacy of the nation-state and which would include the creation of political structures of varying size depending on the scope of the issue to be addressed.[14]

Communitarians call for a radical restructuring of society at all levels, the primary goal of which is to promote the self-reliance and material well-being of every individual: they share a dislike of lifestyles dictated by the norms of Western consumerism, advanced technological solutions to development problems and large-scale centralized political institutions. Third World declarations on self-reliance usually include many of these same aspirations and aversions, yet prescriptions offered by communitarians often encounter a hostile reception from Third World policymakers. Their perception that those in the First World, who already enjoy an affluent life-style, are trying to sell them a second-best, low-growth strategy is an important issue of contention in the North-South debates.

For this second group of writers on self-reliance, whom I shall call statists, and who include more policy-oriented scholars and practitioners from both the Third and First Worlds, national sovereignty is a crucial characteristic of self-reliance. For Third World policymakers sovereignty provides protection against the imposition of often unpalatable prescriptions offered by communitarians and others on the outside; radical internal restructuring is not a solution which is emphasized since it could amount to political suicide for existing elites. Whereas communitarians maintain that the nation-state could be antithetical to the achievement of self-reliance as they define it, statists feel that the nation-state may be the only institution with the capacity to implement a successful self-reliance strategy. Center-periphery formations, which are seen as operating to structure international economic relations to the detriment of the periphery, can only be broken by the existence of strong state structures in the periphery.

The assumption behind this type of state-centered self-reliance is that only in a closed economy can national control be maintained over economic planning. This perspective has a long history in Western economic thought associated with the mercantilist tradition.[15] Lord Keynes offered a similar prescription for Britain in the 1930s[16] and there is evidence that an open world economy was by no means universally perceived as the correct road to national recovery after World War II.[17] Contemporary proponents of self-reliance, who are concerned primarily with using self-reliance as a tool to renegotiate interdependence on more favorable terms for the periphery, maintain that the nation-state is the most appropriate institution for the achievement of this goal.[18] The state must impose tariff barriers and promote the domestic production of intermediate and consumer goods and it must also regulate the selective use of foreign aid and investment. The implementation of this delinking from the international system imposes a heavy administrative burden, however, and is therefore a task that can only be undertaken by the nation-state.[19]

Both statists and communitarians alike stress the importance of building a balanced economy with a mutual complementarity between industrial and agricultural sectors: the necessity of achieving self-sufficiency in food is also stressed by both groups, but there is more willingness on the part of statists to rely on internal markets rather than decentralized local production to assure distribution. Their goals are more state centered: national independence in basic needs to the greatest extent possible, the building of national autonomy, and the capability to control economic decision making are the primary concerns of statists.

While there is agreement between communitarians and statists that conventional liberal models have failed to promote development, they do not always agree on alternative models which might produce better results. Statists often feel that the negative consequences of interdependence can be ameliorated by incremental policy measures such as more national control over the economy to implement selective delinkage from the international system. Some communitarians, however, question whether self-reliance development in the periphery can be achieved at all under capitalism. They point to the fact that all contemporary cases of attempted self-reliance development are socialist:[20] the kind of restructuring necessary to break center-periphery formations, in order to achieve internal redistribution and reduce international dependency, may not be possible in a capitalist framework where there are vested interests in private property and international linkages.[21] Yet for communitarians there is clearly a tension between socialism and self-reliance: the assignment of a large number of important economic functions to the state, which may be necessary for the achievement of a socialist society, could well be as antithetical to the achievement of individual self-reliance as is large scale capitalism. While they often condemn Western capitalism as an impediment to autonomous development in the periphery, their commitment to individuals' autonomy and participation in the development process complicates their attitude toward socialism.

A third group of writers, whom I shall call stage theorists, generally do subscribe to the notion that the transformation to a socialist society is necessary for the achievement of self-reliance. These are academic writers who have undertaken more scholarly, empirically based research on self-reliance in both historical and contemporary settings. They define self-reliance as dependency reversal or the capacity for "autocentric development."[22] Nondependent development in the periphery must be achieved by a three-stage process which involves first, a dissociation from the international system through the erection of tariff barriers and the refusal, where possible, of foreign aid and investment in order to assure that the dynamic for development is located within the economy rather than outside.[23]

After this delinkage has taken place stage theorists propose a restructuring of the domestic economy and internal social relations, usually along socialist lines, in order to assure balanced growth, the domestic production of basic needs and the redistribution of income. Once internal restructuring has taken place, reassociation with the international system on more equitable terms can be reestablished. Self-reliance as stage theory combines many of the ideas of communitarians and statists: with its emphasis on international delinking and internal restructuring, it attempts to incorporate the concerns of communitarians for equality and participation with those of statists for renegotiating interdependence from a position of greater national strength. Clearly the case of China serves as a model.[24]

The third stage of this model calls for the restructuring of international economic relations in such a way that trade and investment will be redirected away from its present North-South axis toward increased interaction between countries of the Third World.[25] Such a strategy is often referred to as collective or regional self-reliance and is prescribed by communitarians and statists also: for the latter collective self-reliance is usually discussed in the context of the NIEO, which has given the Third World a new feeling of group identity and a sense that, with a concerted effort, the system could be changed in its favor.[26] Going well beyond this restructuring of international economic relations, collective self-reliance also emphasizes the duties of less developed countries toward each other, the notion that inter-Third World aid is essential.[27] Regional cooperation is advocated by all three groups in order to strengthen the bargaining position of the South so that North-South relations can become more genuinely interdependent. "The new emphasis on self-reliance implies not a lessening of interest in international cooperation but a striving to make relations between developed and underdeveloped countries reflect genuine interdependence and international economic justice."[28]

Self-Reliance as a Multi-Level Strategy of Development

Drawing on the writings of these various authors, I shall now list what seem to be the characteristic components of a self-reliance development strategy, although it is clear that not all the components are of equal salience for each author. In fact, the integration of all the various components into a coherent strategy may be difficult due to the sometimes contradictory goals that seem to be implied. This survey of the literature suggests that self-reliance must be considered as a multilevel strategy of development the components of which may be contradictory across levels.

The Outline is an attempt to compile all these components of a self-reliance development strategy according to such a multilevel framework. The first level, which I have called individual and local self-reliance, generally but not exclusively defines the concerns most salient to communitarians. Development begins with the individual: its goal must be to assure basic material needs as well as the need for autonomy and political participation for every human being. I have grouped individual and local self-reliance together because those writers most concerned with individual self-reliance generally prefer politically decentralized agrarian communities and small-scale industrial production as being the type of political and economic framework most suitable for its achievement. The tension between individual autonomy and state institutions, which is of crucial concern to this group of writers, is thought to be modified by the primacy of local communities. The resolution of this tension is problematic in any institutional setting, however, and it is not always the case that subnational regions, which are relatively self-reliant, necessarily provide an optimal setting for individual self-reliance.

The components of the second level, national self-reliance, are closest to the concerns of statists who emphasize the necessity of achieving *national* economic self-sufficiency and development in order to decrease dependency on the international system. In order to achieve this goal, national political and economic integration becomes a higher priority than individual participation; an industrial strategy must include the indigenous production of capital goods as well as the satisfaction of consumer demands. While both local and national self-reliance strategies stress the domestic satisfaction of basic needs, there is more willingness among proponents of national self-reliance to rely on internal markets, an approach dictated in part by the priority of national integration. Basic needs satisfaction may rely on a trickle-down strategy with priorities set through national planning.

The differences in the normative bases of local and national self-reliance development strategies suggest that it may not be possible to achieve a consistent definition of development across these two levels. Individual and local self-reliance defines development in terms of universal basic needs satisfaction achieved through widespread local participation, whereas at the national level, development becomes a more state-centered concept with national economic development, measured in terms of increased productive capacity and increased GNP, taking priority. The tension between these definitions of development is of crucial concern in the contemporary development debate.

The third level, collective and regional self-reliance, combines the concerns of the NIEO for developing collective Third World strategies to gain concessions from the North with the concern of most self-reliance advocates for the redirection of economic relations away from their present predominantly North-South axis toward more horizontal intra-Third World linkages. Collective self-reliance is an area that has been strongly supported in Third World rhetoric but has been very weak in practice: likewise, attempts at regional cooperation through the redirection of trade and regional integration schemes have had only limited success.

Outline
Characteristic Components of a
Self-Reliance Development Strategy

1. Individual and local self-reliance:
   Satisfaction of individuals' basic material needs and need for autonomy and participation. Development of a sense of personal efficacy and self-respect. Decentralization of decision making (individual). Preference for a rural economy based on small local production units using locally available resources to the greatest extent possible. Necessary industrial production based on appropriate locally adapted technology. Production only of goods that can be afforded and consumed by all of the population. Preference for small-scale production with worker participation (local).
   Normative basis: Government should serve the basic needs of every member of the

political community, while every member has a right to participate actively in directing that community's affairs.

2. National self-reliance:

Balanced economic growth behind tariff barriers with complementarity of agricultural and industrial sectors. Emphasis on the development of productive powers and capital goods before the satisfaction of mass demands. Large-scale industrialization allowed for efficiency. Tight control and selective use of foreign aid and foreign capital. Augmentation of state power in order to control economic development. Promotion of national integration in order to assure national security and minimize vulnerability with respect to the international system.

Normative basis: National autonomy in economic and political terms.

3. Collective and regional self-reliance:

Less developed country solidarity in order to pressure more developed countries for redistribution of global resources (collective). Priority of trade with and investment in other less developed countries over trade with and investment in more developed countries. Regional cooperation for economic development and regional security (regional).

Normative basis: Priority of international cooperation among less developed countries.

Although the contradictions between these three levels of self-reliance are evident, for the purposes of my analysis I propose that a coherent, well-articulated and successful self-reliance development strategy must be based on such a multilevel conception. A strategy based only at the national level may lead to a concentration of political and economic power that denies widespread individual participation in the gains of the development process. National self-reliance, with its emphasis on national power and international security, may lead also to the emergence of locally hegemonic states that dominate the political and economic interactions within particular regions. The result of both of these tendencies is to reproduce the same dependency relationships at both the internal and regional levels which self-reliance strategies are designed to avoid.

On the other hand, an exclusive focus on a local self-reliance development strategy may enhance local and individual autonomy and prevent the development of center-periphery relations within states, but it does not build national political integration or the economic capacity necessary to gain sufficient strength to fight center-periphery formations in the world economy. There may, therefore, be a fundamental contradiction between the implementation of development practices designed to promote the self-reliance of the individual or region and those which promote the self-reliance of the nation state. In order to pursue the goals of all three levels of self-reliance at once, some reconciliation between levels would seem crucial although problematic.[29]

As I shall attempt to demonstrate, this reconciliation is an important dilemma for self-reliance development strategies. Using this multilevel framework of analysis, I shall now proceed to examine the writings of Jean-Jacques Rousseau, Friedrich List, Thomas Jefferson and Mohandas Gandhi in order to discover what they have to say about the compatibilities and contradictions of a self-reliance development orientation at each of the three levels. While there is evidence of a multilevel conception of self-reliance in their works taken together, they also demonstrate a clear awareness of the tensions between levels.

The two case studies will also include an empirically based discussion of the extent to which self-reliance development contains possibilities for contradictions across levels. The tradeoffs among components of different levels of development in India and the early United States will be examined in order to determine whether some form of self-reliance development, a strategy frequently articulated in the writings of leading statesmen in both countries, was ever a viable or feasible strategy for development. The development of the early United States and India demonstrate that, in both cases, the effects of the international system and a concern with building national power predetermined a strategy of national economic growth and political integration rather than an emphasis on basic needs, local participation or regional cooperation. Through an examination of the works of these theorists and cases taken together, I shall attempt to see whether any resolution of these contradictions is possible.

PART TWO
LOCAL AGRARIAN DEMOCRACY VERSUS NATIONAL POWER POLITICS: TWO CONTRASTING MODELS OF SELF-RELIANCE DEVELOPMENT

In part 2 I shall present two very different models of self-reliance development based on the writings of Jean-Jacques Rousseau and Friedrich List. Representing extreme versions of the communitarian and statist positions which were outlined in chapter 1, they offer a stimulating departure for discussion. Rousseau rejected liberalism because he believed that inequality and dependence tended to arise when individuals were left free to pursue their own political and economic interests. Rousseau's principle concerns, the autonomy of the individual versus the power and interest of the state, the preservation of traditional cultural values in the face of corrupting influences from outside, and the building of an egalitarian society based on autonomous agrarian communities, have much in common with those of communitarians. While his prescriptions for achieving such a society often seem impractical and would presumably, therefore, encounter opposition from many contemporary self-reliance theorists, they raise important issues which must be faced by proponents of the communitarian position.

List, on the other hand, provides a model closer to the concerns of statists. Development is defined in more traditional terms; delinking is not a rejection of the current world order but a strategy designed to improve the terms of a country's participation in that order. List's preference for the primacy of national development, based on increased industrial capacity and guided by state intervention where necessary, over a more decentralized agrarian-based strategy is predicated on an assumption, similar to that made by contemporary statists, that a penetrative international system is the primary obstacle to development in weak states. Much of List's work is a critique of liberalism's belief in the invisible hand and an open world economy, which List believed worked only in the interest of hegemonic states. While List's preoccupation with the enhancement of national economic power and prestige goes well beyond the statist position outlined in chapter 1, the negative effect which such a policy may have on the realization of the goals of local self-reliance is a dilemma that must be addressed by contemporary proponents of national self-reliance development strategies.

CHAPTER TWO

AGRARIAN DEMOCRACY: SELF-RELIANCE THEMES IN THE POLITICAL THOUGHT OF JEAN-JACQUES ROUSSEAU

I HAVE CHOSEN to discuss the writings of Jean-Jacques Rousseau because the issues that they raise about the contradictions between various self-reliance strategies parallel, to a surprising degree, the problems with which contemporary self-reliance theories must contend. Rousseau was concerned with the self-reliance of both the individual and the nation-state. He idealized the self-sufficient peasant who produced for his own basic needs and actively participated in a decentralized political democracy: this is a model that has much in common with local self-reliance strategies favored by communitarians, as discussed in chapter 1. Just as communitarians call for dissociation from a corrupting world order, Rousseau advocated a completely self-reliant nation-state built on the patriotism of its citizens, its democratic institutions and above all its economic self-sufficiency and isolationist foreign policy. Rousseau maintained that such a state should remain poor economically, because he feared that inequalities inherent in growth would lead to dependent political relationships and the expansionist tendencies of growth-oriented societies.

Like twentieth-century self-reliance theorists who are reacting against models of development and cultural values imposed by the West, Rousseau was reacting against very similar phenomena in eighteenth-century Europe. Highly critical of the evolving power of the centralizing nation-state and the new technologies and economic arrangements associated with the beginning of the Industrial Revolution, Rousseau perceived their potential for increasing inequalities among men and for creating new economic and social relationships in which the individual would become powerless and unable to control his own destiny.

The dependence of the individual on the state in the *Social Contract* and the static agrarian economy of *Corsica* are both attempts to avoid the inequalities that Rousseau believed worked against the self-reliance of the individual and the nation-state. Such arrangements, however, create tensions between the individual and the collectivity and between the possibility of the universal satisfaction of basic needs and a preference for a no-growth society. They are dilemmas of which Rousseau was crucially aware and his efforts to resolve them by turning individuals into citizens, thereby compromising their autonomy, and by denying material progress, thereby producing weak states whose survival in the international system would be unlikely, are solutions which are problematic in the contemporary context. Nevertheless they are contradictions that are evident in the theory and practice of contemporary self-reliance.

I shall now analyze Rousseau's concept of self-reliance using the multilevel characterization developed in chapter 1. At the individual and local level I will discuss the political and economic setting in which Rousseau felt that the self-reliance of the individual might best be achieved, the national level will include a discussion of both internal and international strategies for the achievement of national self-reliance. Since Rousseau felt that isolation was the only way of achieving national autonomy, he was not particularly interested in types of policies that would foster collective and regional self-reliance: the focus of discussion will, therefore, be on self-reliance at the local and national levels.

Agrarian Democracy: The Molding of Self-Reliant Citizens

Rousseau was a strong advocate of local autonomous communities because he believed that the achievement of self-reliance for the individual depended crucially on the political and economic framework within which he lived. Only in an environment based on relative economic equality and small-scale democratic political institutions, a setting somewhat similar to that envisaged by contemporary advocates of local self-reliance, did Rousseau believe that the individual could maintain his autonomy.

Since personal autonomy was of such crucial concern to Rousseau, I shall first discuss what he had to say about the relationship between the individual and society for, while Rousseau was concerned with devising the optimal social setting for the individual to retain his self-reliance, he was clearly aware of the difficulty of maintaining individual freedom in any institutional setting.

This problem becomes evident if one goes back to Rousseau's hypothetical portrayal of the state of nature described in the *Second Discourse*. In contrast to other contract theorists, such as Thomas Hobbes,[1] Rousseau painted an idealized picture of man's primitive beginnings because he wanted to show that only in such a state of existence, unencumbered by all institutional restraints, could man be completely independent and hence self-reliant. "I see him satisfying his hunger under an oak, quenching his thirst at the first stream, finding his bed at the foot of the same tree that furnished his meal; and therewith his needs are satisfied."[2]

While men were neither good nor evil in Rousseau's state of nature, they were more content because they were not dependent "having neither harm to fear nor good to hope for from anyone, rather than subjecting themselves to a universal dependence and obliging themselves to receive everything from those who do not obligate themselves to give them anything."[3] Lack of possessions ensured relative equality, "what can be the chains of dependence among men who possess nothing."[4]

While Rousseau seems to admit that man's progress toward becoming a complete human being with faculties beyond those of animals meant that he could not forever remain in this primitive state, his portrayal of the evolution of man beyond the state of nature is not necessarily a happy picture. Once progress began and technology advanced, man ceased to be nomadic and the notion of private property evolved, thus bringing about new social relationships which could potentially contribute to the loss of individual self-reliance:

As long as they [men] applied themselves only to tasks that a single person could do and to arts that did not require the cooperation of several hands, they lived free, healthy, good, and happy insofar as they could be according to their nature, and they continued to enjoy among themselves the sweetness of independent intercourse. But from the moment one man needed the help of another, as soon as they observed that it was useful for a single person to have provisions for two, equality disappeared, property was introduced, labor became necessary.[5]

Rousseau believed that, with the establishment of private property and the evolving complexity of social and economic relationships which led to an increasing division of labor, differences among men were heightened, thus increasing inequality. "So long as one knows only physical need, each man suffices unto himself. The introduction of the superfluous makes division and distribution of labor indispensable."[6]

Given this ever-increasing interdependence of social organization, the dilemma for Rousseau was how men could maintain their autonomy and independence. His writings are particularly concerned with devising a political and economic framework in which inequality would be minimized, thus creating an environment in which men could remain relatively self-reliant as they had been in the state of nature. For this reason Rousseau preferred the simple social organization of a rural subsistence economy: he admired occupations such as agriculture because they promoted self-sufficiency. In spite of his curious condemnation of agriculture in the *Second Discourse*,[7] elsewhere Rousseau was lavish in his praise of an agrarian life-style. "It is in the rustic clothes of a farmer and not beneath the gilt of a courtier that strength and vigor of the body will be found."[8] Rural life produces individuals who are less corrupt[9] and thus rural occupations take precedence over others: "Agriculture is man's first trade. It is the most decent, the most useful, and consequently the most noble he can practice."[10]

The farmer should work hard, using minimal division of labor, and should have very little access to money. Work was important, not only as a means of production, but also for the physical and mental well-being of the worker. "To work is therefore an indispensable duty for social man. Rich or poor, powerful or weak, every idle citizen is a rascal."[11] There should never be surplus production which would enable some people to choose not to work, the duty of government being "to maintain abundance within their [citizens'] reach so that to acquire it, work is always necessary and never useless."[12] Once labor becomes unnecessary, people become idle and for Rousseau this was one of the worst vices.

In spite of his admiration for hard work, Rousseau was against economic growth because he believed that progress inevitably leads to decay. "The equality and simplicity of rural life have, for those acquainted with no other mode of existence, an attraction which leaves them with no desire to change it."[13] Thus Rousseau's ideal agrarian society was static and nonprogressive; he admitted that he was against social mobility; "nothing is more pernicious for mores and for the republic than continual changes of status and fortune among the citizens."[14] Social complexity, usually associated with urban life, erodes the ties of equality that bind men together and breaks down self-reliance.

Rousseau's agrarian peasant society would seem to depend on a large degree of cultural homogeneity and identity of interests; indeed Rousseau was firmly against interest groups as being divisive and undermining the general will.[15] Implicit in his idealized Swiss cantons was an intolerance of minority opinions and a lack of empathy for foreigners;[16] progress away from a rural subsistence economy would contribute to the development of divergent interests. For Rousseau, however, identity of interests, even in his ideal society, did not extend beyond the male population. While self-reliance was his goal for men, it is evident that this concern did not extend to women.

Rousseau never intended women to be self-reliant: as described in the *Second Discourse*, the first stage away from total isolation in the state of nature was the formation of the nuclear family: "Women became more sedentary and grew accustomed to tend the hut and the children, while the man went to seek their common subsistence."[17] In an earlier stage women had been alone and nomadic like men and Rousseau offers no explanation for why women were willing to give up their self-reliance so easily; but clearly his strong concern for equality never included women. After the formation of the family, women were never discussed as complete human beings but rather in terms of their function, which was primarily to serve men and raise their children.[18]

To please men, to be useful to them, to make herself loved and honored by them, to raise them when young, to care for them when grown, to counsel them, to console them, to make their lives agreeable and sweet—these are the duties of women at all times, and they ought to be taught from childhood.[19]

In an agrarian economy the maintenance of relative equality among men, which Rousseau believed was crucial for their self-reliance, depended largely on property relationships, an issue which is also of central importance in many contemporary developing societies where land is often scarce and unevenly distributed. In most of his writings Rousseau advocated the private ownership of property[20] but clearly this arrangement, with its inherent tendency toward creating inequalities, was problematic for Rousseau, just as it is for contemporary writers on self-reliance and his thoughts on this subject changed during the course of his writings. While in *Political Economy* private property exists prior to the foundation of the state and the state is built upon the right of the individual to own property, in the *Social Contract* this view has been modified. Property, although it is still to be owned privately, becomes the creation of the state: "The right which every individual has over his own property is always subordinate to the right which the community has over all."[21]

Rousseau's belief that an individual had a right to only as much land as he could work with his own labor was an attempt to modify the inequalities inherent in private ownership:

Every man has by nature a right to all that is necessary to him; . . . a man must occupy only the area required for his subsistence; . . . he must take possession of it, not by an empty ceremony, but by labor and cultivation, the only mark of ownership.[22]

Rousseau also worked out an elaborate scheme for progressive taxation to ensure that men did not become too unequal through the unequal ownership of property. Taxes were to be levied on commerce and luxuries, rather than on land, so that the burden of taxation would fall primarily on the rich and wealth would not be drained from the countryside to the city.[23] By the time he wrote the *Project for Corsica* in 1765, however, Rousseau had retracted almost completely the right of the individual to own land and seemed to be envisaging a kind of socialism where most property would be owned by the state and as little as possible by the citizens themselves.[24] While this may have seemed like the only way out of the dilemma posed by unequal property relations, it would certainly involve a loss of independence and self-reliance for the individual.

Thus the degree of economic independence and self-reliance posited for men in the state of nature had undergone considerable modification by the time that Rousseau wrote *Project for Corsica:* the maintenance of an egalitarian society depended on the subordination of the will of the individual to a collective will which was judged to be in the interests of all. Clearly, however, this communitarian solution to the problems of inequality and dependence could be a constraint on the autonomy and self-reliance of the individual.[25]

The socialization necessary for the maintenance of this communitarian society was to be achieved through education. Rousseau's views on education demonstrate that he was aware of this tension between the autonomous individual and the citizen who would comply with the norms of an egalitarian society. In *Emile* Rousseau's attempt to create an autonomous man rather than a citizen illustrates the contradiction between these two goals: "Forced to combat nature or the social institutions, one must choose between making a man or a citizen, for one cannot make both at the same time."[26]

In other writings, however, Rousseau advocates the type of education designed to create a citizen rather than an individual. Rousseau suggests in *Poland* that education should be public in order to be widely accessible, as uniform as possible and above all emphasize the learning of virtuous behavior and patriotism. Rousseau devotes considerable attention to this type of education, which he believed was necessary particularly for the citizens of Poland, since it was a nation threatened by foreign domination: it was a question of "getting them [the citizens] accustomed, from an early moment, to rules, to equity, to fraternity, to competitions, to living with the eyes of their fellow citizens upon them, and to seeking public approbation."[27]

This type of education stressed physical exercise rather than book learning; Rousseau believed that education in the arts and sciences led to a corruption of morals and a growth in luxury and dissipation, which he so much despised in eighteenth-century France: "I see everywhere immense institutions where young people are brought up at great expense, learning everything except their duties."[28] The whole of the *First Discourse* is devoted to a condemnation of the corrupting influence of a "scientific" education, although in conclusion Rousseau does acknowledge that a few may need this type of education in order to become rulers.

Rousseau's views on education, which are divided between the desire to shape the autonomous individual and the desire to create the compliant citizen who will serve the interests of the state, illustrate a tension which is evident throughout his writings between his wish for individuals to be self-reliant and the need for uniformity and consensus in order to preserve the type of political community which could enforce equality. Emile's education attempts to create the autonomous man but the education designed for the Poles seems to emphasize collectivism and group conformity. The fate of Emile suggests that Rousseau is unable to solve this tension satisfactorily.[29] The failure to turn Emile into a citizen demonstrates that Rousseau's goals of creating an autonomous man and a citizen are not compatible.[30] In the final analysis men must be citizens rather than individuals.

The strongest evidence for this collectivist solution to the problems of dependency and inequality lies in Rousseau's treatment of the individual's relations with the state. While Rousseau preferred that the individual be as self-reliant as possible in providing for his own basic needs, he was, at the same time, to be excessively dependent on the state in political terms:

[The relation] of the members with one another, or with the body as a whole . . . should, in respect of the first, be as small, and, in respect of the second, as great as possible; so that every citizen may be perfectly independent of all the rest, and in absolute dependence on the State.[31]

Here Rousseau indicates that self-reliance should govern social relationships between individuals; but, at the same time, his fear of dependence led him to a position of excessive reliance on a state whose very existence was dedicated to preventing inequalities which might lead to dependent relationships between individuals.

The social contract means that "since each gives himself up entirely, the conditions are equal for all";[32] it does not destroy equality but "substitutes a moral and lawful equality for the physical inequality which nature imposed upon men."[33]

Although Rousseau was striving for a society of self-reliant individuals, he realized that the physical inequalities between men and the economic inequalities, which were inherent in civil society and which create relations of dominance and dependence, could only be mitigated by a political and economic system which enforced conformity and egalitarianism. The dilemma for the individual then is how to maintain his self-reliance and autonomy in this type of social setting. Rousseau was aware of this dilemma and his preference for small states comprised of subsistence agrarian communities was his attempted resolution of this problem. It is unclear, however, how states, comprised of these local communities, could survive as autonomous units in the international system.

Autarky in the International System: The Self-Reliant Nation-State

Domestic Strategies for Achieving National Self-Reliance

Rousseau's ideal nation-state was small, rural, poor and isolationist with a political system in which each citizen, although strongly conforming to national norms, might become involved in the practice of direct democracy. The emphasis on citizens rather than individuals, as discussed earlier, is a clear indication of Rousseau's preference for a collectivist framework for national institutions. He defined the state as "a body that is organized, living, and similar to that of a man."[34] In using such a metaphor, Rousseau is suggesting a high degree of interdependence of the parts, but the independence and individuality of the whole. In contrast to the individual, however, the ideal state was to be completely independent; there could be no dependence on a higher authority. Domestic strategies for achieving national self-reliance centered on an economic framework which was self-sufficient and egalitarian, the molding of a strong national character, and appropriate political institutions whose forms were dependent on geographic size.

Rousseau's ideal economic system was founded on a dominant

role for agriculture, weak industrial and urban sectors and a relatively progressive tax structure in order to assure equality. Rousseau believed that this type of rural egalitarian society was most likely to produce national as well as local self-reliance. *The Government of Poland* and *Project for Corsica,* his two works that are concerned with real world cases of state building, are both detailed descriptions of self-reliant economies which contain many parallels with contemporary self-reliant development models, particularly the type favored by communitarians. While the creation of a viable economic system, which would be independent of foreign domination, was the major goal of both these writings, clearly both Corsica and Poland were weak entities whose very existence was continually threatened by stronger states. While it seems unlikely that Rousseau's model would enhance their chance of survival, nevertheless his prescriptions raise important issues for strategies of national self-reliance.

Although Corsica was a backward agricultural community, struggling against the imperial designs of France, Rousseau believed that it offered an ideal setting for agrarian self-reliance.[35] "Agriculture is the only means of maintaining the external independence of a state. With all the wealth in the world, if you lack food you will be dependent on others."[36] Rural self-sufficiency was advocated for Poland also: "[if] you wish to be a free nation . . . a nation that is self-sufficient unto itself and happy. . . . Employ the masses of your population in agriculture and the arts necessary for life."[37]

These statements on agrarian self-reliance resemble quite closely the goals of contemporary basic needs development models; in the *Social Contract* Rousseau states that "every man has by nature a right to all that is necessary to him."[38] Universal satisfaction of basic needs is the key to political stability; "the civil State can subsist only so long as men's labor produces more than they need."[39] Like contemporary proponents of self-reliance, Rousseau stressed the importance of a balance between production and consumption; the population should be just large enough to consume all it produces and evenly distributed geographically so that even internal trade is as limited as possible:

It is the men that constitute the State, and it is the soil that sustains the men; the due relation, then, is that the land should suffice for the maintenance of its inhabitants, and that there should be as many inhabitants as the land can sustain.[40]

While Rousseau considered agriculture to be the most important economic sector, he did acknowledge the necessity for some industry even in the backward island of Corsica in order that the economy would be self-sufficient. Fearing, however, that industry would dominate, he suggested that it should be located in the least fertile part of the island so that high transportation costs would keep down the profits of industrial workers, thus ensuring their equality with those employed on the land. He advised against industry producing a surplus for export since this would increase its overall productivity and profits and balance with the rural sector would be lost.

Another critical factor in rural-urban balance was the role of towns in economic life. Rousseau was highly critical of urban living because it promoted idleness, luxury and money, attracted foreign influence and drained surplus from the country, thus creating an imbalance of wealth. "For every palace that I see rising in the capital, I seem to see a whole rural district laid in ruins."[41] To avoid domination of the capital over the rest of the country, Rousseau suggested in the *Social Contract* that it should rotate.[42] For Corsica he selected a capital in the geographic center of the island, a site whose possibilities for expansion were limited by physical restrictions but which was, most importantly, far away from the influence of foreigners.[43]

Rousseau preferred that agricultural production be as near subsistence level as possible in order to prevent dependence, which would lead to inequality.[44] In both *Poland* and *Corsica,* Rousseau raised the possibility of doing without money at all, even for purposes of taxation. He cited Switzerland as an example of a country where payment of public officials was usually made in kind and where work necessary for the state was performed by conscripted labor.[45] While in *Political Economy* Rousseau talked about more complicated tax structures, which were better suited to existing conditions, in *Poland* he envisaged a proportional tax on land levied in kind; commodities thus produced would be sold abroad to raise money the state might need—a somewhat curious solution in light of his dislike of foreign trade, but one which avoided the handling of money by the citizenry.[46] In *Corsica* as well he suggested a tax in the form of commodities[47] and a system of corvée or conscripted labor; but, since the state was to own a large portion of the land, this presumably would give it a substantial resource of its own.

The molding of a strong national character was another method of achieving national self-reliance. If Rousseau's proposals for a self-reliant agrarian subsistence economy insulated from urban penetration were already anachronistic in his own time, his ideas on national identity have been considered just the opposite[48] and they too are crucial for national independence and self-reliance. Rousseau admitted that patriotism must usually be taught, for it cannot be assumed: "each people has, or ought to have, a national character; if it did not, we should have to start by giving it one."[49] Rousseau chastized Peter the Great for his attempts at modernization which turned Russians into Germans or Englishmen;[50] his views on the importance of national identity for ensuring independence were most highly developed in *Poland* mainly because of existing political conditions. Poland, a state whose independence was continually theatened, was sufficiently vulnerable for Rousseau to suggest patriotism as a substitute for territorial autonomy,

to establish the republic in the Poles' own hearts, so that it will live on in them despite anything your oppressors may do. Those hearts are, to my mind, the republic's only place of refuge: there force can neither destroy it nor even reach it.[51]

Patriotism must be taught through public education, ceremonies, public games and the revival of ancient Polish customs and dress: "The newly born infant, upon first opening his eyes, must gaze upon the fatherland, and until his dying day should behold nothing else."[52] In short, indoctrination should be complete. Rousseau's views on patriotism are consistent with his antimaterialism: in *Poland* Rousseau contrasts the patriotism of the ancient Greeks with the decadence of modern Europeans who think more of their passion for luxury than love of their country.[53]

Rousseau was also concerned with building the kind of political institutions which would contribute to the maintenance of national independence and self-reliance. For this reason he argued that each country should have a government suited to its own particular needs. "Do not draw conclusions about your own nation from the experience of others; rules drawn from your own experience are the best by which to govern yourselves."[54]

Just as contemporary local self-reliance theorists are concerned that political institutions be designed to decrease alienation and permit widespread participation in decision-making processes, the most important determinant of appropriate political institutions for Rousseau was geographic size. In order that all citizens might participate in the formulation of the general will, Rousseau preferred direct democracy, "troops of peasants regulating the affairs of the State under an oak and always acting wisely,"[55] an arrangement which would afford maximum participation for all male citizens. He realized, however, that direct democracy was only suitable for small rural states; the pyramid of government would become too complex in a large state for widespread political participation and citizens would have less identification with more distant institutions.[56] Rousseau believed that Corsica had the potential for democracy but, even in such a small island, he advocated further decentralization into twelve districts, none of which would have more power than any other.[57]

Large populations, vast territories! There you have the first and foremost reason for the misfortunes of mankind, above all the countless calamities that weaken and destroy polite peoples. Almost all states, republics and monarchies alike, prosper, simply because they are small.[58]

Rousseau's real-world models for small states, which were successful according to his criteria, were Switzerland and the Greek city-states. It is hard, however, to draw from his work any generalizations about what type of political system would best foster self-reliance in cases any larger than Swiss cantons.[59] In advising the Poles to keep their monarchy it is clear that Rousseau felt that republican democracy was untenable in a large modern state. The larger the state, the more difficult it would be to preserve liberty and equality; to govern such a state more repressive power would be needed for executing the laws if not for legislating them.[60] Rousseau advocated an aristocracy as the executive in medium-sized states and a monarchy in large ones, although the people would still be represented via an elected legislature; clearly, then, widespread direct political participation was limited to small states. Rousseau's advice to the Poles was to get smaller territorially or, failing that, to adopt a federal system:[61] "If Poland were what I should like it to be, namely, a confederation of thirty-three tiny states, it would combine the strength of a great monarchy with the freedom of a small republic."[62]

While Rousseau was pessimistic about the potential for direct democracy in large states, he makes it clear that he perceived the dangers for self-reliance inherent in nondemocratic government: "A good and sound constitution is one under which the law holds sway over the hearts of the citizens";[63] "obedience to a self-pre-scribed law is liberty."[64] In other words the people should be the authors of the laws and the law, not the people, should rule. Truly virtuous citizens obey only the law, thus ensuring that every citizen, neither commanding nor obeying other men, remains free and independent.[65]

The fear that rulers rather than rules could dominate the citizenry caused Rousseau to dislike even representative democracy. Representatives might soon forget the wishes of the people and succumb to the corruptions of office: "So soon as the service of the State ceases to be the principal business of the citizens, and they prefer to render aid with their purses rather than their persons, the State is already on the brink of ruin."[66] Moreover, the general will could not be represented. Rousseau maintained that in England the people were only truly free on election day: his ideal models were ancient Greece and Rome where representation was unknown.[67]

Rouseau's admiration for the ancient Greeks and Romans is also consistent with his belief that all political systems tend to decay. Rousseau feared change and incremental lawmaking since he felt that such change could only weaken any constitution;[68] the ideal constitution, if it could be devised, would be difficult to maintain, since any body politic bears in itself causes of its own destruction.[69] The preservation of a truly self-reliant nation-state, with the kind of political and economic institutions that Rousseau preferred, was no easy task and he accurately predicted the dangers inherent in the nineteenth- and twentieth-century European state system, where the expansionist tendencies of some have continually threatened the self-reliance of others both within Europe and beyond.

International Strategies for Achieving National Self-Reliance

Rousseau's views on the foreign policies of states conform to his belief in the necessity of isolation in order to resist corrupting influences from outside and maintain a truly self-reliant state with the type of economic and political system most suitable for the molding of self-reliant citizens. While Rousseau apologizes at the conclusion of the *Social Contract* for not considering international relations, "a new subject too vast for my limited scope,"[70] his opinions on this subject can readily be deduced from references which are interspersed throughout his writings and which are entirely consistent with his belief in national self-reliance and his fear of the tendency of some states in the international system to dominate others. Given the existing nation-state system, Rousseau preferred isolation over internationalism since the latter would invite domination of the weak by the strong either in the form of a direct military threat or the more subtle guise of economic or cultural penetration.[71]

This desire to avoid economic and cultural penetration, which Rousseau understood so well, is often an important motivating force behind contemporary self-reliance strategies. Rousseau's views on trade, defense and imperialism evoke themes which are evident in various dependency-reducing strategies in the Third World today and are evidence of his preference for national isolationism. His opinions of trade were somewhat ambiguous, but generally he was against it: "if you occupy extensive and convenient coasts, cover the sea with vessels and foster commerce and navigation; you will have a short and brilliant existence."[72] Rousseau recognized that commerce benefited some states, but only in the short run and usually at the expense of others.[73]

Even though Rousseau was writing during the mercantilist era, his antitrade position stemmed from quite different assumptions from those of mercantilists; Rousseau maintained that trade creates wealth, which is undesirable because it invites dependency on material goods which are themselves undesirable because they promote inequality. Rousseau's advice to the Poles was that, while their agricultural commodities would be highly lucrative on the international market, the wealth they would bring would not be desirable so trade should be avoided: "They [foreigners] need your wheat more than you need their gold";[74] and "produce will, as a matter of course, bring you more money than you need."[75]

In short, national wealth causes dependence because it promotes inequality and locks nations into interdependent relationships that erode their autonomy and self-reliance.[76] Avoidance of trade and wealth ensures national independence.[77] A nation-state should therefore try to attain self-sufficiency through the achievement of a balance between population and production; when this balance is broken dependency will result.

Rousseau's views on defense are aimed, at most, at ensuring the integrity of the nation-state. The type of nationalism he espoused was in no way aggressive or expansionist: for Rousseau the cause of war was rooted in the nation-state system and the pursuit of power promoted by interdependencies and the desire for national aggrandizement. The poor but autonomous state that Rousseau preferred would not have had such aspirations.[78]

The only kind of war that Rousseau believed to be legitimate was that of self-defense in the face of foreign aggression against a state's territory or citizens.[79] To repel such an attack, Rousseau acknowledged the need for a defensive force; however, he strongly disliked standing armies staffed by professionals which, he maintained, were created for the expansionist ambitions of despotic rulers and in no way reflected the interests of the people. In their place he advocated a nonprofessional citizens' militia: "The state must not be left without defenders. . . . But the state's true defenders are its individual citizens, no one of whom should be a professional soldier but each of whom should serve as a soldier as duty requires."[80]

Using the Swiss model Rousseau's militia would rely primarily on the rural population, which he believed to possess ideal qualifications for the makeup of soldiers: "Tilling the soil makes men patient and robust, which is what is needed to make good soldiers."[81] Strong defense depended on rural self-reliance and the spreading of the population as evenly as possible over the territory rather than in urban concentrations. In *Poland*, Rousseau describes the ideal training for Polish soldiers, suggesting that they should excel at guerrilla warfare in order that they be able to move swiftly through the countryside attacking the enemy at many points,[82] a strategy that shows striking parallels with some twentieth-century colonial liberation movements.

If, however, the Poles should be unable to prevent Russian conquest, Rousseau maintained that they could still keep their identity within their hearts.[83] For the Poles nationalism need not even rely on territorial integrity should that prove impossible in the face of the ambitions of stronger states. Liberty, a most cherished goal for Rousseau, was equated with peace;[84] he was strongly opposed to a nationalism that was in any way expansive. Consistent with his preference for small states, Rousseau maintained that they have more vigor than large ones: "Public spirit does not grow with territory; as territory expands, that spirit erodes, movement becomes weak and such a large body, overburdened by its own weight, sinks down, falls into apathy and decays."[85]

In the *Social Contract* Rousseau maintained that governments without colonies are those that prosper the most;[86] there are always reasons for expansion, however, but one way to guard against it is by ensuring "that the land should suffice for the maintenance of its inhabitants, and that there should be as many inhabitants as the land can sustain."[87] Rousseau realized that imperialism could be caused by pressure on resources, but his aversion to economic growth negated the necessity of expansion for this reason. This static balance between population and resources, which was crucial for Rousseau's ideal democracy, would produce a state which could be both self-sufficient and poor enough not to incite the envy of its neighbors. It was for such a state that Rousseau envisaged total isolation from the international system.

This preference for total isolation meant that Rousseau did not display any interest in international or regional cooperation of the kind that would be characteristic of a strategy of collective self-reliance. His portrayal of international relations as a system characterized by the domination of the strong over the weak would seem to make international cooperation impossible. Rousseau cautioned against states entering into international alliances; a state best adapted for the kind of democratic government envisaged in the *Social Contract* is one that does not enter into disputes with its neighbors and is self-sufficient.[88] In the conclusion to *Poland*, Rousseau maintained that he attached "no importance to the external security that is won by means of treaties";[89] treaties are always broken when it serves the interests of the signatories to do so and thus the only route to survival is to be truly self-reliant. Collective self-reliance favors agreements among weak states in order to counter the domination of the strong. Rousseau never proposed such arrangements; rather he relied on the weak not to attract the attention of the strong. There would seem to be strong evidence, however, for the impracticality of such a policy both in the state system of eighteenth-century Europe and in the global order of today.

Conclusion

In an important sense Rousseau raises many of the dilemmas and contradictions faced by theorists and practitioners of self-reliance development today: the issues that have been raised in this discussion are themes that will be reiterated in most subsequent chapters.

Rousseau's agrarian subsistence economy, where the individual produces most of his own basic needs using a minimal division of labor, in many respects resembles the kind of development model favored by communitarians. His rural participatory democracy, built on widespread small property holdings, would seem like an ideal setting for individual autonomy and self-reliance. But Rousseau was keenly aware of the inherent contradictions in such a model once the possibility of economic growth was introduced: pursuit of material gain would lead to inequality, which could erode individual self-reliance even in local communities and create chains of dependencies that could constrain personal freedom and diminish local self-reliance—a process that often occurs, particularly when development strategies encourage national integration.

By the time he wrote *Corsica*, Rousseau's static economy required a great deal of state intervention which would presumably work against individual self-reliance, a dilemma noted by some contemporary theorists, who are wary of socialist solutions precisely for this reason. Nevertheless Rousseau's collectivist solution to the problems of maintaining equality and minimizing dependence could be of more relevance to resource-scarce societies of the contemporary Third World than Western liberalism, which was built upon the assumption of the possibility of continued and expanding growth. Although a no-growth solution would not be acceptable in the Third World today, Rousseau's antimaterialist themes are often evoked by contemporary communitarians. Just as some of Rousseau's ideas on economic organization were anachronistic in his own time, contemporary communitarians must question the feasibility of their preferred kind of development given the aspirations of Third World states and their populations to become self-reliant through modernization. It seems dubious to assume that the individual is willing to forego the fruits of a modernization strategy, particularly when he is being encouraged to be self-reliant.

Rousseau's locally self-reliant peasant economy depended on a high degree of cultural and economic homogeneity. His dislike of minority or interest groups suggest that it would be hard to practice this type of local self-reliance in larger or more complex societies, a problem that is particularly relevant for hierarchical or multiethnic societies today. Rousseau must have realized this since he advocated democracy only for small rural states; anything larger or more diverse contained a stronger potential for disintegration, which Rousseau countered through his advocacy of a much more powerful executive branch of government than in his peasant democracies. However, this does not solve the problem of the practice of decentralized participatory self-reliance strategies in states larger than Swiss cantons: those contemporary proponents of self-reliance who stress the importance of local participation must deal with the issue of size and democracy. Devising appropriate political institutions to ensure local participation *and* national integration is a crucial problem for self-reliant development and one of which Rousseau was well aware.

The kind of political participation which Rousseau envisaged for his ideal citizen might be hard to practice in a more progressive economy with a more refined division of labor. Rousseau was lavish in his praise of the direct democracy of the ancient Greeks, although production in their economy was highly dependent on the slave labor of which he so strongly disapproved. Presumably, for Rousseau, his preference for productivity at no higher than subsistence level would free the citizen for his political tasks; however, this is not a model that would have much applicability in more complex or growth-oriented societies.

While Rousseau was a strong supporter of political participation and direct democracy, he was well aware of the difficulty of allowing for widespread participation and individual self-reliance without sacrificing equality and thus promoting dependence. Rousseau's solution was that individuals should be independent of each other but highly dependent on the state; the concept of the general will, which assumed an identity of individual interests and the type of socialization necessary to mold citizens whose interests would coincide would, however, seem to impose a high degree of conformity, which could produce some tension with the practice of individual and local self-reliance even in Rousseau's preferred local communities. For Rousseau, personal self-reliance could only be achieved by turning individuals into citizens.

In spite of Rousseau's emphasis on decentralized democracy, his sense of nationalism was highly developed. While his type of nationalism would probably not be compatible with the contemporary communitarian or statist positions, the type of nation-state he envisaged might not be totally unacceptable to communitarians. Rousseau was not in favor of national power. His state was to be an autonomous and self-reliant whole, but the rationale for its existence was the collective well-being of its individual citizens rather than the aggrandizement of state power. Since Rousseau did not believe in economic growth, there was no need for the nation-state to be aggressive or expansionist; his preference for national isolation was a policy aimed at preserving his ideal self-reliant citizen from foreign influence rather than one of promoting the interests of the state.

A crucial problem for this kind of state, which may be weak in its institutional structure, is its survival as a self-reliant entity in the international system. While the case of Switzerland might have provided one such example of survival, Rousseau's advice to the Poles to preserve national identity in their hearts is an indication that he realized that such a problem existed. However, the preservation of national autonomy, through the centralization of state power and an increase in wealth and defense capabilities, must always involve some sacrifice of decentralized democracy, and it was a sacrifice that Rousseau was unwilling to make. Nevertheless, this issue raises the important question of whether the type of development favored by Rousseau and the communitarians can ever be compatible with strategies designed to increase autonomy at the national level. This is a dilemma that is critical in any multilevel theory of self-reliance and is an issue that is central to subsequent discussion. I shall turn next to an examination of a very different kind of self-reliance development strategy, one that is aimed primarily at the enhancement of national autonomy with respect to the international system, illustrated through the writings of Friedrich List.

CHAPTER THREE

FROM AGRARIAN DEMOCRACY TO INDUSTRIAL POWER: THE SACRIFICE OF LOCAL SELF-RELIANCE IN FRIEDRICH LIST'S THOUGHT

ALTHOUGH BOTH were critical of liberal theory, Friedrich List's views on self-reliance provide a sharp contrast with those of Rousseau. List's primary concern, decreasing international dependency and peripheralization through strategies designed to enhance the autonomous development of the nation-state, fits quite closely with the issues of foremost importance to statists. The Listian model provides a useful and provocative introduction to a discussion of the issues that arise when a self-reliance development strategy focuses on the national level. Like Rousseau, List preferred a collectivist model for society over liberal individualism but, in contrast to Rousseau, his rationale for self-reliance was not reactive nor was it concerned primarily with devising the kind of social structure in which the individual could be self-reliant. List was not questioning the legitimacy of the prevalent world order nor the effect of that order on the individual: instead he was concerned with devising a national development strategy whereby a nation-state might participate in the international system on more advantageous terms. Such a position is quite compatible with the statist version of the contemporary discussion of self-reliance, although List's goal, a development strategy whereby states such as Germany might catch up with the hegemonic position held by Britain in the nineteenth century, led him to espouse a version of national self-reliance which went considerably beyond the goals of the contemporary statist position.

List is best known for his theory of productive powers, which suggests that a nation should develop its manufacturing capability behind tariff barriers; it is an early example of a school of thought which, following the mercantilist tradition, used economic analysis to challenge liberal theories of international interdependence, the dominant position in the mid-nineteenth century.[1] Free trade and development, via diffusion of ideas and resources through what has generally been viewed as a benign international environment, has remained the dominant paradigm of the conventional liberal approach to development, although recent disillusionment with this model has resulted in a revival of interest in theories that support delinking from the international system. Those who use List to support such theories generally advocate his strategy for building productive powers, certainly an important component of a self-reliance strategy.[2] But List's work raises certain problems for a strategy of self-reliance when it is defined in the multilevel terms outlined in chapter 1. His emphasis on building a national economy and national economic power leaves unresolved the question of devising the optimal social setting for the self-reliance of the individual or of other states that may be exploited in the process.

List spent six years (1825–1831) of his life in the United States. Although this stay was brief, it had a major influence on his principal work, *The National System of Political Economy*.[3] This chapter will concentrate on that work and on List's American publications, because they are concerned with many of the same issues faced by Thomas Jefferson and the early United States. Most of the secondary writings on List in the English language acknowledge the important influence on his work of both the American experience as a new nation and American economists of the protectionist school.[4] List had been involved with early attempts to found the German Zollverein before going to the United States but it is probable that it was America's international economic relations in the early nineteenth century which converted him to protectionism.[5] It has also been suggested that he acquired his views on building productive powers through the protection of infant industry from Alexander Hamilton.[6] While List admired the United States it was for his native Germany that he most wished his model to succeed.

The achievement of national power and prosperity were List's foremost goals; List believed that the strategy most likely to further these goals was the development of productive power behind tariff barriers and balanced growth of all sectors of the economy. Such a strategy parallels contemporary models of national self-reliance but its heavy emphasis on building a national economy neglects many of the crucial features of self-reliance as a multilevel concept, such as individual participation, local satisfaction of basic needs and regional cooperation. For List, the role of the individual was to contribute to the growth of national economic power, a role which is inconsistent with certain aspects of the concept of self-reliance as I have defined it. An analysis of List's views on self-reliance, using a multilevel framework, reveals an emphasis on building self-reliance at the national level and much less concern with the norms associated with either individual and local or collective and regional self-reliance.

The Erosion of Local Self-Reliance: The Individual's Contribution to National Development

Unlike Rousseau, List was not concerned with the effect of size or scale of production on the self-reliance of the individual. In fact List was extremely critical of small states in general and agrarian societies in particular:

A large population, and an extensive territory endowed with manifold national resources, are essential requirements of the normal nationality; they are the fundamental conditions of mental cultivation as well as of material development and political power. . . . A small State can never bring to complete perfection within its territory the various branches of production. (NS 142)

In a speech given in Philadelphia in 1827 List congratulated Americans for not heeding the advice of Rousseau and other European philosophers who argued that democracy could only be successful in small states. List went on to say that he believed that "democratic government is only possible in a large country."[7]

Many of the negative aspects of progress, such as personal alienation, dependency and powerlessness, which were noted by Rousseau, were discounted by List who did not believe that development would be problematic for the individual: in fact he argued that the more developed the society, the more prosperous and therefore content its members. Like Rousseau, List believed that men could be improved by society but, whereas Rousseau's ideal society was devised primarily to provide the necessary social structure for the self-reliant citizen, List expected that, when necessary, the citizen would sacrifice his personal interests to the development of the nation.

We have shown that only where the interest of individuals has been subordinated to those of the nation, and where successive generations have striven for one and the same object, the nations have been brought to harmonious development of their productive powers. (*NS* 132)[8]

While Rousseau was against development because it promoted inequality, thus weakening the individual and making him dependent, List was committed to economic growth primarily because it was the road to national power. The national interest took priority over the individual:

In national economy, the effect of measures and of events, of the condition and of the arts of individuals, is as different as the circumstances are, in which the different nations are existing; and all that in general can be said is this, that if they are promoting the productive power of the nation, they are beneficial; if not—not.[9]

List believed, however, that in such a social setting the individual would also prosper. He argued that a vision of the material prosperity of a manufacturing economy would induce individuals to work harder, thus contributing to the productive powers of the nation.[10] List also maintained that the larger the political association, the better off the individual members; the negative effect of size on the individual's sense of participation was discounted:

Alone and apart from his fellows the individual is weak and helpless. The greater the number of those to whom he is socially united and the more complete the union, the greater and more complete is the resulting moral and physical welfare of the individual members.[11]

One of the principal reasons for List's anti-individualism was his desire to attack English liberalism, particularly its most prominent spokesman Adam Smith. List disliked England because of its predominant position in the world and its consequent ability to dictate the course of other states' development.[12] But at the same time, List greatly admired English power and realized that emulation of its path to development was the way in which countries such as the United States and Germany could also become powerful economic actors. Liberalism was a creed well suited to a country whose supremacy was already secured but a poor strategy for less powerful "catch-up" states. List correctly suggested that England itself had only subscribed to laissez-faire liberalism in the nineteenth century when its predominance was already secured.[13]

List's writings contain numerous attacks on Adam Smith and the English liberal school: Smith, he states, was concerned only with the welfare of the individual, not of the nation, and List notes that the two may not be coincidental.[14] For Smith the key to the increase in productivity and hence individual prosperity was the division of labor, an economic arrangement which was seen by Rousseau as being potentially undermining of the individual's self-reliance. In spite of his disagreements with Adam Smith, List also supported the division of labor extending it to the agricultural sector and turning it into a larger, more organic model which emphasized sectoral interdependencies where the primary contribution of the individual was to the welfare of the nation:

In order to create such a result, [increase national productivity] the different individuals must co-operate bodily as well as mentally, and work together. . . . It [English liberal school] has not perceived that the same law [division of labor] extends its action especially over the *whole manufacturing* and *agricultural power,* over *the whole economy of the nation.* (NS 122)

List was against a decentralized agrarian economic system, of the type favored by Rousseau and contemporary communitarians, where the individual would produce most of his basic needs and where the division of labor would be minimal, because such an arrangement would lower total national wealth (*NS* 159). Instead of creating dependencies and alienation, which were of primary concern to Rousseau, List believed that, in a large integrated manufacturing economy where the division of labor was most refined, the individual would be most resourceful, intelligent and energetic. Individuals engaged in manufactures were more competent and progressive than farmers (*NS* 160). Contrary to Rousseau, List maintained that city dwellers were a beneficial influence on those living in the country; "The country derives energy, civilisation, liberty and good institutions from the towns" (*NS* 167). City dwellers "pursue instruction and new ideas instead of stags and hares" (*NS* 168).

Societies that were predominantly rural produced individuals who were at a lower stage of social development:

In a country devoted to mere raw agriculture, dullness of mind, awkwardness of body, obstinate adherence to old notions, customs, methods, and processes, want of culture, of prosperity, and of liberty, prevail. (*NS* 159)

Men need not necessarily be such dull, clumsy and unintellectual beings as we perceive them to be when occupied in crippled agriculture in small villages. (*NS* 179)

Since rural man was an inferior being, he was less able to take part in his own governance or become self-reliant:

Owing to the isolation in which the agriculturalist lives, and to his limited education, he is but little capable of adding anything to general civilisation or learning to estimate the value of political institutions, and much less still to take an active part in the administration of public affairs and of justice, or to defend his liberty and rights. Hence he is mostly in a state of dependence on the landed proprietor. (*NS* 164)

It is somewhat curious that List noted this dependence on the landed proprietor but never the dependence of wage labor engaged in manufacturing. However, List's negative references to agricultural society were based primarily on examples derived from the social system of feudal Europe. While Rousseau was lavish in his praise of the Polish people, List used Poland as an example of a semifeudal society with an institutional structure that inhibited development. Without the benefit of a manufacturing sector, List believed that Polish society was unlikely to produce self-reliant citizens (NS 177). List does admit, however, that in any society, after the introduction of manufacturing, the rural individual could become more energetic and productive, led by the superior culture of the towns (NS 167). This in no way opposes his negative view of farming (List himself tried farming in Pennsylvania for the first year after his arrival in the United States but he was not very successful at it).[15] Yet he maintained that "the conduct of his [the farmer's] ordinary business require but little mental exertion and bodily skill" (NS 159).

For List, therefore, the introduction of manufactures would also have a beneficial effect on the rural sector. He maintained that agriculture was improved when carried on close to towns, since it would be more receptive to modern techniques of cultivation and stimulated to increase its productivity in order to satisfy urban demand (NS 128). It is an important distinction, therefore, that List was a supporter of capitalist agriculture, which could contribute to a modernizing economy, but not of an agrarian life-style. In trying to reconcile List's negative views on rural life with his support for a balanced economy, which included a rural sector, it is necessary to distinguish between agriculture as List described it in semifeudal Poland and modern agriculture as it was evolving in Western Europe and the United States. Led by significant technological and economic changes in agriculture, which were underway in England by the first half of the eighteenth century and which for the first time created the possibility of producing an agricultural surplus, this agrarian revolution was an important stimulus for the industrial revolution that followed. It has been argued that agricultural modernization was a necessary precondition for industrialization[16] and it seems that List was keenly aware of this interrelationship.

For List, then, the agricultural sector was viewed in positive terms only insofar as it contributed to national development. His comparisons between the dependent rural individual and his self-reliant urban counterpart were intended to contrast the potential power of a nation-state engaging in manufactures with the relative weakness of a solely agrarian economy. Unlike Rousseau, List assessed agriculture in terms of its contribution to national self-reliance, rather than as an environment which might contribute to the self-reliance of the individual; it was probably for this reason that he was so critical of rural society.

While List condemned the *economic* organization of a liberal society as being a poor strategy for building national economic power, he was strongly in favor of liberal political institutions that enabled the individual to be given as much *political* freedom as possible. Relying on the British model to support his conclusions, List suggested that liberal democracy was dangerous for lesser peoples far down the scale of development but essential for the achievement of national power and prosperity.[17] List used Machiavelli's writings to demonstrate a need for autocratic rulers in the early stages of nation building, which he believed must be completed before the enlargement of individual freedoms could take place (*NS* 265). Once national integration was assured, however, List maintained that political freedom was essential for stimulating the kind of creativity and industriousness needed for economic development (*NS* 113). But if the individual were to be given this political freedom it must always be used in the national interest:

As individual liberty is in general a good thing so long only as it does not run counter to the interests of society, so is it reasonable to hold that private industry can only lay claim to unrestricted action so long as the latter consists with the well-being of the nation. (*NS* 139)

Contextually this passage was a criticism of Adam Smith; while List supported political freedom, he always justified state intervention in the economy where it was dictated by national interest. There was no invisible hand that ensured that the good of every individual was synonymous with the good of the whole nation (*NS* 132ff).

It seems then that List's individual was progressing through stages of enlightenment which might coincidentally lead to a greater potential for self-reliance. These stages were closely associated with the evolution of the political system toward democracy and the development of the productive powers of the economy through industrialization; it might be supposed therefore that the truly self-reliant individual could be found in a nation where:

> all the factors of material prosperity, agriculture, manufactures, and trade, have been equally and harmoniously cultivated; whether the power of the nation is strong enough to secure to its individual citizens progress in wealth and education from generation to generation and to enable them not merely to utilise the natural powers of their own country . . . but also, by foreign trade and the possession of colonies, to render the natural powers of foreign countries serviceable to their own. (*NS* 111)

Yet even at this highest stage of development, the individual never seemed to escape from his role as a cog in the wheel of national development. Moreover the self-reliance of some depended for List on the denial of the self-reliance of others. List believed that individuals living in "torrid zones" could never be self-reliant; they would live in the perpetual dependence of their colonial status since they were not capable of developing manufactures and therefore not capable of independence. Justified by a somewhat curious climatic theory about the superior energies of individuals living in temperate zones, List's writings are full of implicit statements on the superiority of European peoples.[18] Clearly, self-reliance was not a state that could be achieved by all races and societies.

List's belief in the potential for self-reliance of the individual was limited by geographical and cultural considerations. He made the assumption that the individual could only become complete through the social conditioning of an advanced urban society and liberal political institutions. Yet these assumptions were made less out of concern for individual self-reliance than to support a strong commitment to the power and prosperity of the nation-state. The effect of size, the division of labor and the alienation of manufacturing occupations, so crucial to Rousseau and contemporary communitarians, were not of central concern to List in his desire to build a strong national economy. He never considered that progress toward building a self-reliant nation-state might be problematic for the self-reliance of the individual.

The Primacy of National Power:
Self-Reliance Transformed

Domestic Strategies for Achieving National Self-Reliance

While the development of the self-reliant individual was not of
central concern for List, the development of the self-reliant nation-
state was crucial and it was with devising a strategy for autonomous
national development that most of his writings and political activities were concerned. List maintained that the discipline of political economy should focus on the economy of the nation-state.
Political economy is a science that teaches:

how by means of those national productive powers the national
resources can be utilised in the wisest and best manner so as to
produce national existence, national independence, national prosperity, national strength, national culture, and a national future.
(*NS* 285)[19]

So strong was this sense of national identity in List's writings that
the nation-state became anthropomorphised, a complete being, the
organic unity of its individual members:

A being which elects presidents and representatives . . . which has
separate interests respecting other nations, and rights as well as
obligations respecting its members, [it] is not a mere *grammatical
contrivance*; it is not a *mere grammatical being*; it has all the qualities
of a *rational being* and real existence. It has a body and real possessions; it has intelligence, and expresses its resolutions to its members by laws.[20]

The interests of the nation should take precedence over the selfish interests of the individual: "an individual, in promoting his own
interest, may injure the public interest; a nation, in promoting the
general welfare, may check the interest of a part of its members. . . . Individuals without the regulations of a community are
savages."[21] If the prevailing ideology were one of excessive individualism, List feared that individuals would "trouble themselves but

little about the power, the honour, or the glory of the nation" (*NS* 140). List attributed such a state of affairs to Adam Smith's liberal society but, in a well-functioning integrated national economy of the type proposed by List, he expected that the interests of both the state and the individual would coincide:

The economy of the people becomes identical with *national economy* where the State . . . embraces a *whole nation* fitted for independence by the number of its population, the extent of its territory, by its political institutions, civilisation, wealth, and power, and thus fitted for stability and political influence. (*NS* 157)[22]

For a nation-state to become completely self-reliant, it would have to pass through various stages of development culminating in the most crucial of all, that of the development of "productive powers." For List a set of uniform stages unfolded consecutively: "In national economic development we must distinguish the following stages: the savage, the pastoral, the agricultural, the agricultural and manufacturing, the agricultural, manufacturing and commercial."[23]

List concentrated his analysis on the last three stages; all of the stages constituted an upward progression from the most primitive to the final stage where agriculture, manufacturing and commerce were mutually interdependent and mutually sustaining of one another. Any nation that was striving for autonomy and self-reliance could not be successful until it had reached this final stage of development. "The highest degree of civilisation, power, and wealth can only be attained by a combination of manufactures and commerce with agriculture" (*NS* 90).

The crucial "take-off" point for the achievement of national autonomy was the introduction of manufactures; an agricultural state was acceptable during early stages of development (*NS* 125), but ultimately "an agricultural nation is . . . an individual with *one* arm . . . an agricultural-manufacturing nation is an individual who has *two* arms *of his own* always at his disposal" (*NS* 146).

For agriculture to contribute to the increasing productivity and growth of the economy, it must be complemented by the internal production of manufactures; when manufactures are introduced the agricultural sector can begin to specialize and exchange its products for those of the town, thus becoming integrated into the national economy while also improving its efficiency, an important consideration for List. List had a Malthusian attitude toward a solely agricultural economy since he believed that, without some external demand apart from the agricultural sector itself, increased productivity would merely result in increased population and hence eventual poverty (*NS* 185). Contrary to Rousseau, who believed that agrarian economies had a greater potential for self-reliance, List maintained that they were prone to scarcities and famine due to price fluctuations and variations in weather (*NS* 210). The introduction of manufactures, however, would raise effective demand and thus increase profits and wages, ultimately raising the price of land, which would then no longer be susceptible to these unstable fluctuations (*NS* 123).

For List, therefore, the key to autonomous national development was the creation of coherent internal markets. While List was critical of international exchanges because of the ability of powerful states to dominate weaker ones, he was a strong proponent of national markets which, he maintained, would result in a "perfect unity of interests" (*NS* 219). Balanced growth, List's mutual complimentarity between agriculture, manufactures and commerce, is an important goal of most contemporary self-reliance strategies; yet proponents of local self-reliance are critical of the tendency of internal markets to create uneven development and to reproduce dependencies at the domestic level. While List maintained that agricultural production, which was not integrated into the market, could not prosper, Rousseau and contemporary communitarians argue that a market economy, with its tendency to increased specialization, inequality, and the division of labor, may not be the best method of satisfying the basic needs of all the population. This may be especially true today in Third World countries with large agricultural sectors which are not fully integrated, as List prescribed, into the national market.

In spite of List's emphasis on a balanced economy in the final stage in development, there is much evidence in his writings that he felt that manufacturing was the most important and dynamic sector. England, the only country in List's view which had reached this final stage, depended quite heavily on the importation of raw materials: List was quite critical of the English Corn Laws, protectionist measures which were intended to decrease England's reliance on grain imports. List also cautioned against the westward expansion of the United States lest capital, manpower and talent be drained away from the eastern states where trade was flourishing and manufacturing was most likely to succeed (*NS* 84, 85).

A successful manufacturing sector depended on strengthening the domestic means of production. List's theory of productive powers has been considered to be one of his most important contributions to economic thought. In short it stated that "*the power of producing wealth* is infinitely more important than *wealth itself.*"[24] While the accumulation of national productive power depended on the social system and the creativity and industriousness of the population, more importantly, a nation builds its productive power through the protection of manufactures behind tariff barriers. List was particularly critical of liberal economic theory's emphasis on the accumulation of individual wealth through exchange: where necessary he believed that consumption must be deferred to future generations for the sake of building the means by which wealth could be created. With the framework of a strong national economy in place, the political freedom of a nation is also assured (*NS* 3); the achievement of both was the ultimate goal for every self-reliant nation.

The most important issue which this raises for strategies of national development is how a nation can begin to develop its productive powers. List tells us that nations should make the transition from agriculture to manufactures when they reach the capability to do so.[25] Capability depended on political and economic integration or national unity,[26] an advanced state of agriculture and a well-developed infrastructure and internal system of transportation.[27] But none of these conditions was as important as free institutions (*NS* 87) and a favorable intellectual climate, which generally must be acquired from outside.[28] It is important to remember that List believed that not all nations had the capacity to reach the higher stages of development. More than anything else, this capability was determined by geography and climate; "torrid zones" lying outside areas with temperate climates were doomed to perpetual backwardness and dependency.

At times List seemed to be saying that the beneficial influence of manufacturing and urban living caused people to behave in a way that would stimulate further progress; at other times he argued that a favorable social climate would then give rise to manufactures. The circularity of the argument makes problematic an adequate explanation of the *causes* of development.[29] About one aspect of this argument List was consistent, however; since all countries were at different stages, development was a process which, in its early stages, depended on influence from the outside. Contrary to Rousseau, List believed that foreign influence could be invigorating and stimulating for development when it came from superior civilizations. The statesmen whom List admired most were those political leaders, such as Colbert, who recognized the importance of borrowing skills, manpower and technology from more advanced nations and using them for the creation of national economic power (*NS* 57); dependency issues associated with such a strategy, which are of overriding concern to most contemporary theorists of self-reliance, were generally not an issue for List and other nineteenth-century writers.[30]

The development of its manufacturing sector, therefore, was the key to any nation's success in terms of power and prosperity; as it developed, it was expected that this crucial sector would increase its returns to scale in the interests of efficiency and productivity. Just as economic development was synonomous with larger scale production, so also would political development result in larger political institutions. The logical conclusion of this trend was the eventual union of all mankind, about which List often wrote, although only hypothetically.[31]

Nowhere was List explicit about what this universal society would look like: for the immediate future the most efficacious political organization was the nation-state; only when nation-states became equal in power and prosperity could universal union be contemplated. This, however, was a condition that List admitted was almost impossible to achieve, for he correctly hypothesized that in any open world system, the powerful would threaten the autonomy of the weak (*NS* 330).

Within the boundaries of the nation-state, List assumed that progress meant the development of centralized political institutions: the negative effect of large-scale institutions on the development of the individual, noted by Rousseau and contemporary communitarians, was of no concern to List; the disassembling of national unity into small-scale political units would be to commit national suicide and expose the nation to conquest by some lesser state (*NS* 288). The possibility of local objection to a centralized national strategy of development or the desire to protect local autonomy were not considered; it was assumed that, as nations develop their economic strength, so too would they increase their capacity for political integration.

List maintained that government intervention in the economy was a necessary aspect of development which would increase as development proceeded; he believed that, in the early stages, a policy of economic laissez-faire was advisable but that, as a nation advanced, widespread intervention in the economy would become more desirable (*NS* 144). The most crucial area for government expenditure, according to List, was internal improvements, especially transportation. List was particularly interested in the building of canals and railroads because of its potential for increasing national economic integration and national markets:[32] after his return to Germany in 1831, he worked to promote a German railroad system which would serve as a means to economic and political unification.

The national government, therefore, was the institution best suited to provide the necessary infrastructure for the development of productive powers;[33] List showed none of the concern over the extension of national power which Rousseau feared could be detrimental to the self-reliance of individual citizens. List's strategy was quite consistent with his overriding goal of promoting the self-reliance of the nation-state in order that it might achieve autonomy with respect to the international system.

International Strategies for Achieving National Self-Reliance

Unlike Rousseau, List never advocated isolation in international relations for ideological reasons. Withdrawal from the international system behind tariff barriers was specific to the early manufacturing stage of development for the purpose of building national economic power, which List believed could not be accomplished in an open world economy containing more powerful economic actors. Prior to the establishment of manufactures, nations should follow a policy of free trade, for List believed that industrial development was usually stimulated by contact with other nations and that the free importation of manufactures was the surest method of "inducing their landowners and nobles to feel an interest in industry, of arousing the dormant spirit of enterprise among their merchants, and especially of raising their own civilisation, industry and power" (*NS* 90).

Once established, manufactures should receive protection until they were able to withstand foreign competition; like contemporary stage theorists of self-reliance, List believed that a nation, in its final stage of development, should revert back to free trade, a policy which he noted was always advantageous to highly developed states; it is important to note, however, that the dynamic for development must always be internal. Therefore, strategies for achieving national self-reliance must center on the *domestic* economy: a reversion back to an open economy could only be undertaken once this dynamic was assured.

Countering what List saw as the ahistoricism of the liberal school, Part I of the *National System* examines the historical development of various European countries and North America in terms of their relationship with the international system, which for List was a crucial determinant of their political and economic development.[34] It is a challenging critique of the liberal free trade position. In arguing that free trade over time tends to work to the detriment of producers of raw materials, it is surprisingly similar in its assumptions to the arguments against free trade made by the dependency school today.[35]

The degree of association or dissociation with the international system that List thought to be appropriate at various stages of development was clearly based on the British model (*NS* 29–46). According to List, English supremacy was achieved by many centuries of judicious commercial policies which could be traced back to the fourteenth century when the roots of English manufacturing were established by Edward III's encouragement of the domestic wool industry. Thereafter manufactures continued to receive protection along with support for commercial interests begun under the Tudors and climaxing with the passage of the Navigation Acts. Only in the nineteenth century, when England had achieved a position of dominance, did it revert back to the policy of free trade which it had pursued in the thirteenth century. Yet, argued List, the English liberal school was advocating a policy of free trade for all nations regardless of their stage of development (*NS* 295). This historical analysis also suggests that English supremacy was achieved at the expense of the development of other nations; for example, Portugal's failure to develop into a manufacturing power was due primarily to the signing of the Methuen Treaty in 1703, which gave Portuguese wine preference in English markets in exchange for English manufactures. List believed that the importation of English cloth and other manufactured goods prevented Portugal from developing its own cloth industry, which had taken root in the seventeenth century, thus thwarting the development of its productive powers in general (*NS* 47–53).[36]

The nascent manufacturing sector would be assured continuous growth through the existence of an internal market. Even if manufactures could be purchased more cheaply from abroad, List argued that the development of productive powers was of greater importance than short run gains in exchange value for the consumer. Importing manufactures invites dependency; their export signifies power: for List, history showed that "nations are richer and more powerful the more they export manufactured goods, and import the means of subsistence and raw materials" (*NS* 176).

As mentioned earlier, List frequently stressed the importance of a balanced economy, but he also approved of importing raw materials, at least for nations with a well-developed manufacturing sector; he did not feel that foreign raw materials would cause dependency in the same way that foreign manufactures would. It seems likely that List was again using the English model. Yet nineteenth-century England was in a unique position due to its control of the seas through its superior naval power: List emphasized the possible disruption of foreign trade by war and advocated that Germany, in cooperation with other continental nations, build naval power to counteract the supremacy of the British if it wished to be successful as a significant economic actor (*NS* 332). Clearly, then, reliance on imported raw materials could not be a prescription for every country's growing economy were it not in a strong enough position to protect its commerce. Nevertheless List was perfectly consistent in never advocating protection for agriculture: he argued that the protectionist Corn Laws were detrimental to England because they lowered agricultural imports. The more agricultural

products England imported, the more manufactures it would export in exchange, and hence the more prosperous the manufacturing sector (*NS* 175).[37] Contrary to his position on manufactures,
List worked out his rationale for free trade in agriculture on the
basis of comparative advantage, for he argued that, if a country
were forced to produce all its agricultural needs, it could not benefit from specialization and the division of labor (*NS* 173).[38] List also
maintained that agricultural protection would cause inefficiencies,
an argument which he never used in the case of manufactures.

In spite of these views, which supported free trade in agriculture,
the inferences which can be drawn from List's discussions of international trade have many themes in common with contemporary
dependency writers and are much more compatible with strategies
of self-reliance development than with the liberal interdependence
model. For example, List noted that free trade works for the benefit
of *both* trading partners *only* when they are at a similar level of
development, producing goods at similar levels of processing when
"competition is not overwhelming, destructive, or repressive, nor
tending to give a monopoly of everything to one side" (*NS* 260).
List felt that such a condition existed between some of the continental nations of Europe and that it would be to their advantage to
cooperate against the superior power of England (*NS* 339).[39]

When trading partners are not at a similar stage of development,
free trade benefits only the leader: it is "a universal subjection of the
less advanced nations to the supremacy of the predominant manufacturing, commercial and naval power" (*NS* 103). Nations of the
second rank with manufacturing capabilities must use protection in
order to catch up with the leader: "The system of protection . . .
forms the only means of placing those nations which are far behind
in civilisation on equal terms with the one predominating nation"
(*NS* 103). This strategy for the development of catch-up states was
one that List advocated for both the United States and Germany:
his *Outlines of American Political Economy* contains many references
to the detrimental effects of free trade on American development.
Although Anglo-American trade fitted exactly the classical liberal
model of comparative advantage, List, in an analysis which parallels contemporary dependency-reversal strategies to a remarkable
degree, argued that American export of primary products, in ex-

change for English manufactures, placed the United States in a position of dependency:

Because the exports of the agricultural nation are directed to a few manufacturing nations, which themselves carry on agriculture, and which indeed, because of their manufactures and their extended commerce, carry it on on a much more perfect system than the mere agricultural nation; that export trade is therefore neither certain nor uniform. (NS 210)

List's prescription for America was to diversify its exports both in terms of products and in terms of markets.[40] The fluctuations in agricultural trade could be avoided when a nation developed the capability to work up its own raw materials and export manufactures; List of course felt that both Germany and the United States possessed such a capability. The skill, capital and labor-saving machinery, which would go into producing manufactures, would raise the productivity of labor and thus manufactures would do better in the international market in terms of exchange value. List frequently noted that great nations always export manufactures and that the international division of labor always benefited the leader: it would also be good for countries of the "torrid zones" because they could never develop a manufacturing capability of their own (NS 211). Self-reliant development then becomes a strategy that is possible for some but not for all.

List's views on trade are quite compatible with national self-reliance strategies, but since his ideal model of national development was based on the English case, it is questionable whether it was a self-reliance model in the complete sense. England's development relied on a strategy that included protection during the early stages of development but involved expansion and the exploitation of others at the same time. The achievement of English autonomy was won through managed but continuous association with the international system and through the denial of self-reliance to others.

The English model might therefore be called mercantilist rather than self-reliant since England, as List noted, had used a variety of international economic policies over time, all of which were designed to project national power rather than encourage self-sufficiency. List was quite critical of classical mercantilism because of its emphasis on the amassing of precious metals rather than on the development of productive powers.[41] Yet List was sympathetic to many other facets of mercantilism and his writings have often been seen as a contribution to the transition of mercantilism from its classical to its more modern version. Mercantilism, in its complete sense, is a system of power in which the state is the focal point: its economic activities are intended to enhance this power, if necessary at the expense of others. The nineteenth-century version of mercantilism, of which List was an important proponent, was considerably enlarged from its original meaning: it was a development strategy that involved the building of productive capacity behind tariff barriers and other state interventions to promote a balanced economic growth that did not rely on foreign resources. It was often associated with the building of national security capabilities in order to project an image of national power in international politics.[42] For List, national power was an important means by which national wealth could be protected "because national wealth is increased and secured by national power, as national power is increased and secured by national wealth."[43] The overriding goal of development, therefore, was the increase in the wealth *and* power of the nation-state; international trade could contribute to this goal, not if left to regulate itself as advocated by the liberal school, but only if managed by wise, self-interested commercial policies.

The imports and exports of independent nations are regulated and controlled at present not by what the popular theory [liberalism] calls the natural course of things, but mostly by the commercial policy and the power of the nation, by the influence of these on the conditions of the world and on foreign countries and peoples, by colonial possessions and internal credit establishments, or by war and peace. (*NS* 219)

Commercial restrictions could be vital to a nation's security interests also. Consistent with a mercantilist perspective, a judicious commercial policy was linked with national defense in List's writings: "It is the principle of self-maintenance, of self-defence, which counsels the nations to work up their agricultural products themselves, and to dispense with the manufactured goods of the enemy" (*NS* 242).

While List acknowledged the destructive forces of war, he frequently noted that war could also provide a stimulus to national development, particularly for countries entering the "takeoff" stage in manufactures:

War acts on it [an agricultural nation] like a prohibitive tariff system. It thereby becomes acquainted with the great advantage of a manufacturing power of its own, it becomes convinced by practical experience that it has gained more than it has lost by the commercial interruption which war has occasioned. (*NS* 147)

In times of war "every nation must endeavour, without regard to its economical conditions, to be sufficient to itself" (*NS* 248). French manufactures had been stimulated by the Continental blockade during the Napoleonic Wars, as had American industry by the War of 1812 (*NS* 59, 79), but according to List, the French policy of imposing tariffs after the conclusion of the war was more judicious than America's reverting back to a more liberal trade policy. List also noted that England had always benefited from the stimulus which wars, never fought on its own territory, gave to its productive power (*NS* 44).

War's beneficial effects on development are often gained by some nations at the expense of others; that wealth must be acquired by taking it away from someone else is an important aspect of mercantilist philosophy both in its classical and modern versions.[44] Imperialism is also an expression of this zero-sum aspect of development that goes well beyond the goals of national self-reliance.

This link between mercantilist development and imperialism is evident in List's writings: while expansion may not be a necessary condition for the development of an autonomous state, List certainly believed that states with large territories or states with expansionist tendencies had a greater capacity for economic power and prosperity. List argued that a state lacking in territory, natural resources or access to the sea must first remedy these deficiencies before proceeding to the development of manufacturing powers.[45] List used this argument to advocate the incorporation of Holland into a united Germany (*NS* 327). A small nation such as England depended on territorial conquest for its greatness (*NS* 143). Colonies assume an important function in the development of the productive powers of the mother country by providing a market for manufactures and a source of raw materials:

> The mother nation supplies the colonies with manufactured goods, and obtains in return their surplus produce of agricultural products and raw materials; this interchange gives activity to its manufactures, augments thereby its population and the demand for its internal agricultural products, and enlarges its mercantile marine and naval power. The superior power of the mother country in population, capital, and enterprising spirit, obtains through colonisation an advantageous outlet, which is again made good with interest by the fact that a considerable portion of those who have enriched themselves in the colony bring back the capital which they have acquired there, and pour it into the lap of the mother nation, or expend their income in it. (NS 216)

List's discussion of the strategy by which England achieved its position of supremacy indicates that he attributed an important place to British imperialism in this strategy: List pointed out that the maxims of English state policy had always been to direct any surplus productive power to colonization, to monopolize colonial markets for British manufactured goods, to continually expand colonial possessions and to protect these commercial advantages through the maintenance of naval power (NS 294). More generally List argued that the countries of the temperate zone have a responsibility for supplying manufactures to the "torrid zone," since the latter could never achieve this capability for themselves. Contrary to the ethic of self-reliance, List continually emphasized the more intangible beneficial effects of colonialism, such as the transmission of enlightenment to uncivilized peoples:

> Wherever the mouldering civilisation of Asia comes into contact with the fresh atmosphere of Europe, it falls to atoms. . . . In this utter chaos of countries and peoples there exists no single nationality which is either worthy or capable of maintenance and regeneration. Hence the entire dissolution of the Asiatic nationalities appears to be inevitable, and a regeneration of Asia only possible by means of an infusion of European vital power, by the general introduction of the Christian religion and of European moral laws and order, by European immigration, and the introduction of European systems of government. (NS 336)

In arguing that the mother country is beneficial to the colony, it is possible that List was looking for a moral justification for expansion; he was extremely interested in a scheme for German expansion which he felt was essential if Germany were to become a great power like England. To achieve such a goal, the German Zollverein, which List saw as a forerunner to political unification, must "extend over the whole coast, from the mouth of the Rhine to the frontier of Poland, including *Holland* and *Denmark*" (*NS* 143). While England achieved national expansion through territorial conquest, List felt that Germany could achieve similar results through the free commercial association of a customs union. It is important to note, however, that since List was primarily interested in the expansion of German influence on the European continent, his arguments about the civilizing effects of European colonialism would not apply in this particular case.

Prophetically, List predicted the day when Europe would be united in one commercial union. But, on the other hand, the history of the twentieth century has contradicted List's belief that "the more that industry advances, and proportionately extends over the countries of the earth, the smaller will be the possibility of wars" (*NS* 101). While List argued that commercial union and colonization were preferable to war for channeling a nation's energies (*NS* 101), he admitted that the goal of creating a powerful economic actor, to which he aspired for Germany, might be a justification for war in itself (*NS* 330). Even if German expansion were to be achieved peacefully, it would be done at the expense of small European states with temperate climates and presumably a high enough level of civilization to allow them to pursue an independent course of national development of their own. List's scheme for a powerful, self-reliant Germany, which was his most cherished goal, is problematic for a strategy of local self-reliance, such as Rousseau's, which advocates small states as being more promising frameworks for the achievement of individual self-reliance. List's focus on large political units, as a means to assure the viability of national self-reliance through larger economic markets, does not take into account the aspirations of smaller states that may be exploited in the process.

Nevertheless, List's support for the commercial union of continental European states has some parallels with policies associated with collective self-reliance. Yet there are important differences that tend to emphasize the tensions between the norms associated with genuine collective self-reliance and List's more mercantilist strategy. List favored European union in order to challenge British economic supremacy, both in Europe and the rest of the world (*NS* 332). List was well aware of the realities of international power politics, and commercial and political cooperation was advocated in order to challenge the power of the hegemon with the desired result being the reproduction of the existing international system with different states on top. Besides proposing such a policy in the interests of creating a more powerful Germany, List clearly had such a strategy in mind for the United States. In advocating policies that would serve to capture the commercial markets of South America and compete for commercial advantages with the British, List was prescribing strategies for a future hegemon rather than a cooperative regional partner (*NS* 339). Since List's prescriptions for building viable autonomous economies depended on both commercial and political expansion, conflictual rather than cooperative relations were likely to result.

Conclusion

The dilemmas and contradictions that arose out of Rousseau's attempt to achieve self-reliance for the individual *and* the nation-state have been resolved by List in favor of the latter. This resolution ignores many of the problems associated with the role of the individual in the developmental process that are noted by Rousseau and contemporary communitarians. More importantly, however, it raises questions about the feasibility of any self-reliance strategy that focuses at the national level, an issue that is also of primary concern for the statist position.

Although for different reasons, neither Rousseau nor List believed in liberal individualism: List's individual, like Rousseau's, was to be a citizen who was part of an organic whole; but the foremost goal for List's collectivist framework was to enhance national economic power and prosperity rather than to reduce personal dependency. List considered the individual primarily in terms of his contribution to a national development strategy with which he was assumed to concur. Rousseau's communitarian society has been turned upside down in order to serve the collective interests of the nation rather than those of its individual citizens.

List believed, however, that these two sets of interests could be coincidental. The social structure most conducive to the achievement of industrially based national economic power was one in which the individual was also presumed to function most effectively. In such a society basic needs would be satisfied through the creation of a balanced economy that was critically dependent on the linkage between the manufacturing and agricultural sectors. For List, a prosperous manufacturing sector was the key to the success of this type of economy: only with the development of manufactures could agriculture be pulled up out of a primitive state and turned into an efficient productive sector which could contribute its share to national prosperity. List's strong antirural bias reflects his belief in the benefits of a modernizing economy which depended crucially not only on a thriving manufacturing sector but also on a division of labor and coherent internal markets. There was also a strong commitment in List's work to scientific and technological progress which would drive toward larger institutions and a more refined division of labor. The negative effects of this type of political and economic framework, such as personal dependency, alienation and inequality, so important to Rousseau, were discounted. However, they are salient issues for many contemporary Third World states with large populations which are only marginally integrated into the developmental process.

Large geographical size was preferable, therefore, both for a prosperous national economy and the prosperity of its individual members. The size of government most appropriate for individual participation and self-reliance was not a central issue for List as it was for Rousseau and contemporary communitarians. But in general large states with more centralized institutional structures were considered preferable to small ones, national integration being crucial for a well-functioning national economy. Since the interests of the nation took precedence over the individual, centralization was assumed to be a mark of both political and economic development and therefore the goal of any modernizing state.

The case for List as a self-reliance theorist rests on his theories of balanced growth and the development of productive powers behind tariff barriers, along with his critique of the internationalist associative liberal model of development. His analysis of the historical development of various European states in these terms is the most provocative aspect of his work in terms of its contribution to a strategy for dependency reversal and self-reliance development.

But List's failure to develop a model consistent with a multilevel definition of self-reliance is due to the fact that his principal aim was to discredit the English liberal school while at the same time emulating the English path to development. The fact that these goals may be contradictory raises important issues for national self-reliance strategies. Balanced growth was not the primary goal of the English model, which relied heavily on the importation of raw materials: England's development was actually a case, not of self-reliance, but of colonial expansion and managed association with the international system. In spite of his commitment to balanced growth, List was never against the importation of agricultural products. Food self-reliance is a goal of all contemporary self-reliance strategies but those that support a policy similar to List's, which emphasizes the primacy of protected industrialization, may also end up importing food, as will be demonstrated in the case of India in part 4.

List's model of development might more accurately be called a mercantilist model of dependency reversal. Such a model stresses national autonomy and self-reliance but it can be excessively nationalistic and therefore lead to expansionism and exploitation of others. List greatly admired England for its position of predominance in the international system and his "catch-up" strategy was based on emulating England's path to greatness. Even though List believed that more than one nation could achieve this superior position, it would seem that the success of such a strategy must be limited to only a few, since British supremacy had always depended on the denial of such a position to others. List believed that European races alone were capable of advanced civilization and thus it became their duty to transmit this civilization to others, certainly a denial of the ethic of self-reliance and a position that can justify imperialist policies or, at least, a reproduction of the same dependency relationships that a strategy of national self-reliance is originally designed to combat.

Such issues are highly relevant to a discussion of self-reliance since they illustrate many of the dilemmas that can arise when self-reliance focuses at the national level. The case of India, to be discussed in part 4, and to some extent that of the early United States, demonstrate that national strategies of self-reliance can all too easily evolve toward this type of model which then becomes inconsistent with a multilevel definition of self-reliance and which may even defeat the goals of self-reliance at the national level.

This conclusion will be further elaborated upon and illustrated in subsequent discussion. I shall now turn to a comparative analysis of the early United States and contemporary India in order to illustrate the tensions that can arise when the theoretical premises of the communitarian position are faced with the realities of national development and the imperatives of the international system.

PART THREE
UNITED STATES DEVELOPMENT, 1776–1829: THE VICTORY OF FEDERALIST POLICIES OVER JEFFERSONIAN PRINCIPLES

In part 3 I shall first examine Thomas Jefferson's views on self-reliance and then link them with the historical development of the United States from 1776 to 1829, the period during which Jefferson played such an important role both through the influence of his political thought and as a national policymaker.

Although Jefferson's political thinking was rooted in the British liberal tradition, and thus differed in many respects from Rousseau's, his preference for agrarian democracy has some important similarities with the type of local self-reliance preferred by Rousseau and contemporary communitarians. When Jefferson became a national policy leader, however, he moved away from supporting local agrarian democracy and toward policies designed to build a strong nation-state.

Although Jefferson was an influential political figure during most of this period, the actual development path taken by the United States between 1776 and 1829 was governed by the imperatives of building national integration and autonomy, priorities that have much in common with those of List and contemporary statists. That List's prescriptions for national development were not followed more closely in the case of the United States was probably due to the good fortune of the American environment rather than to alternate policy preferences.

Important illustrations of the tensions between local and national self-reliance development, in both theory and practice, are found in the evolution of Jefferson's political thinking, as its emphasis shifted from individual rights to national power, and in the surrender of decentralized democracy to the priorities of nation-building in the early United States.

CHAPTER FOUR

BETWEEN THEORY AND PRACTICE: THE TRANSFORMATION OF SELF-RELIANCE THEMES IN THOMAS JEFFERSON'S THOUGHT

THOMAS JEFFERSON'S early political thought shows a strong concern for the self-reliance of the individual, which he believed, like Rousseau and contemporary communitarians, could best be achieved in a decentralized, relatively egalitarian agrarian democracy, a social setting similar to that which existed in the United States at the time of independence. Yet, when Jefferson became President in 1800, the precarious position of the United States in the international system compelled him to change his views and to support policies designed to promote national integration and national self-reliance even when they compromised his earlier preferences.

Although committed to the ideals of agrarian democracy, Jefferson proved to be a pragmatic political leader in responding to the swift movement of events during America's early years of independence. The evolution of his political and economic thinking, which transformed his views on self-reliance, can best be explained by changing circumstances—from America's role as a colony in the British Empire to its position of political and economic independence at the time of Jefferson's death in 1826.

Jefferson's political thought was grounded in the context of the English liberal school which emphasized individual rights, government by consent, and liberal institutions and which differed in many important respects from the more collectivist orientation of Rousseau, List and contemporary communitarians.[1] The emphasis on the primary importance of the collectivity over the individual, expressed in Rousseau's concept of the general will and in List's organic model of national power, has no place in Jefferson's political philosophy: Jefferson recognized the legitimacy of self-interest and felt that republican government was the best form for the representation and reconciliation of the different interests which are bound to arise in any society.

I propose now to examine Jefferson's views on self-reliance at the local, national and collective levels. The inconsistencies in Jefferson's political and economic thought will be discussed in terms of an apparent tension between the decentralized political, economic and social structure most advantageous for the practice of individual self-reliance and the greater degree of centralization and control needed for building a strong self-reliant nation-state with the ability to act autonomously in the international system.

Jeffersonian Democracy:
The Idealism of a New Nation

Even though their political thought was rooted in substantially different traditions, Jefferson's self-reliant individual shared many characteristics with Rousseau's. Jefferson idealized rural life, feeling that agricultural pursuits fostered the development of the individual: "Cultivators of the earth are the most valuable citizens. They are the most vigorous, the most independent, the most virtuous, and they are tied to their country and wedded to its liberty and interests by the most lasting bonds."[2] "Those who labour in the earth are the chosen people of God."[3] In these passages, which echo Rousseau, Jefferson was debating whether Americans should engage in manufacturing occupations; in contrasting agricultural employment with manufacturing, dependency, a characteristic of urbanization, was of crucial concern to Jefferson: "Dependence begets subservience and venality, suffocates the germ of virtue, and prepares fit tools for the designs of ambition."[4] Jefferson believed that those who worked for wages, particularly in an urban setting, would lose their self-reliance and become subservient and corrupt;

agricultural occupations, however, would build character and self-reliance and universal private ownership of property would lessen dependence even further.

For Jefferson, the right to own property was crucial for the freedom of the individual. Like Rousseau, Jefferson believed that property should be owned privately, not in the form of large estates, but distributed as widely as possible, sufficient for each individual to satisfy his own basic needs and produce a surplus which could be traded for manufactures and other necessary products. Jefferson advocated male suffrage based on a property qualification, but he also suggested that the propertyless be given land from the vast tracts available in eighteenth-century America.[5]

This scheme for dispensing land to those without property would ensure the continuation of an agrarian society;[6] a nation of small property holders would prevent dependencies caused by a wage economy, a condition which Jefferson saw and deplored in France during his years there as the United States minister. This preference for an agrarian life style was undoubtedly based on personal considerations: Jefferson's favorite pursuit was farming and throughout his political career he often expressed a desire to retire from public life and devote himself exclusively to his estate at Monticello.

While Rousseau feared private property ownership's tendency to foster inequality, Jefferson believed that inequality and dependence could be prevented by distributing property as widely as possible, creating a society of owners of small farms. Jefferson continued to idealize rural life throughout his career, but his strong preference for an agricultural economy is most apparent in his earlier writings, before he became President; after 1800 Jefferson began to entertain the possibility of Americans' engaging in manufacturing, preferably of the domestic kind, in order to prevent urban concentrations. As he became increasingly concerned with politics on the national level, nation building took precedence over devising an economic and social framework designed to promote the self-reliance of the individual; Jefferson's primary focus was always on politics rather than economics, a decisive factor in the shift in his economic thought after 1800.[7]

Consistent with his belief in a type of personal self-reliance based on individual freedom and rights, Jefferson advocated a more limited form of government than did Rousseau, one that acted only to protect natural rights and to prevent any encroachment on civil liberties:

A wise and frugal government, which shall restrain men from injuring one another, shall leave them otherwise free to regulate their own pursuits of industry and improvement and shall not take from the mouth of labor the bread it has earned.[8]

Government itself must be restrained in order that it not threaten individual freedom: "the natural progress of things is for liberty to yield, and government to gain ground."[9] Jefferson advocated the separation of powers for the purpose of ensuring liberty; he felt that, in the United States of his time, the legislative branch, being the one chosen directly by the people, was the most representative and hence the least susceptible to abuses of power.[10]

Jefferson did not support the making of permanent constitutions; like Rousseau he argued that authority should be vested in the individual who has the right to make government as he pleases:

I consider the people who constitute a society or nation as the source of all authority in that nation, as free to transact their common concerns by any agents they think proper, to change these agents individually, or the organisation of them in form or function whenever they please.[11]

Jefferson's dislike of permanent constitutions and his support for the right of revolution against unjust government structures would seem to lend further support to the importance of the individual as the source of authority:

No society can make a perpetual constitution . . . The earth belongs always to the living generation. They may manage it then, and what proceeds from it, as they please, during their usufruct. *They are masters too of their own persons* [my emphasis], and consequently may govern them as they please.[12]

In contrast to European contract theorists, who postulated a hypothetical state of nature in order to explain the rationale for civil government, Jefferson's experience with making the social contract was immediate and real in eighteenth-century America and it was further reinforced by his stay in France during the years immediately preceeding the Revolution. Even during his later years, Jefferson never lost his belief in the uniqueness of the American experiment and the superiority of the American environment. Government should function only to ensure the security needed by citizens in order to pursue their individual private enterprises: in short a policy of laissez-faire built on a predominantly agrarian economy.[13]

The social structure most favorable for the type of government advocated by Jefferson was a homogeneous population of small landowners with wealth distributed as widely as possible. Like Rousseau and List, Jefferson believed that any social system depended for its cohesiveness and stability on its cultural homogeneity; in eighteenth-century America, therefore, it is doubtful whether his concept of the ideal self-reliant farmer extended much beyond white males, preferably of Anglo-Saxon origins.[14] Jefferson's views on other racial groups, such as blacks, left them little room to function as self-reliant individuals in American society and, in Virginia's slaveholding economy, the self-reliance of some was clearly achieved through its denial to others. In spite of his ownership of slaves, however, Jefferson was a strong advocate of emancipation, although his support was rooted in the view that any society is corrupted by the existence of slavery, rather than in a desire for blacks to become part of American society. Jefferson advocated the deportation of freed slaves back to Africa, or possibly to the West Indies, since he believed that prejudice was too deeply rooted for them to become free American citizens on equal grounds with whites. Jefferson also believed that blacks were inferior to whites in reason, imagination and other characteristics of body and mind.[15]

Of American Indians, Jefferson had a higher opinion; he admired their bravery and powers of reason[16] and maintained, at least in 1791 when *Notes on Virginia* was written, that no white man should encroach on their territory without their consent. Clearly this would be quite consistent with the practice of individual and local self-reliance but, when Jefferson became President, his attitude toward Indians underwent a shift motivated by his vision of America's westward expansion. The Indians' nomadic existence, which was in itself a challenge to Jefferson's belief that individual

self-reliance required an agrarian life-style, depended primarily on
hunting for the satisfaction of basic needs and thus required a great
deal of arable land; in a Confidential Message to Congress, Jefferson noted this inefficient use of land and suggested that the Indian
should be encouraged to give up hunting and taught to pursue a
more sedentary existence, raising agricultural crops, producing domestic manufactures and ultimately participating in the benefits of
the white man's government and civilization.[17] It is evident that, in
this scheme, white Americans were to be the teachers and Indians
the learners, a plan that parallels the classic pattern of Western
colonization and one which would seem to deny self-reliance to
indigenous populations.[18]

Recently freed from colonial rule themselves, the ties of white
Americans with their European heritage was still strong in eighteenth-century America. But Jefferson continually emphasized the
differences that separated European and American peoples and
their institutions. He took pride in distinguishing Americans from
their European ancestors. Americans, he believed, were less corrupt, more ingenious and more self-reliant:

It is part of the American character to consider nothing as desper-
ate, to surmount every difficulty by resolution and contrivance. In
Europe there are shops for every want; its inhabitants, therefore,
have no idea that their wants can be supplied otherwise. Remote
from all other aid, we are obliged to invent and to execute; *to find
means within ourselves, and not to lean on others.* [my emphasis][19]

In this letter to his daughter, Jefferson went on to exhort Martha
to conquer her Livy and not to rely on her teacher, since it was a
task that no one else could do for her. For a woman in eighteenth-
century America, learning Latin was primarily an exercise in sur-
mounting difficulties rather than one that could be expected to
have many practical benefits. Jefferson believed that skills of utility
for women were those of "the needle and domestic economy," for
"in the country life of America there are as many moments when a
woman can have recourse to nothing but her needle for employment."[20] Jefferson would have been in advance of his time had he
advocated equality for women but, since women were not included
in his proposals for state donations of property and extension of

the suffrage discussed above, self-reliance of the individual in the complete sense would be limited to the white male population.[21]

In his ideal agrarian society, Jefferson advocated that each such individual be left as free as possible to manage his own property and production, with government playing a minor role limited primarily to the security function. Freedom was to be ensured by a representative republican government based on as wide a suffrage as possible, and on freedom of religion and equality of opportunity through free access to education.

Jefferson's strong commitment to religious freedom, a reaction against the privileged position of the Anglican church in eighteenth-century Virginia,[22] was an essential part of his concept of individual self-reliance. He introduced a Bill for Religious Freedom into the Virginia Assembly as early as June of 1779, although it was not passed until 1786:[23] it was as the author of this bill that Jefferson wished to be remembered at his death.[24] Consistent with these views of freedom of expression, Jefferson was a strong supporter of the insertion of a Bill of Rights into the Constitution.

For Jefferson the way in which an individual could best be prepared for his role as a self-reliant citizen was through education. Like Rousseau, Jefferson proposed that free education be available to everyone but, whereas for Rousseau education was socialization into correct thinking as a citizen, for Jefferson the emphasis was on independence and the ability to order one's own life. Universal education was desirable in order that people "would be qualified to understand their rights, to maintain them, and to exercise with intelligence their parts in self-government."[25]

In 1779 Jefferson outlined his plan for public education;[26] it included three years of free education in basic subjects for all children, both male and female, and then further education at the expense of the parents. Free education at the primary level would ensure that all citizens be literate and hence have access to information on which to order their lives, judge the errors of rulers, and guard the public liberty.[27] Jefferson did not believe that all people were endowed with equal mental or physical capacities, but he believed that talent was distributed among rich and poor alike: free primary education would serve to search out talent from among the poor, the most gifted of whom would be selected for further education at a grammar school and possibly at the university, at the expense of the state. Education was the guardian of liberty and the mechanism by which people could learn to govern themselves: "Every government degenerates when trusted to the rulers of the people alone. The people themselves therefore are its only safe depositories. And to render even them safe, their minds must be improved to a certain degree."[28]

Jefferson's plans for universal education did not assume equality of each individual's mental capabilities but rather equality of opportunity to develop them. Neither was it intended to promote uniformity and patriotism, as was the case with Rousseau's educational schemes, but rather to produce informed citizens capable of questioning and checking the actions of their rulers. There was, however, between Jefferson's self-reliant individual and a society committed to progress a certain tension which was to compromise his preferred agrarian social structure. While Jefferson idealized rural life there was a contradiction between maintaining this rural society and promoting economic growth and progress: his self-reliant individual was also a citizen of a developing nation-state committed to growth and prosperity.

Agrarian Self-Reliance Compromised: The Imperatives of National Power
Domestic Strategies for Achieving National Self-Reliance

The economic base on which Jefferson's ideal agrarian republic was founded was quite different from the self-sufficient subsistence economy, isolated from the rest of the world, that Rousseau advocated for Corsica. In his earlier years Jefferson was strongly committed to free trade and an open economy, with the United States producing an agricultural surplus which would be traded for manufactured goods primarily from Europe, an economic system which had been characteristic of the colonial era in general and colonial Virginia in particular. Jefferson believed that Americans had acquired a taste for luxury[29] through English imports in colonial times, and therefore could not be expected to be self-sufficient after independence: there was no outright condemnation of foreign luxury as a perpetrator of dependence as there was in Rousseau's work.

The more crucial distinction between Rousseau's closed economy and Jefferson's commitment to free trade, however, was that while

Jefferson preferred an agrarian economy for the cultivation of virtuous citizens and saw it as most suited to conditions in eighteenth-
century America,[30] he never envisaged that it would be static and
self-sustaining. When American export markets and foreign sources
of manufactured goods were threatened, Jefferson moved away from
his support of free trade and toward the promotion of domestic
manufactures in order that America's growth and prosperity would
not be undermined. This switch led Jefferson to compromise his
ideal agrarian society. The tension between the self-reliant individual, living in a relatively decentralized agrarian society, and
the self-reliant nation-state was eventually resolved in favor of the
latter.

The immediate cause of Jefferson's evolution toward a preference
for an economy that included the domestic production of manufactures was the protracted conflict in Europe at the turn of the nineteenth century. As his free trade strategy proved increasingly
untenable during the Napoleonic Wars, Jefferson moved to support an isolationist position for the United States based on the
principle that America should remain aloof from European quarrels and rivalries. Frequent references to the corrupting influence
of European politics echo Rousseau but, unlike Rousseau, Jefferson
was not willing to sacrifice America's growth and potential as an
independent actor in world politics.

The first hint of Jefferson's turn toward the support of domestic
manufactures came as early as 1791 when, as Secretary of State, he
was primarily occupied with the impact of European events on
American policy:

Our best interest would be to employ our principal labour in agriculture, because to the profits of labour which is dear this adds the
profits of our lands which are cheap. But the risk of our hanging
our prosperity on the fluctuating counsels and caprices of others
renders it wise in us to turn seriously to manufactures. . . . [31]

In other words the self-reliant nation must not depend on others
for its prosperity. During the 1790s Jefferson continued to advocate
domestic manufacture but only of the household kind, which could
be undertaken on the farm, thus avoiding the growth of cities which
he regarded as breeding grounds for poverty and dependence.

When Jefferson assumed the Presidency his outlook became

more nationalistic and, as disruptions of commerce and threats to American neutrality increased, the evolution toward a more mercantilist strategy became evident in his thinking. The Eighth Annual Message to Congress of 1808 called for the enlargement of public factories for the domestic production of armaments; by this time Jefferson had accepted the permanence of American manufactures of both the household and factory type. At the conclusion of his presidency in 1809, Jefferson was supporting a Listian strategy of balanced growth and simultaneous development of all sectors of the economy:[32]

I trust the good sense of our country will see that its greatest prosperity depends on a due balance between agriculture, manufactures and commerce, and not in this protuberant navigation which has kept us in hot water from the commencement of our government, and is now engaging us in war.[33]

A national development strategy, based on the development of the agricultural sector alone, had become endangered by the instabilities of the international system. Effective protection for American manufactures reached its height during this period at the time of the War of 1812; in 1813 Jefferson indicated his approval of the changes in the economic structure brought about by the war:

The continuance of the war will fix the habit [of manufacturing] generally, and out of the evils of impressment and of the orders of council, a great blessing for us will grow. I have not formerly been an advocate for great manufactories. . . . But other considerations entering into the question, have settled my doubts.[34]

Noting with approbation that the domestic manufacture of cloth had almost excluded English imports, a condition which he hoped would be permanent, Jefferson concluded in 1813 that "this revolution" in the domestic economy "was well worth a war."[35]

For Rousseau, national self-reliance was best pursued in a small static agrarian community insulated from the corrupting influences of modernity: for Jefferson and List national self-reliance included the mercantilist goal of wealth and power.[36] But even if the rural community had to be sacrificed for this goal, Jefferson never lost sight of the importance of keeping the United States isolated from Europe. America's identity depended on its separation from the corruption of European politics. Even in his earlier years, when he favored free trade, Jefferson was conscious of the necessity of distancing America from its colonial past against which the War of Independence was fought:

I sincerely join you in abjuring all political connection with every foreign power; and tho I cordially wish well to the progress of liberty in all nations . . . yet they are not to be touched without contamination from their other bad principles. Commerce with all nations, alliance with none, should be our motto.[37]

Whereas for Rousseau national identity seemed to take precedence over economic growth, for Jefferson the two went together; national identity depended on the foundation of a strong and prosperous nation-state.

While Rousseau believed that the ideal political unit should be small so that all citizens could participate directly in its governance, Jefferson's views on this subject are more complex and reflect an attempt to work out the tension between the self-reliance of the individual and the international autonomy of the nation-state.

Jefferson has generally been interpreted as an advocate of states' rights in opposition to the Federalist position of support for a stronger federal government. Jefferson was fairly consistent in his belief that states should maintain a large degree of control over their own affairs, but he always assumed that the federal government should regulate foreign affairs, one of the important reasons for his support for a stronger federal constitution in 1789:

The politics of Europe render it indispensably necessary that with respect to everything external we be one nation only, firmly hooped together. Interior government is what each state should keep to itself . . . insult and war are the consequences of a want of respectability in the national character.[38]

Jefferson's attitude toward size of government might better be characterized as a preference for various levels of government appropriate to the size of the task, an approach to which he subscribed throughout his political career. States should preserve their sovereignty in intrastate affairs but interstate concerns should be dealt with by the federal government.[39] Even so, Jefferson never envisaged the federal government playing the role that it does today and his long dispute with Hamilton illustrates his reluctance to see federal powers enhanced.[40] Nevertheless he did come to accept many of the Federalist programs after he became President, in part due to the increasing impingement of foreign affairs on domestic policy. Jefferson, as President, was committed to a vigorous foreign policy in order that the United States could overcome its dependencies and win respect abroad.

Also consistent with his levels-of-government approach, Jefferson proposed that units smaller than states should have a role in the administration of local issues such as education. Jefferson greatly admired the New England system of town meetings: "[they] are the vital principle of their governments, and have proved themselves the wisest invention ever devised by the wit of man for the perfect exercise of self-government and for its preservation."[41] Jefferson frequently extolled the virtues of ward government, as he called this smallest unit. Wards, which were smaller than counties, should be given control "in all things relating to themselves exclusively."[42]

In 1786 Jefferson proposed that the western states be kept small since people wish to have a just share in their own government. "Considering the American character in general, that of those people particularly, and the inergetic nature of our governments, a state of such extent as 160,000 square miles would soon crumble into little ones."[43] In 1800, shortly before assuming the presidency, Jefferson wrote: "our country is too large to have all its affairs directed by a single government. Public servants at such a distance, and from under the eye of their constituents, must . . . be unable to administer and overlook all the details necessary for the good government of the citizens."[44]

Thus Jefferson's political philosophy seemed predisposed in the direction of limited government, at the national level at least, and government over as small a physical space as possible. An ideal republican government would have meant direct participation by all citizens; a practical compromise was representative government, with representatives chosen directly by the people for short terms, in order to ensure expression of the popular will.[45] But Jefferson was also aware that in small geographic units, conflicts could arise: "It seems that the smaller the society the bitterer the dissensions into which it breaks."[46] Jefferson believed that the United States, in contrast to the Italian republics, for example, was saved from disintegration by its large geographic size, which countered the destructive tendency of local dissent. The necessity of a strong federal structure to counter local dissent and also local prejudices is a problem for any theory of self-reliance and one which most strikingly illustrates the tensions between the local and national levels.

But foremost among Jefferson's dilemmas about the appropriate size of government was his desire to see the United States become a strong autonomous actor in world politics. Agrarian self-reliance, with its decentralized participatory government structures, is not necessarily conducive to nation building. Even before he became President, Jefferson believed that foreign policy was a federal concern, and his desire to strengthen the federal government was motivated by his wish that the United States might project a strong image abroad. Rousseau, List and Jefferson were all concerned with national identity and national independence; for Jefferson, as for List, this was strongly linked with economic growth and national power.

International Strategies for Achieving National Self-Reliance

Jefferson was an isolationist, like Rousseau, but his free trade position led to a greater involvement in foreign affairs than Rousseau would have approved of. However, even if free trade was to be encouraged, there were to be no alliances or other entanglements with foreign powers that might compromise America's unique experiment. Jefferson's writings display a continual attempt to differentiate the United States from Europe culturally, politically and economically, and to assert its independence in all these areas. America's moral superiority is emphasized: America is pacific, Europe warlike;[47] Americans are upright while Europeans are corrupted by bad government.[48]

Jefferson was well known for his anglophobia, which he often discussed in terms that resemble themes of contemporary leaders from various newly independent states. Jefferson frequently spoke of his dislike of the continued English influence on the domestic affairs of the United States even after independence:

By all these bearings on the different branches of government, they [the English] can force it to proceed in whatever direction they dictate, and bend the interests of this country entirely to the will of another; . . . it is impossible for us to say we stand on independent ground.[49]

Rousseau was satisfied with countering foreign influence by keeping patriotism alive in the minds of citizens; for Jefferson foreign influence must be fought by means of strong political institutions and a prosperous economic base. The Declaration of Independence was a declaration of war by a people desiring to free themselves from a state of colonial dependency. It affirmed the right of a nation to govern itself, the right of peoples to choose the form by which they wished to be governed and also the right to national equality and independence.[50] The War of Independence severed the political ties with Britain while the Constitution of 1789 laid the framework for international autonomy by ensuring that the states would be unified in their foreign policy at least and thus strengthened in their dealings with foreign nations.

But even if political relationships with England had been severed in 1776, economic ties remained strong; just as with many newly independent nations of the twentieth century, the bulk of foreign trade continued to be with the former mother country in spite of English discriminatory practices, which were carried over from the colonial era. Jefferson's support of free trade, a position that is quite contrary to self-reliance strategies in general, was in part motivated by his desire to reduce economic dependence on England even before independence: it stemmed less from economic theory than from the belief that the right to trade without discrimination is a natural right of all peoples which had been taken away from the colonists by Britain's imperial trade restrictions.[51] Jefferson was aware of the colonies' dependence upon England, which was reinforced by practices such as that of shipping American raw materials to England for manufacture and reshipment back to America, and also that of denying the colonists the right to sell their products in other foreign markets.[52]

If trade is to take place on a more equal basis, it must involve a diversification of both export markets and sources of imports. Jefferson was aware of this and spent much of his time in France negotiating trade treaties with various European nations.[53] During his years as Secretary of State, Jefferson continued to advocate the diversion of trade away from England, a strategy similar to some contemporary dependency reversal strategies.[54] However, Britain's supremacy on the seas and its interference with the rights of neutral shipping during the Napoleonic Wars, as well as its long-established trade patterns with its former colony, ensured that this policy of diversification would have only limited success.

Another important reason for Jefferson's commitment to free trade was his reluctance to see the United States become a manufacturing nation. Jefferson believed that only farmers could be free and hence self-reliant; if America should become a manufacturing nation in order to ensure national economic independence and self-reliance, it would be forced to give up the moral independence of the individual.[55]

Jefferson continued to support free trade in principle throughout his first term as President, but the Napoleonic Wars made this position increasingly difficult in practice. Jefferson's imposition of the trade embargo in 1807 was, he maintained, the only alternative to war with England;[56] thereafter his commitment to free trade declined and he began to support policies that encouraged domestic manufactures. Self-reliance theory suggests that political autonomy is hard to manage when economic interdependence is high: Jefferson's difficulties with commercial policies while he was President are proof of this. The shift toward protection, during the War of 1812, is said to have marked America's effective economic independence from England and the foundation of its manufacturing capability.

Once he had been forced to abandon his free trade position, Jefferson's support of domestic manufactures evolved considerably beyond his original intention of trying to enforce sanctions against the British: "Nothing more salutary for us has ever happened than the British obstructions to our demands for their manufactures."[57] Besides the obvious benefit of breaking dependent relationships with England, Jefferson was becoming increasingly aware of the complementarity of American regions in supplying each others' needs without depending on the instabilities of the international system. This evolution toward supporting a policy of balanced growth is consistent with a more self-reliant development strategy.

While Jefferson continued to favor the promotion of agricultural

exports, he never suggested that manufactures should also be produced for export. Even after the Embargo he maintained that manufactures should be limited to the extent of domestic need: "My
idea is that we should encourage home manufactures to the extent
of our own consumption of everything of which we raise the raw
material."[58] Were the principle of comparative advantage to be applied to the United States, therefore, it would be the producer of
raw materials.[59] The economic supremacy of England, so admired
by List, which was due in large part to its leading position as supplier of finished products to much of the world, was not something
Jefferson envisaged for the United States; perhaps the contradictions between his ideal agrarian community and the imperative of a
powerful industrial nation such as England were too great.

Any new nation committed to independence and autonomy must
be concerned with issues of security. Since Rousseau's ideal state
was to be nonexpansive and play a minimal role in the affairs of
Europe, he advocated that it be defended by a small citizens' militia.
Jefferson's earlier views on defense and security were quite similar
to Rousseau's, but along with the evolution of his economic policies
toward a more nationalistic focus, and because of the impact of
events in Europe, his views on defense changed also. Early in his
political career Jefferson was strongly against a standing army: "two
favorite ideas of mine [are] of leaving commerce free, and never
keeping an unnecessary souldier."[60] As late as 1799, when European events were threatening, Jefferson still hoped that any necessary preparations for internal defense could be undertaken by a
citizens' militia.[61] His opposition to a standing army stemmed in
part from the possibility of its being used to suppress civil liberties.[62] But, by the mid 1780s, Jefferson was willing to consider the
establishment of an American naval force to retaliate against vio-
lations of its commercial rights as a neutral.[63]

Jefferson's Eighth Annual Message to Congress emphasized the
necessity for measures to increase the domestic production of arms
and called for complete control by Congress over the organization
of state militias:[64] by 1808, with tensions over foreign commerce
increasing, Jefferson's attitude toward American security was
changing. He was still committed to staying out of Europe's wars
but for reasons of America's relative weakness rather than as a
matter of principle:

If we go to war now, I fear we may renounce for ever the hope of seeing an end of our national debt. If we can keep at peace eight years longer, our income, liberated from debt, will be adequate to any war, without new taxes or loans, and our position and increasing strength put us "hors d'insulte" from any nation.[65]

When the United States was finally drawn into war with England in 1812 Jefferson, in his retirement, supported it for its beneficial effects on America's economic development even though its outcome was not politically advantageous to the United States.

Our progress in manufactures is far beyond the calculations of the most sanguine. . . . insomuch that were peace restored tomorrow we should not return to the importation from England. . . . even of the finer woolen cloths. Putting honor and right out of the question therefore, this revolution in our [domestic] economy was well worth a war.[66]

Indeed I consider the most fatal consequence of this war to England to be the transfer it has occasioned of her art in manufacturing into other countries. From this and her impending bankruptcy, future history will have to trace her decline and fall as a great power.[67]

Jefferson anticipated England's decline by a hundred years but, like List, he did perceive the link between manufactures, war and national power, and the mercantilist strain in his thinking is clearly evident in these passages. He understood that the United States was embarking on the road to national power, based on a vigorous industrial economy, and that it was stimulated by the imperative of war.

It is our business to manufacture for ourselves whatever we can, to keep our markets open for what we can spare or want; and the less we have to do with the amities or enmities of Europe, the better. Not in our day, but at no distant one, we may shake a rod over the heads of all, which may make the stoutest of them tremble.[68]

While Jefferson still advocated isolation in 1815 he raised the possibility of America's participation in world politics from a position of economic independence and political autonomy.

That the United States was to remain relatively isolated from European politics for another one hundred years was in part due to the seemingly limitless possibilities for expansion within the American hemisphere itself. Jefferson's writings indicate a strong interest in the expansion of the United States to its geographical limits and even beyond into the Caribbean and Central America. The type of agrarian society that Jefferson envisaged, which depended on as wide a distribution of private property as possible, could only be sustained through the possibility of expansion in order to meet the needs of a growing population and of economic growth and prosperity.

Jefferson realized the vital importance of the West for American commerce, revenue and territorial expansion: he was aware of the importance to Virginia of its western lands and he advocated retaining control of its navigable rivers in order to reap the benefits of western and Indian trade.[69] But Jefferson also understood that this commitment to expansion could severely compromise his support for small units of government and republican democracy: "the moment we sacrifice their [people living in the West] interests to our own, they will see it is better to govern themselves."[70]

Jefferson's attitude toward expansion demonstrates tensions between all three levels of self-reliance. While he was committed in principle to small self-reliant agrarian communities Jefferson realized that the agricultural surplus, generated by western lands and exported abroad via the Mississippi River, was vital to American national development and was the only way that it might grow and prosper without turning to manufactures:[71]

I think our governments will remain virtuous for many centuries; as long as they are chiefly agricultural; and this will be as long as there shall be vacant lands in any part of America. When they get piled upon one another in large cities, as in Europe, they will become corrupt as in Europe.[72]

Besides being a vital contribution to overseas commerce, western agriculture was also to be a part of intra-American trade, thus providing balance and complementarity between various regions of the country. Jefferson believed that balanced internal growth must be facilitated by internal improvements designed to promote internal communications and interregional trade:[73]

I experience great satisfaction at seeing my country proceed to facilitate the intercommunications of it's several parts by opening rivers, canals and roads. How much more rational is this disposal of public money, than that of waging war.[74]

Jefferson always believed, however, that internal improvements should be undertaken by the individual states[75] rather than the federal government, which probably explains why this issue was not much discussed during his years in national office.[76] Money for such improvements should come from taxes on trade because the burden of these taxes fell disproportionately on the rich who could afford imported products.[77]

During Jefferson's later years, when he was President, the imperative of the nation-state seemed to take increasing precedence over the ideal of decentralized agrarian communities:

It is impossible not to look forward to distant times, when our rapid multiplication will expand itself beyond those limits, and cover the whole northern, if not the southern continent, with a people speaking the same language, governed in similar forms, and by similar laws.[78]

The vision of the unlimited potential for American expansion was behind the launching of the Lewis and Clark expedition in 1803 at Jefferson's instigation. Clearly Jefferson's vision was of the expansion of a relatively homogeneous population of European inhabitants across America regardless of its effect on native peoples or other nation-states.[79]

During Jefferson's second term as president, western expansion was becoming increasingly intermeshed with international politics. As it encroached on the interests of European powers in America Jefferson's western policy began to sound more belligerent. If necessary the Floridas must be seized from Spain in order to punish it for boundary disputes along the Mississippi.[80] At all costs commercial rights of passage through New Orleans must be maintained, if necessary by the use of gunboats.

Shortly before his death, Jefferson raised the possibility of adding Cuba to the United States: "for, certainly her addition to our confederacy is exactly what is wanting to round our power as a nation to the point of its utmost interest."[81] One of Jefferson's final statements to James Monroe shortly preceded the Monroe Doctrine:

Our first and fundamental maxim should be, never to entangle ourselves in the broils of Europe. Our second, never to suffer Europe to intermeddle with cis-Atlantic affairs. America, *North and South* [my emphasis] has a set of interests distinct from those of Europe and peculiarly her own. She should therefore have a system of her own, separate and apart from that of Europe.[82]

The Monroe Doctrine marked the end of an era that had been dominated by America's attempt to assert its independence from Europe. It was proclaimed near the end of Jefferson's life and it was a statement that rested, in part, on his influence and his policies while in national office: it proclaimed a policy of national and regional self-reliance.

While the Monroe Doctrine has often been interpreted as a statement of regional self-reliance, there is little evidence, in Jefferson's writings or policies, of support for the type of collective and regional self-reliance defined in chapter 1. His preference for regional separation from the affairs of Europe was motivated by the desire to create a region in which the United States was to assume the role of dominant power rather than cooperative partner.

If Jefferson was determined to push back European claims in North America, in order to allow for the expansion of the United States, he did not view the liberation of South America in quite the same light. He recommended friendship with Latin America, but not to the extent of joining its wars of independence, for Jefferson feared that a free Latin America would threaten the United States with commercial rivalry. An independent Latin America, composed of many small nations, was preferable since one large state might become too powerful a force in the American hemisphere.[83]

We must conclude, therefore, that Jefferson would not have deemed collective self-reliance in the best interests of the United States in its bid to become a regional power, a goal which Jefferson, as President, wholeheartedly supported.

Conclusion

This analysis of Jefferson's writings, in terms of the multilevel definition of self-reliance developed in chapter 1, raises a number of contradictions that offer some important insights into the tensions with which any multilevel theory of self-reliance must contend.

Jefferson's ideal self-reliant individual, like Rousseau's, was a rural landowner producing for his own basic needs, free from the dependencies associated with wage-earning occupations and educated to participate effectively in his own governance; but the type of social and economic structure in which he functioned was not truly self-reliant. The economy of early Virginia, the prototype of Jefferson's ideal society, involved the exchange of agricultural goods for manufactures, and was thus part of a worldwide division of labor, a connection that Jefferson was unwilling to relinquish due to his commitment to economic growth and prosperity. In any such system the self-reliant individual can become vulnerable to the international economy while at the same time being self-reliant at the expense of the self-reliance of others, in this case the Europeans who worked for wages in urban manufacturing industries.[84] Moreover, both Jefferson's self-reliant citizen and the Virginian economy depended on a system of slavery: his dilemma over this issue and his conclusion that slaves, even if freed, could never become a part of American society is further evidence that, for Jefferson, the self-reliance of some depended on the denial of self-reliance to others.

This denial of self-reliance to certain ethnic groups, along with his desire to limit immigration in order to prevent corrupting principles from contaminating the American experiment, suggest that Jefferson, like Rousseau, preferred cultural homogeneity for the practice of local self-reliance. But, in a nation as large as the United States, the problem that confronted Jeffersonian democracy was that of building larger political structures to protect the rights of others and ensure that their self-reliance was not denied while, at the same time, maintaining the degree of decentralization necessary for the individual to retain his sense of efficacy and control over his own destiny.

Jefferson's support for a political system that included federal control over foreign policy as well as ward management of local issues was an attempt to construct a multilevel framework for government in order to solve this dilemma. This multilevel framework, together with a social and economic system based on an expanding frontier and a population of owners of small farms would seem like a possible resolution of the contradictions between local and national self-reliance.

But when this type of social and economic system, which was preferred by Jefferson in his earlier years, became vulnerable to threats from the international system and issues of national integration became more pressing, the tendency was to move toward strengthening national institutions at the expense of the individual. Jefferson's evolution toward a policy of supporting domestic manufactures and balanced growth, a strategy that had some similarity to the Listian model, increased the division of labor within the American economy and hence compromised his ideal self-reliant individual. Jefferson's support for strengthening federal political structures often arose in the context of issues relating to international politics, and such policies were usually preferred when autonomy vis-à-vis the international system was threatened.

When the autonomy of the nation-state is in jeopardy, national strategies for dependency reversal may further compromise structures that encourage local self-reliance and policies that allow for the self-reliance of other nations. Such strategies tend to become mercantilist and Jefferson's writings show evidence of mercantilist themes such as economic nationalism, the association of war with growth, the domestic production of armaments and the idea that America's prosperity might have to be gained at the expense of others. Mercantilist strategies raise the issue of whether national economic growth is reconcilable with the self-reliance of the individual. In Jefferson's America, growth was critically dependent on lateral expansion; Rousseau's solution, a static economy which he felt was least likely to compromise the self-reliance of the individual or other states, was not acceptable to Jefferson, who was strongly committed to America's potential for power and prosperity.

The tension evident in Jefferson's writings between the desire for an egalitarian participatory democracy and the desire to build a strong nation-state capable of autonomy with respect to the international system is a universal phenomenon evident in the aspirations of both statesmen and citizens living within the framework of the modern nation-state. Jefferson's evolution toward increased support for Federalist policies was evidence of the intractability of this problem: the development path taken by the United States, to which I shall turn next, demonstrated the priority of nation-building over the ideals of Jeffersonian democracy, a priority which even Jefferson himself was forced to acknowledge in practice.

CHAPTER FIVE

THE VICTORY OF NATIONAL AUTONOMY OVER LOCAL SELF-RELIANCE IN THE EARLY UNITED STATES

HAVING EXAMINED self-reliance themes in the works of Thomas Jefferson, I shall now turn to the political and economic development of the United States from 1776 to 1829, the period during which Jefferson was writing, and examine it in terms of self-reliance. While the United States never practiced self-reliance development in the complete sense, there is strong evidence of its concern with the problems, which are faced by many newly independent nations, of association with the international system; moreover, the tensions between individual and national self-reliance are strongly evident in the constitutional debates during the period of the Confederation, debates which were later reproduced in the disputes between Jeffersonian republicanism and Hamiltonian federalism.

The international context in which the United States found itself in 1776 resembled in many ways that of contemporary Third World nations. Making policy for a relatively weak new nation, facing an international system dominated by superior political and economic forces, American political leaders understood the dangers that openness with respect to the world system might bring:

The United States are, to a certain extent, in the situation of a country excluded from foreign commerce. They can, indeed, without difficulty, obtain from abroad the manufactured supplies of which they are in want; but they experience numerous and very injurious impediments to the emission and vent of their own commodities. . . .

In such a position of things, the United States cannot exchange with Europe on equal terms; and the want of reciprocity would render them the victim of a system which should induce them to confine their views to agriculture, and refrain from manufactures. A constant and increasing necessity, on their part, for the commodities of Europe, and only a partial and occasional demand for their own, in return, could not but expose them to a state of impoverishment.[1]

The concerns expressed here by Alexander Hamilton were shared by most of the leading statesmen of his time; evidence suggests that they were well aware of the constraints that the international system could impose on nation building and economic development. This chapter will highlight concerns of policymakers regarding the issue of self-reliance and will attempt to see whether and to what extent these concerns were acted upon, and if not, why not. It is hoped that such an analysis will also contribute to the questioning of some implicit assumptions about Western development which tend to underlie Western prescriptions for contemporary development strategies.

While the United States did not pursue a self-reliance development strategy in the sense in which self-reliance is usually defined today, the need for policies designed to manage association with the international system was accepted by most policymakers of varying political perspectives. Moreover, attempts were made to implement such policies within the constraints of a written constitution based on the liberal principle of individual property rights in an era before widespread management of the economy was accepted.

Self-reliance as an issue in early American development will be discussed using the multilevel definition developed in chapter 1. By searching for self-reliance themes and policies at the individual, and local, national, and regional levels, I shall show that, in the case of the United States, there were strong contradictions inherent in pursuing self-reliance at all three levels at once, contradictions which are also evident in contemporary self-reliance development strategies. Jeffersonian agrarian democracy, which was the basis of Republican philosophy if not always of Republican practice well into the nineteenth century, evidences strong parallels with some contemporary local self-reliance strategies, but it was a philosophy that contradicted Federalist desires to build a strong centralized nation-state. The latter goal, which eventually won out among Republicans and Federalists alike, is closer to a nationalist development strategy than to either decentralized participatory democracy at the local level or collective self-reliance at the regional level.

There is strong evidence, in the American case, that government intervention to promote economic growth was more widespread than has often been assumed and that it was undertaken with the clearly stated objective of building a strong, self-sufficient, balanced national economy.[2] However, it was by no means assured in 1776 that this goal was either possible or desired by a majority of the population: the United States was a collection of thirteen weak, almost sovereign states with no assurance of political integration or of the legitimacy of any kind of federal government.[3] As a colony, its economic development had been determined by its position as a supplier of raw materials and market for manufactured goods within the British Empire, a situation which parallels the colonial experience of many contemporary Third World nations. This economic arrangement was particularly advantageous to a small class of merchants and planters on the Eastern Seaboard whose economic interests and cultural identity were closely tied with those of the mother country but did not necessarily coincide with the interests of the growing agricultural subsistence population in the West.[4] Later these tensions would be reenacted in the political rivalry between Federalists and Republicans, although the desire to minimize dependency with respect to the international system was one goal that pushed toward a consensus on policy issues after Jefferson became President in 1800.

Analogies with the contemporary Third World must not be overdrawn however: clearly the United States in the late eighteenth century, with an abundant resource base and a scarcity of labor, was in a vastly different position from most contemporary developing countries. The majority of the population had strong ties to the former mother country, which eliminated the cultural confrontation evident in ex-colonial nations of the contemporary world. Moreover, the United States was relatively isolated from the rest of the world after 1815, although it was able to absorb a great deal of foreign capital, particularly after 1840.

It is also important to remember that, by contemporary standards, economic growth was quite slow. While data are scarce for this period, no reliable estimates put annual growth per capita above 1.5 percent before 1840.[5] As mentioned above, while government intervention may have been more widespread than previously thought, neither its scope nor its involvement in promoting rapid growth rates approached the levels expected of governments today.

With these reservations about the contextual uniqueness of early American development possibilities strongly in mind, I shall attempt to reanalyze some of the major issues in the political and economic development of the early United States in terms relevant to self-reliance in its contemporary context. Some concluding remarks will draw together this analysis and discuss the tensions between the various levels.

The Erosion of Local Self-Reliance in Early America

Political, economic and social conditions at the time of American independence were strongly predisposed toward both the ethic and practice of local self-reliance defined in terms of political decentralization, citizen participation and the meeting of basic needs locally through a decentralized system of production. Distrust of a distant government's intrusion into people's lives, expressed through a strong commitment to liberty and individual rights, and an aversion to political centralization were important values in eighteenth-century America and have remained as such to the present in spite of an ever-increasing divergence between these ideals and the reality of American political development.[6]

The British heritage of the first settlers brought with it a strong tradition of local government which was reinforced by Britain's laissez-faire attitude toward colonial government, at least until 1763 when its costly imperial wars compelled Britain to extract a greater surplus from its colonies through a more vigorous policy of taxation. By 1776 two quite different forms of local government, the New England township and the county government of Virginia, were firmly established, differences between the two can be accounted for by geography and by the different types of landholding patterns most appropriate for subsistence farming in New England and for plantation agriculture in the South.[7] The Puritan religious tradition, which had grown out of religious persecution, reinforced the spirit of individual self-reliance and the principles of local self-government. New England towns were closely knit communities in which religious and political participation were mutually reinforcing; geography impeded linkages with other areas of settlement.

Writing in 1838 about the United States, Alexis de Tocqueville was impressed by the strength of what he termed the principle of sovereignty of the people which, he maintained, derived from this earlier colonial tradition of local self-government. His explanation for this uniquely American phenomenon was that, before independence, popular sovereignty was not applicable at the national level and was therefore preserved in townships that had become close to independent nations.[8] De Tocqueville felt that the tension between centralization and local democracy, which continued well into the nineteenth century, and its attempted resolution through a federal system of government could not have been tolerated in Europe. Such a system, which he thought might be more beneficial for individuals, could only be maintained in a state where geographical isolation from international politics decreased the need for a strong central government.[9]

De Tocqueville also noted the high level of political participation in early America relative to eighteenth-century Europe: Americans were involved in the destiny of their nation.[10] Since land tenure was widely distributed and suffrage was generally based on a fairly low property qualification, the franchise was considerably broader than in Europe. At independence, land in some states was promised to those who enlisted in the Continental Army or was given outright to army veterans. Subsequent federal and state government policies of selling land cheaply for revenue-raising purposes ensured a continued extension of the suffrage into the nineteenth century. While the disestablishment of the Anglican church did cause controversy in some southern states, religious toleration was written into most state constitutions without question, thus removing a barrier to political participation which existed in Europe. The late eighteenth century saw the rise of a large number of democratic republican societies which provided an institutional base for political education and political participation.[11] Education in early America was relatively widespread; by 1830 the proportion of the population enrolled in school was second only to that of Germany and would probably have ranked first had slaves been excluded from the population count.[12]

The economic conditions that prevailed in the United States at the time of independence, and remained basically unchanged well into the nineteenth century predisposed the country toward the necessity of meeting basic needs locally. In 1763 nine-tenths of the population were farmers who lived in settlements of 2,500 or less;[13] by 1790 only 3.3 percent of the population lived in cities of 8,000 inhabitants or more.[14] There was an abundance of fertile virgin land which was rapidly being placed in the hands of small landowners due to state and federal policies of raising revenue through land sales. Communications were poor, transportation often being limited to river routes on the western boundaries of settlements, thus necessitating the practice of subsistence farming supplemented by home manufacture of other necessary products such as tools and clothing. Interstate transportation around the time of independence was often conducted by sea, reflecting the early development of ocean transportation routes tied to the mother country.

The self-reliance ethic of the American frontier has been widely documented.[15] Abundant land and a scarcity of labor created a situation where labor was relatively expensive, thus making Americans a "do-it-yourself" people.[16] As long as land was fertile and abundant, demands made on government for aid in raising productivity were minimal; thus early American agrarian self-reliance was founded on individual initiative and self-help which, together with widespread ownership of land, produced political philosophies emphasizing liberty rather than a demand for government intervention. The American Revolution was an expression of this political tradition and the Articles of Confederation, by which America was governed during the first twelve years of independence, were a reaction against increased governmental intrusion during the last decade of British rule. The powers given to the Confederation under the Articles were so limited that the federal government became nothing more than a coordinating body between almost sovereign states that managed their own monetary supplies and taxation and commercial policies.

Antifederalism, the doctrine of those who preferred a weak central government, was strong in 1776. Labeled Antifederalists by their opponents, this group was not opposed to the Confederation: they were, however, extreme decentralists who represented the local or individualist ethic of eighteenth-century America. Support for this position came primarily from owners of small farms, many of whom lived at or near subsistence level and who wanted democratic control of government: they were often debtors who opposed any increase in government taxation. Antifederalism was particularly strong in the less affluent, usually western portions of various states: its followers advocated widespread political participation through reduced property qualifications for voting, annual elections, the location of political power in popular legislatures and a reduction of executive authority.[17]

The issues that provoked the most debate during the years of the Confederation were primarily political questions pertaining to the tension between centralization and local self-reliance. While there was general agreement about the need to fund the national debt, supporters of the congressional power to tax directly, rather than through requisitioning state governments, were seen by Antifederalists as a threat to state sovereignty: the possibility of creating a federal army was also opposed by Antifederalists for similar reasons. Antifederalists maintained that only in small states could liberty be preserved and representatives be responsible to the people: efforts to strengthen the central government were perceived as an attempt to solidify upper class rule by removing government further from the people.

When ratification of the Constitution came in 1788 it was supported by barely half the population but, since it was the more affluent and influential who generally supported ratification, they were able to mobilize enough resources to ensure its passage.[18] While this struggle was in part a continuation of a long history of social conflict which extended back into colonial times, it is particularly significant that almost all segments of the population that were dependent on commercial activities, even less affluent urban workers, were in favor of ratification. The division was largely between those who were integrated into the market and those who lived at subsistence level, an alignment that foreshadowed the support for increased centralization by those interests that would rely on a strong nation-state to protect both domestic and international markets against a penetrative international system.

After ratification the small property owning farmers, who had been the main supporters of antifederalism, together with southern plantation owners, whose economic interests were already beginning to diverge from Federalist policies, formed the core of the early Republican party. A commitment to participatory decentralization, minimal government, the preservation of individual liberty rights and an agrarian life style, which characterized the political philosophy of this group, continued the tradition of antifederalism. The subsequent struggle of this type of republicanism with Federalist principles is an example of the tension between this version of self-reliance, with its antigovernment ideology, and the imperative of building a strong self-reliant nation-state.

One of the basic statements of this early American version of individual self-reliance was the Declaration of Independence itself, written by Thomas Jefferson. The Declaration specified that all men were created equal and endowed with certain rights; thus there could be no single ultimate authority, apart from the institutions that expressed the authority of all citizens on which Americans could rely for just decisions. Jeffersonians maintained that, whereas all men were basically equal, they were highly differentiated from other species by a superiority which enabled them to overcome their natural boundaries and to become a nation of pioneers in both the scientific and territorial sense. This strong belief in the potential of individuals to shape and improve their environment was grounded in the specific context of early America, where citizens believed that they were building a new and better world highly differentiated from the old world of Europe.[19] This sense of uniqueness, combined with an emphasis on the individual and his rights, formed the basis of American nationalism in the eighteenth century.[20] Private property was crucial for the practice of this philosophy, for it allowed the pursuit of an agrarian life-style free from dependence and formed the basis for the American conception of liberty.

The political philosophy of the early Republicans was one of minimal government whose purpose was to be limited to the protection of property and private economic transactions; while government intervention to promote economic development should be kept to a minimum, support for the Constitution was based on the need to build institutions to protect liberty, defined in part as the right to own property, from disorder.[21] Natural rights theory, on which this philosophy was based, was more concerned with setting strict limits on the functions of government than with specifying the duties of citizens or the moral ends of the state. According to Thomas Paine, government was a necessary evil, a construct that arose because of the inability of moral virtue to govern the world;[22] its goal was the freedom and security of the individual.

As mentioned earlier, in 1789, the strongest reaction against a weak decentralized political system came from those segments of the population which were integrated into the market. Their support for a stronger federal government was reinforced by the economic depression of the 1780s, which was caused in part by America's vulnerable position as a new and powerless nation in the international economy. An inundation of foreign imports together with a loss of foreign markets within the British imperial system contributed to a severe shortage of specie.[23] While economic necessity broadened the basis of support for a stronger federal government, a commitment to agrarian democratic decentralization remained as the basic philosophy of the Republican party into the nineteenth century.

In practice, Jeffersonian republicanism prior to 1800 took the form of opposition to the Federalist program, which was conceived in large part by Alexander Hamilton and implemented during the administrations of George Washington and John Adams. While Republicans reluctantly went along with Hamilton's proposal that the federal government assume the debts of the states in 1790, in exchange for moving the federal capital to Washington, Jefferson later maintained that it was the worst error of his political career.[24] The rift widened over the creation of the Bank of the United States which was chartered in spite of Jefferson's opposition. Expressing some of the same concerns as the earlier Antifederalists, Republicans saw both these measures as favoring commercial and business interests over those of agriculture and also believed that they exceeded the powers given to the federal government under the Constitution. The third prong of Hamilton's program, the Report on Manufactures, which proposed raising tariffs on many manufactured imports in order to foster domestic industrial growth, was also strongly opposed by Republicans who, initially at least, were strongly committed to free trade in the belief that only by importing necessary manufactures could America remain rural and agrarian.

The Republican electoral victory in 1800 signified a reaction against the centralizing policies of the Federalists. The Alien and Sedition Acts of 1789, which divided Republicans and Federalists on the issue of liberty, raised a storm of protest, particularly in the South, and led to the drafting of the famous Kentucky Resolutions which, until the Civil War, formulated the basic arguments behind states' rights theory and the doctrine of nullification.[25] But with the Republican victory came a gradual shift in Republican philosophy which led to the incorporation of most of the Federalist programs already enacted into Republican practice and to an increased attention, on the part of subsequent Republican presidents, to the necessity of building a strong national economy.

Antifederalism prior to 1789 and the Republican opposition to Federalist programs prior to 1800 manifested many of the previously mentioned tensions that can exist between local self-reliance and the imperatives of building a self-reliant nation-state. That Jefferson, and subsequently Madison, Monroe and John Quincy Adams, once in office, accepted most of these Federalist programs suggests that these tensions were eventually resolved in favor of national autonomy.[26] Nevertheless, early Republican theory and practice evidence both strong parallels and important differences with contemporary strategies of local self-reliance. The meeting of basic needs locally by means of a decentralized agrarian economy supplemented by domestic manufactures, a strategy that minimizes the division of labor and slows the development of an interdependent economy (both of which can create dependencies) has some similarity to the Gandhian tradition, which will be discussed in chapter 6. However, the strong individualist streak in Republican thought is quite at odds with Gandhism and other contemporary local self-reliance strategies which, in quite different economic contexts, often emphasize collectivization.[27] Nor is a minimal definition of federal government powers consistent with contemporary Third World strategies, although the desire to scale down government intervention is often strong in rhetoric supporting self-reliance in the First World today.

There were, however, certain important flaws in the Republican theory of local self-reliance that might contribute to an explanation for the Republicans' later defection to Federalist policies. First, free trade, an important aspect of early republicanism, was generally not consistent with a local basic needs strategy since it encouraged concentration on single cash crops for export rather than diversification for domestic consumption: it also proved unrealistic in the context of the trade rivalries of the major protagonists in the Napoleonic Wars. Second, the practice of agrarian self-reliance depended on a large class of property-owning farmers who demanded an ever-growing supply of fertile land and thus led Republicans to support the continued expansion of United States territory, a policy that worked against local self-reliance since it necessitated the augmentation of national power. The increasingly nationalist focus of Republican presidents after 1800 can partially be explained by the need to prevent the political disintegration of newly acquired lands and to promote political centralization in order to manage those conflicts with European powers toward which expansion inevitably led. The Louisiana Purchase of 1803, which required a broad interpretation of federal powers, was quite out of the tradition of Jeffersonian political thought but was strongly supported by Republicans in office.

Although Jefferson himself returned to his early views on states' rights once he had left national office, the trend away from local self-reliance had begun by the early 1800s. The Jeffersonian tradition stayed alive throughout this period, however, particularly in the South. Southern support for free trade during the tariff debates of 1827 reactivated the issue of states' rights in the form of the nullification controversy, which echoed the earlier Kentucky Resolutions. The leading figure in this controversy, John Calhoun, appealed to the Jeffersonian position on states' rights but Calhoun's political philosophy broke with that of his predecessors in denying the equality of man and the doctrine of natural rights.[28] Calhoun regarded himself as a Jeffersonian,[29] but Jeffersonian democracy had been turned upside down in order to protect the sectional interests of the South which, although it continued to prosper until the Civil War, was already to some extent outside the mainstream of American political thought and the national political economy.

The erosion of local self-reliance in the United States progressed

as markets widened and the states' economies became more interdependent due to an improvement in internal transportation and
communications. The political theory and practice of early republicanism, which had been a justification for the political economy of local self-reliance, was highly specific to its context and
became anachronistic as soon as a national economy began to take
shape. Republicanism adapted to circumstances and gave its support to an expansionist state and Federalist policies designed to
enhance political and economic integration, as the logic of state
building took precedence over localism soon after the first decade
of America's independence.

Building National Autonomy in the Early United States

The Theoretical Basis for a National Political Economy

The growth of a national economy during the first years of independence was severely inhibited by the fact that the American states
were practically independent of one another both politically and
economically. The tradition of decentralization and states' rights
was a potent political force, and participation in the British mercantilist system had steered commercial activities toward overseas
transactions with the mother country rather than toward the development of a domestic economy. In spite of this lack of political and
economic integration, Federalists were making a strong case for
building a national economy capable of ensuring the autonomy of
the United States with respect to the international system.

The Federalist position was not inconsistent with the prevailing
economic doctrine of the time. British liberalism, upon which
American political thought was founded, had existed alongside the
mercantilist tradition of economic development, in which economic policies were specifically designed to promote the interests
of the state, and which was still an important force in eighteenth-
century Europe.[30] Laissez-faire individualism in *economic* affairs
was a doctrine of the nineteenth rather than the eighteenth century. Mercantilism, which preceded it, was a more interventionist
state philosophy committed to the principle that government

should be responsible for the welfare of citizens but, more importantly, for the welfare of the nation.

Mercantilism has often been described as a strategy for backward or "catch-up" states seeking to achieve wealth and welfare in a potentially hostile international environment dominated by more powerful nations.[31] In modern terms it is analogous to a strategy of dependency reversal which seeks to balance the development of agriculture and industry in order to achieve an integrated national economy that can assure self-sufficiency, particularly in necessities such as food. Mercantilism also favored the promotion of exports to ensure a favorable balance of trade which, it was believed, would promote the national welfare. Most Americans of the late eighteenth century had been raised in the mercantilist tradition and it was not until the 1830s that this ideology died out in the United States.[32]

In theory at least, it seems that most American policymakers of this period supported this notion of government responsibility for the general economic welfare. That the state was not more involved was probably due to the constraints of a written Constitution, with its Lockean philosophical underpinnings, and to the frontier tradition and the relatively abundant resource base on which the American economy developed. It does seem, however, that government intervention in economic development was more widespread in early America than has frequently been supposed but that it often took place at the state rather than the national level.[33]

An analysis of statements made by leading American policymakers in national office during this period suggests that they were well aware of the perils of a weak, newly independent nation in an international system dominated by more powerful states and that they attempted to take measures to avoid dependency within the constraints of their interpretation of the Constitution. If we examine this mercantilist ideology of economic development, which existed alongside the individualist natural rights theory embodied in documents such as the Declaration of Independence, we can trace a continuous overriding concern among leading national statesmen with building a balanced national economy, a prerequisite for any self-reliant nation-state. This goal is strongly evident in

Federalist policies which won out over the more decentralized strategies of early republicanism.

It is evident from the statements of postrevolutionary American
leaders, such as Hamilton, Madison and Washington, that they
were crucially aware of the vulnerability of the United States in
1789, which was caused largely by its dependence on England, and
that they realized that this dependency threatened its existence as
a sovereign state. The immediate need, in 1789, for a stronger
federal government arose out of an economic depression caused in
part by America's international economic relations, but the deeper
rationale was the necessity of creating a national economy capable
of achieving balanced economic growth and thus assuring autonomy vis-à-vis the international system:[34]

> But whatever may be our situation, whether firmly united under
> one national government, or split into a number of confederacies,
> certain it is, that foreign nations will know and view it exactly
> as it is; . . . If they see that our national government is efficient and
> well administered, our trade prudently regulated, our militia
> properly organized and disciplined, our resources and finances
> discreetly managed, our credit re-established, our people free, con-
> tented and united, they will be much more disposed to cultivate our
> friendship.[35]

The Federalist Papers, of which the first appeared in 1787, argued consistently for the enlargement of federal powers in order
that the United States might win respect abroad. The principal
authors, Hamilton and Madison, probably favored increasing
federal powers beyond those stipulated by the Constitution but in
The Federalist they defended compromise, there being no hope of
getting a stronger constitution. Hamilton's contributions to the
Federalist Papers pointed to the dangers of weak confederacies,
frequently illustrated by the case of the Greek city-states which fell
prey to internal disintegration and humiliation from abroad.[36]

During the tariff debates in the First Congress of 1789 Madison
called for the creation of a balanced national economy with town
and country complementing each other through the promotion of
internal commerce and interdependence. While Madison favored
free trade in principle, he noted that this principle frequently
broke down in practice when nations discriminate: the United

States, therefore, should be prepared to retaliate through its own commercial restrictions in order to promote its national interest and security:

I am a friend to free commerce, and at the same time a friend to such regulations as are calculated to promote our own interest, and this on national principles.[37]

Madison noted also that British independence and power stemmed from its flourishing manufactures and commerce which had been built up under its mercantilist system of special privileges. When two countries enter into a commercial relationship where one discourages the manufactures of the other, as was the case of the early United States and England, the benefits are not mutual but one-sided: "Our own experience has taught us that, in certain cases it [free trade] is the same thing with allowing one nation to regulate it for another."[38]

Some of the strongest statements in favor of national self-reliance came from George Washington. Washington supported the development of domestic manufactures; having developed an aversion to European products earlier in his life, he pledged in 1787 to wear nothing but American garments. Cloth, shoes and milled flour were produced on his estate at Mount Vernon.[39]

In his first annual address to Congress Washington sounded a mercantilist theme:

A free people ought not to be armed, but disciplined; to which end a uniform and well-digested plan is requisite; and their safety and interest require that they should promote such manufactories as tend to render them independent of others for essential, particularly military, supplies.[40]

Washington went on to outline a plan for a balanced national economy through the simultaneous promotion of agriculture, commerce, and manufactures, the encouragement of inventions from abroad in order to stimulate domestic productivity and the promotion of internal trade through improvements in communication and transportation.[41]

The most complete exposition of Washington's strategy for balanced national economic growth can be found in his Farewell Address, which evokes striking parallels with today's Third World national self-reliance strategies. Washington warned of the dangers of "an attachment of a small or weak, towards a great and powerful nation, [which] dooms the former to be a satellite of the latter."[42] Besides its fame as the first document of American isolationism,[43] the Farewell Address also urged the development of an integrated national economy with the North supplying manufactures which would be exchanged for raw materials from the South and food from the West. Washington noted that the West and South would benefit equally from the creation of an internal market for their primary products and an internal source for their manufactures, thus making these regions less vulnerable to the international system.[44] Washington warned repeatedly of the dangers of sectionalism and party division, the chief threat of such strife being that it would impede the building of a national economy capable of withstanding foreign influence.[45]

These themes, evident in the pronouncements of the Founding Fathers, predate the actual establishment of a national economy in the United States and were therefore quite revolutionary in their orientation:[46] the implementation of such policies had its beginnings in the Federalist program of the 1790s associated with the political career of Alexander Hamilton, first Secretary of the Treasury. Hamilton's vision of the United States as an industrial power was years ahead of its time and his program for its achievement was equally farsighted in the context of eighteenth-century America. Hamilton's goal for the United States was the achievement of national power comparable to that of England; like List, his strong admiration for England was based on its hegemonic position in the international system.[47]

In contrast to Jeffersonian philosophy, Hamilton maintained that, where there was tension between individual self-interest and the interest of the state, the state would take precedence. Since he believed that men were basically selfish and driven by their passions, the test of a viable government would be to harness these passions and enlist them in the service of the common ends of society.[48] As the general welfare of the state took precedence over the individual, the state would become an organic whole striving for unity and power. Hamilton was no democrat; he believed that those with superior talents should be in positions of authority to prevent the erosion of state power.

Contrary to prevalent thinking in eighteenth-century America, Hamilton maintained that loyalty to the nation should transcend attachment to the individual states:

There is something noble and magnificent in the perspective of a great Federal Republic, closely linked in the pursuit of a common interest, tranquil and prosperous at home, respectable abroad; but there is something proportionately diminutive and contemptible in the prospect of a number of petty states, with the appearance only of union, jarring, jealous and perverse, without any determined direction, fluctuating and unhappy at home, weak and insignificant by their dissensions in the eyes of other nations.[49]

While the kind of centralized government that Hamilton envisaged before independence did not come into being under the federal Constitution, most of the program that he presented as Secretary of the Treasury was successfully implemented and was a significant step toward the creation of a national economy and the development of the kind of national integration that he sought for the United States. Hamilton's Report on Public Credit, which was adopted during Washington's first administration, was based on the assumption that, in order to enhance national power, financial interests must be attached to the national government which itself needed credit for industrial development and commercial activity. To this end Hamilton proposed that the federal government fund the domestic and foreign debt using taxes and import duties to finance interest payments. The Report also recommended that the war debts incurred by the states be assumed by the federal government, again to bind creditors to the national interest.

The other prong of Hamilton's fiscal program, the Bank of the United States, was chartered in 1791 and a national currency was established by the Mint Act of 1792. These latter measures passed over strenuous opposition by Republicans, who felt that they exceeded the constitutional powers of the federal government and that, echoing the earlier fears of Antifederalists, they would promote the interests of an elite commercial class centered in the Northeast.

The third aspect of Hamilton's plan for building a strong, balanced national economy was contained in his Report on Manufactures, although this was not implemented during his lifetime. The Report contains parallels with contemporary strategies of national self-reliance and also with eighteenth-century mercantilist thought. The rationale for promoting American manufactures was "to render the United States independent on foreign nations for military and other essential supplies."[50] States should produce from their own soils "the articles of prime necessity requisite to their own consumption and use, and which serves to render their demand for a foreign supply of such articles, in a great degree, occasional and contingent."[51] Thus the basic needs argument was linked with the issue of national security.

In contrast to the Republicans, Hamilton believed that manufacturing gave greater scope for a diversity of talents and a greater stimulus to the human mind than did agrarian pursuits. Like List and dependency writers of today, Hamilton noted that agricultural nations were placed at a great disadvantage in international trade since foreign demand for agricultural products was generally "rather casual and occasional."[52] Through the establishment of a manufacturing sector, however, agriculture would have a more reliable domestic market for its products: "If Europe will not take from us the products of our soil, upon terms consistent with our interest, the natural remedy is to contract, as far as possible, our wants of her."[53] Hamilton noted also that the international demand for manufactures was more consistent and that single commodity exporters were particularly vulnerable in international trade.[54]

Having argued for the necessity of building a balanced economy, Hamilton assumed that this would not take place without the intervention of government, which must intercede with the provision of bounties, protective tariffs and other financial aids to infant industries. The government should also encourage immigration, the employment of women and children and the introduction of machines in order to alleviate the labor shortage.[55]

Hamilton's Report on Manufactures is quite consistent with many of the pronouncements of other national leaders of this era, particularly those of President Washington; it is also one of the most detailed expositions of a national strategy for self-reliance. While it was not immediately acted upon, its arguments were reconstructed during the tariff debates of 1816 and used by supporters of the

American System as a basis for protectionist thought throughout the 1820s.

While Jefferson's accession to the presidency in 1800 marked the end of the Federalist era, Republican commitment to an agrarian, decentralized economy was gradually eroding, and most of Hamilton's policies were continued under Jefferson's and subsequent Republican administrations. The views of Albert Gallatin, Jefferson's Secretary of the Treasury, who had represented the agrarian West's strong opposition to Federalist policies during the Adams administration, evolved to a position that was not much different from that of Hamilton.[56] While the Jefferson administration was pledged to a reduction of the national debt and internal taxes, by 1805 the federal budget was back to Federalist levels. Like Hamilton, Gallatin supported commercial capitalism, the growth of manufactures and the right of federal government to promote balanced national development; he often argued in favor of a broad interpretation of implied powers under the Constitution as had the Federalists.

Gallatin was a strong supporter of internal improvements although he felt that, on this particular issue, government involvement in such projects would require a constitutional amendment:

No other single operation, [building of roads and canals] within the power of Government, can more effectually tend to strengthen and perpetuate that Union which secures external independence, domestic peace, and internal liberty.[57]

Gallatin's Report on Manufactures of 1810 contained many of the same ideas as Hamilton's;[58] industrialization would increase domestic markets for farmers and thus reduce their dependence on foreign trade. Gallatin proposed a government loan of $20,000,000 to assist manufactures because he regarded the lack of investment capital as the most serious obstacle to their development.

In contrast to Jefferson, Gallatin strongly supported the renewal of the charter of the Bank of the United States which was to expire in 1811. But, by 1809, three quarters of the capital of the Bank was held by foreigners, a fact which strongly argued against renewal and highlighted issues of dependency. Gallatin proposed making the Bank more truly national by issuing new shares only to American citizens and state governments, a policy that would also promote the Bank as a bond of national unity in the Hamiltonian tradition. While the recharter effort failed in 1811, it passed in 1816 during another Republican administration.

By the end of Jefferson's presidency in 1809 the mercantilist principles of the demised Federalists had been thoroughly incorporated into the Republican party. In spite of a decrease in the importance of international relations to the domestic economy after the conclusion of the Napoleonic Wars in 1815, the commitment to a policy of balanced national growth continued to be promoted by subsequent Republican presidents.

After the Second Bank of the United States received its charter in 1816, much of the national debate centered on the tariff issue and the extent to which the federal government should become involved in internal improvements. Most policy leaders were committed to internal improvements as a means of promoting national growth, but the degree of government intervention centered on the issue of constitutionality. In 1822 President Monroe argued strongly that Congress must have the right to build roads since roads were indispensable to the conduct of war;[59] he argued also for the "incalculable benefits" of creating a communications infrastructure between all parts of a varied economy which could thus complement each other through internal trade. Monroe believed, however, that the federal government could only undertake internal improvements with a constitutional amendment, but this was denied him by lack of Congressional support.[60]

In his seventh annual message to Congress of 1823, Monroe recommended a review of the tariff; he proposed added protection for articles of manufacture that "are more immediately connected with the defense and independence of the country."[61] John Quincy Adams continued this mercantilist tradition established by his predecessors and, of all of these Republican presidents, Adams was probably the most committed to a broad interpretation of the welfare function of government and its role in building a national economy:

The great object of the institution of civil government is the improvement of the condition of those who are parties to the social compact, and no government, in whatever form constituted, can accomplish the lawful ends of its institution but in proportion as it improves the condition of those over whom it is established. Roads and canals, by multiplying and facilitating the communications and intercourse between distant regions and multitudes of men, are among the most important means of improvement.[62]

John Quincy Adams has been considered the last American President in this tradition. 1829, therefore, marks the end of an era in American history: the philosophy of mercantilism as an economic doctrine was giving way to that of laissez-faire and the national consensus on political and economic development was beginning to show the strains of sectional strife.

The commitment to greater political and economic centralization at the expense of local autonomy during this period was reinforced by the rulings of the Supreme Court under John Marshall, Chief Justice from 1801–1835. Like Hamilton, Marshall's goal for the United States was national power founded on an expanding empire. Marshall regarded the development of both agriculture and manufactures as the means to national prosperity; he particularly admired George Washington's Farewell Address as an important precept for American statesmen.[63]

The decisions of the Marshall Court consistently advanced the cause of nationalism and centralization over states' rights and local democracy. The implication of the famous principle of judicial review, established in Marbury versus Madison, ensured that judicial veto would offer a protection against the instability of popular government.[64] On the issue of implied powers of the federal Constitution versus states' rights, a dispute that had consistently divided Federalists and Republicans, Marshall took the Federalist position that the Constitution must be interpreted broadly.[65]

Marshall believed that the Court must maintain national cohesion and authority through its interpretation of the Constitution. The Court under his leadership was also a strong supporter of individual property rights: Marshall defined property broadly, in terms of capital as well as land, a definition that conformed with earlier Federalist principles. Like Hamilton, Marshall was a social conservative who believed that one of the functions of government was the protection of private property in all its forms.[66]

This strong commitment to the rights of private property, evidenced in Marshall's Court, was also shared by most of the policy leaders of this period, Republicans and Federalists alike. While I have emphasized their support for a coherent strategy of balanced national growth, through government intervention if necessary, this mercantilist philosophy existed alongside a firm commitment to private property. The role of government as a protector of individual property rights in the Lockean tradition, together with the particular economic circumstances of an abundant resource base, probably explain why government intervention in the economy was not even more extensive given the prevailing mercantilist ideology.

In some sense the frontier saved early American leaders from making a choice between the protection of property rights and greater government intervention to promote the general welfare: nevertheless the assumption of the Founding Fathers seems to have been that government should intervene *where necessary* to promote the growth of a balanced national economy capable of autonomy in the international system.

The Growth of a National Economy, 1776–1829

Throughout this period the American economy remained primarily agricultural although the trend toward industrialization and commercialization, both factors that were to erode agrarian local self-reliance, were already evident by 1830. The percentage of the labor force in agriculture began a small downward trend after 1820 which continued throughout the century while the percentage employed in manufacturing, which was negligible at the beginning of the century, began to rise very slowly, most notably in the textile industry.[67]

The relatively large percentage of the labor force that was self-employed in early nineteenth-century America was due to the widespread distribution of land. But, while subsistence farming continued on the frontier until 1860, rural households in the older communities began to be incorporated into the market through the evolution toward a merchant capitalist type of economy. The merchant capitalist supplied the artisans, often members of a farming family, with raw materials and then moved the product directly into the market; the producer was not yet a wage earner but this "putting-out" system of manufacture in the home did have the effect of widening the market, particularly in clothing. The merchant capitalist system contributed to the decline of artisans and craftsmen producing for the local market.[68]

The only perceptible shift to factory production before 1830 was in the area of cotton textiles, where industries sprang up in many cases in response to the interruption of trade due to the Embargo and War of 1812. Large-scale manufacturing of cotton textiles was also stimulated by the introduction of machinery and the beginnings of a transportation network. By 1830 the power loom system was well established: even though the British attempted to stop the export of technology, most of the technological innovation came from England, often via the emigration of skilled artisans. A famous example is Samuel Slater who, having memorized the complete design of a new textile mill in England, emigrated to the United States in 1789 and constructed an Arkwright machine in a factory in Pawtucket.

The principal advance in weaving came in 1814 when Francis Lowell of Boston devised a power loom, also after studying English machines: the Boston Manufacturing Company in Waltham, which began operation in 1815, is considered a breakthrough in the emergence of the factory system. American technological development was marked by a high degree of ingenuity and adaptation, partly because the restriction that the British put on the export of machinery forced Americans to make their own machines: the strong utilitarian bent of American society, in part fostered by a scarcity of labor along with an absence of inhibiting institutions, produced a steady increase in technological progress in the early years of the nineteenth century.

It seems, however, that the shift to factory production in the cotton industry was due primarily to a sharp increase in demand which in turn drove technological change.[69] A population increase of about 3 percent per year, accompanied by a rise in per capita income, accounted for this growth in demand for manufactured products, but the crucial variable was the steady increase in the development of transportation and communication which greatly increased the size of the market.

The War of 1812 stimulated the demand for government involvement in the building of roads and canals, based on the argument that communications during the war had not been adequate for national defense. The most significant outcome of internal improvements during this era was the building of roads from the East to the West. An important example of federal involvement was the construction of the Cumberland Road, which was completed by 1818. The Erie Canal, built in 1819, initiated an era of canal building which lasted until about 1840. The Erie Canal was built by the state of New York: generally canals were owned by the states or were under private ownership with capital supplied by the states. Before the railroad era, river navigation was an important form of transportation: by 1830 this was dominated by the steamboat, which was first introduced on the Mississippi in 1811. The importance of the Mississippi as a commercial route, as well as improvements in road and canal transportation between the East and West, tended to discourage the growth of manufacturing in the West; New England and the mid-Atlantic states became the chief locus of manufacturing with products exchanged for western agriculture.

The role of the state in the development of a national economy is a subject of increasing debate among economic historians; as mentioned earlier, state intervention in the economy was probably more widespread than is often believed. The Federalist programs of the Hamilton era established a precedent for state involvement for the purpose of stimulating private initiative and investment. In the transportation field, considered so crucial for economic growth, government was always heavily involved during this period,[70] although that involvement more often took place at the state rather than the federal level, the Cumberland Road being an important exception.[71] State involvement was particularly important during the planning stages of transportation enterprises as states were often the major suppliers of capital. Once they were built, transportation systems were usually handed over to private enterprise which ran them on a toll collection basis.

During the administration of John Quincy Adams a boom in state involvement in internal improvements began which was to continue into the 1830s and beyond. The Adams administration spent almost as much on internal improvements as had been allocated during the previous twenty-four years and, by 1826, the government was the largest single entrepreneur in the country.[72] It was also quite heavily involved in regulatory activities such as setting transportation rates, hours of work and the inspection of food.[73]

The consensus among revisionist economic historians seems to be that government did play a significant role in the creation of a national economy and that the prevailing mercantilist ideology fostered an expectation that it should do so. The responsibility of government for economic conditions was generally taken for granted, the major question being whether that responsibility should be at the state or federal level. The government's role was generally limited, however, to that of supporting private enterprise through the creation of an infrastructure, such as transportation facilities and a fiscal system, and the supplying of investment capital and regulation where necessary. Federal government assistance to private economic ventures was widely accepted in an era where private capital was quite limited.

The peculiar economic circumstances of the early United States ensured that government involvement would be limited to the encouragement of private enterprise. An abundant resource base and a relatively small population comprised of small property owners, reinforced by a moving frontier, all contributed to widespread support for private property rights and private enterprise. While the existence of the frontier contributed so strongly to the ethic of local self-reliance, its incorporation into the national economy also contributed to its demise. If economic growth in the early United States depended so crucially on the widening of the market, territorial expansion drove this extension of the market and the development of a national economy, thereby sowing the seeds for the destruction of local self-reliance, a philosophy and way of life upon which the frontier had been founded.

The Role of the International System in Determining National Development

I shall now turn to an analysis of the international relations of the United States during the period 1776–1829 in order to see how far the international system and the management of international affairs contributed to the building of national self-reliance. This analysis will include an examination of America's westward expansion: while this issue was not always strictly international, the extent to which it involved the United States in controversy and negotiations with European powers suggests its relevance to this discussion.

International relations during that time fall into two quite distinct periods, the division occurring around 1815 with the conclusion of the Napoleonic Wars in Europe. While the United States was committed in principle to nonintervention in foreign affairs, its twin goals of maintaining commercial ties with Europe and expanding to the West and South brought it into conflict with most of the powers of Europe at some time before 1815. While the tensions with Europe related to expansion continued after 1815, the United States was more detached from European affairs during this period and more concerned with hemispheric relations. The internal economy became the mainspring of economic expansion, whereas earlier American economic development took place largely in the context of the Atlantic economy.[74]

Prior to 1815 events in the United States were conditioned to a considerable extent by the actions of the belligerents in the Napoleonic wars: much of the debate on both domestic and foreign policy was conducted in the context of the need to strengthen federal institutions and conduct foreign relations in a way that could effectively increase American autonomy in a hostile international environment.

As mentioned earlier, the overriding impetus for amending the Articles of Confederation came from the need to strengthen the federal government's ability to conduct foreign affairs. The perception of America's powerlessness in the international system and its continued dependence on Britain for manufactured imports encouraged a nascent nationalism which was an important element of support for a stronger federal government in the 1780s. Independence had shut the United States out of the mercantilist trading system of the British empire, which included lucrative trade with the British West Indies and Canada.

By 1790 American exports had decreased; deterioration of the export trade was intensified by a decrease in foreign demand for staple products such as rice, tobacco and wheat.[75] The most sweeping change in postwar commerce was the decline of the tobacco trade which, in colonial times, had been the largest source of export to England. A British tax on foreign tobacco precipitated this decline and an excessive importation of European goods further contributed to a negative trade balance.[76] Pro-tariff movements were springing up in states such as New York, Massachusetts and Pennsylvania to counter this postwar depression.

Debates in Congress reveal both a commitment to universal free trade, which was based on liberal principles, and a reaction against British commercial restrictions during the colonial period, as well as a realization that free trade could result in unequal benefits for trading partners.[77]

After Madison had opened the tariff debate in the first Congress by urging the passage of a tariff bill, primarily for revenue purposes, a demand for industrial protection arose, led by the state of Pennsylvania. The Tariff Act of 1789 was intended both for revenue and protection; its objectives were proclaimed to be "the support of the government, the discharge of the debts of the United States, and the encouragement and protection of manufactures."[78] In addition to the Tariff Act, the First Congress also passed a Tonnage Act which gave an important boost to the American shipping industry.[79] While the debate over these two measures clearly signaled a note of national economic independence, American commercial relations were too deeply tied to England for economic independence to become a reality for some time.

Throughout this period Britain remained by far the largest market for American exports and supplied most of its imports. Merchants were used to trading with England and customers were used to British products.[80] Citing arguments similar to those of Third World leaders today, American policymakers after independence were aware of the need to diversify sources of trade. Jefferson and John Adams both attempted, with limited success, to negotiate trade treaties with various European countries during the 1780s.

It has been estimated that, in 1793, nine tenths of total government revenue was raised from tariff receipts and that three fourths of this amount came from commerce with England, which meant that this relationship, although difficult, was of vital importance; this is a dilemma that confronts many newly independent nations today in their relationships with their former mother countries. It was an issue that, more than domestic policies, vehemently divided Federalists and Republicans. While Hamilton argued that commercial relations with Britain were financially necessary, Republicans believed, somewhat unrealistically, that retaliation against England would force it to concede on issues of commercial disagreement.[81]

The vulnerability of America's position vis-à-vis England was borne out by the signing of Jay's Treaty in 1795, which yielded little in terms of commercial concessions and continued the exclusion of the United States from the lucrative British West Indies trade: the only American gain was British evacuation of the northwest posts on the Canadian border, which had actually been agreed to in principle at independence but never implemented due to American weakness. American acquiescence to the Treaty, over strong Republican opposition, was an admission of its vastly inferior power in relation to England.

In short-run economic terms the outbreak of war in Europe in 1793 was a stimulus for American economic growth. As the major source of supply for both belligerents, American commerce began to prosper once more: the reexport trade between Europe and the American hemisphere became so great that, during the 1798–1807 period, the value of goods, reexported through American ports, exceeded the value of domestic products sent abroad.[82]

In spite of this commercial prosperity political issues, such as the restrictions on neutral trade imposed by both Britain and France and the particularly sensitive issue of British impressment, overwhelmed the short-run economic rationale for open association with the international economy. Political weakness meant that the United States was unable to negotiate these issues and was forced to resort to the Embargo of 1807. Enacted by a Republican administration, whose sympathies lay primarily with agrarian free trade interests, the Embargo was justified as a measure necessary for the preservation of national independence, thereby indicating the priority accorded to political over economic considerations.[83]

The Embargo, which lasted for two years, seriously disrupted the American economy, which was highly dependent on commerce; the most drastic effect was on the cotton trade.[84] Since a large proportion of government revenue came from trade, this type of disruption revealed the high level of vulnerability to which an associationist commercial policy could lead; that the effects were not more disastrous was partly due to a treasury surplus of $17 million in 1807 and partly to widespread evasion of the Embargo.[85]

The War of 1812 was a further assertion of America's quest for political autonomy and economic independence which had been frustrated by its commercial relations with England. While New England was bitterly opposed to the war, as it had been to the Embargo, support came largely from western states whose expansion was causing border disputes with England. Although the

Treaty of Ghent, which ended the war in 1814, yielded few of the objectives for which the United States had fought,[86] America emerged from the war with a nascent manufacturing industry and a firmer consensus on building a national self-reliant economy. A temporary decline in factionalism was accompanied by the rise of a new nationalism, which was embodied in the American System and associated with political figures such as John Calhoun and Henry Clay.

Before 1815, therefore, America's development was highly dependent on the vicissitudes of its commercial relationships with Europe: like contemporary commodity producers, the United States experienced great prosperity when export prices of commodities were high and a sharp decline when they fell or when markets were cut off. A commitment to both free trade and isolation proved to be an impossible strategy for the Republican party, which it in effect admitted with the imposition of the Embargo. Jefferson's changing commercial policies contributed to the consolidation of a Republican and Federalist consensus on building a national economy—a consensus that remained more or less intact, in terms of party politics, until 1829.

After 1815 there was a strong break in the pattern of American economic development. Before the Embargo, commercial centers and exporting regions had experienced the greatest prosperity and growth but there was little development in terms of national integration.[87] After 1815 the United States turned inward with more emphasis on western expansion and the development of internal communications; commercial policy continued to be significant, however, with the protection controversy being one of the most important issues in national politics for the next twenty years.

The Embargo and War of 1812 had been important stimuli for American manufacturing, particularly for the establishment of the cotton industry, but also for wool, iron and glass.[88] The Tariff Act of 1816, the first such act since 1789, was intended to protect these industries, which had grown up during the war, but the continued flood, mainly from England, of manufactured imports in 1817 and 1818 and a severe depression in 1819–1820 created a persistent demand for a further increase in duties on manufactured goods.

Due to good European harvests, American agricultural prices dropped in 1819 and, for the first time, the demand for protection became a national movement supported by both industry and agriculture. When industrial unemployment rose, agricultural interests, realizing the vulnerability of relying on foreign markets, began to lobby for protection in order to increase the domestic demand for agricultural products: for the first time since independence a consensus on protection and balanced sectional growth was emerging, signifying a shift away from export-led growth.[89] That this consensus held more or less throughout the 1820s, when tariffs were increased in 1824 and 1828, was partially due to the fact that, although the physical volume of exports increased throughout the decade, export values actually declined due to a deterioration of prices.[90]

The 1820s saw the publication of numerous pamphlets supporting the tariff movement; the first systematic academic treatise on protection appeared in 1820 when Daniel Raymond published his *Thoughts on Political Economy*. An admirer of Hamilton, Raymond made a similar argument that the state is an organic entity rather than an aggregate of individuals; rather than promoting individual interests, as liberals suggested, the state must therefore build up national wealth behind tariff barriers through the development of productive powers, an argument that sounds similar to List's.[91] This position had also been taken earlier by Tench Coxe who maintained that, even when agriculture was the dominant sector of the American economy, industry must be encouraged through protection in order to provide a more reliable market for the agricultural surplus.[92] More importantly, Coxe believed that a balanced economy, with a well-developed transportation system, would be less vulnerable in war, an issue that was particularly salient during the 1790s. Supporters of the protectionist school were centered in the mid-Atlantic states where a number of societies promoting domestic manufactures grew up and flourished during the 1820s.[93]

The leading politician associated with the proponents of this "American System" was Henry Clay. Clay, a Kentuckian who occupied the influential role of Speaker of the House of Representatives from 1811 to 1825, was important in uniting western farmers and eastern manufacturing interests in favor of protection. Clay was the leading proponent of the 1824 tariff, which he hoped would make the United States self-sufficient in necessary items: he proposed that the revenues from the tariff should be used specifically for internal improvements. The American System was to be separate and distinct from Europe, and was to include South America but with the United States in a predominant position.[94] An ardent nationalist like Hamilton, Clay saw the potential for the United States as an industrial self-reliant nation-state with a predominant position in the hemisphere, through which it could play an important role in world affairs.

Protection, balanced growth and internal improvements, were the means by which proponents of the American System felt that the United States could achieve this position of supremacy. The Tariff Act of 1824 was passed by a coalition of western and mid-Atlantic states with the partial support of New England. Rates on imported manufactures and farm products were increased, with protection on cotton manufactures raised to one hundred percent on cheap grades. With the 1828 Tariff Act, protection reached its highest level before the Civil War, including high rates on textiles and iron and a forty-five percent rate on raw wool, which was particulary objectionable to New England.

Although perceived by protectionists of the time as necessary for the growth of manufactures, the effect of the tariff on American industry is a subject of much debate among economic historians. Most seem to believe that, while the tariff may have contributed to the growth of manufacturing, it was not the decisive stimulus for its development. There does seem to be agreement, however, that the Embargo and War of 1812 were extremely important in the establishment of the cotton textile industry.[95] Taussig, in a detailed analysis of the rise of the cotton and woolen industries, agrees with this conclusion, but he argues that the influence of subsequent protection was much less decisive.[96]

An important factor in the growth of American manufactures after the war was a sharp increase in demand due to a population increase and improved communications, which widened the domestic market. Zevin estimates the annual growth rate of the cotton industry between 1816 and 1860 to have been 15.4 percent which, he argues, was due primarily to an increase in demand and to a lesser extent to an improvement in machinery with tariff effects being fairly insignificant.[97]

Even if its effects on domestic manufacturing are disputed, the tariff was undoubtedly an extremely salient political issue after the war; this in itself justifies the argument that laissez-faire economic growth was not taken for granted. The statements of leading American policymakers make it clear that they were concerned with the issue of protection for reasons of building a strong, self-reliant national economy .

Although all sections of the country had supported the Tariff Act of 1816, the South began to break away from this consensus during the 1820s; the defection of Calhoun from his earlier support for the American System and the nullification controversy of 1828 marked the climax of the erosion of southern support for the tariff.[98] The South, lacking an indigenous manufacturing capacity, was paying a high price for imported necessities due to tariff protection.

Although southern interests were already out of step with the national consensus in the 1820s, revisionist historians portray the antebellum South as a much more prosperous economy than had previously been believed. With per capita income growth about equal to that of the rest of the country, slavery appeared to be a viable institution and the decision not to diversify into manufacturing was a rational response, in the short run, to increasing profits from plantation agriculture.[99]

For this prosperity the South depended almost entirely on the export of cotton, a commodity in which the region enjoyed an enormous comparative advantage in international trade.[100] The South was not well integrated into the national economy, however, and the extent of the region's participation in interregional trade may not have been as great as that of the rest of the country. There was a lack of urbanization and inland communication, transportation routes being directed toward coastal centers for export purposes, and also a lack of investment in human capital, the promotion of education and progress generally not being in the interest of the dominant planter class.

To a considerable degree, the antebellum southern economy resembled that of one-crop primary exporters in the contemporary Third World. The goal of short-term growth through comparative advantage in international trade hampered the building of a diversified economy; the Civil War was largely a result of the South's peculiar position in the national economy, and the fact that the South lost the war was due in part to its lack of productive capacity.[101] Thus the South was already on the periphery of the nascent national economy in 1830. Ironically, the section of the country upon which Jefferson had built his vision of agrarian self-reliance had become extremely dependent on the fortunes of the international system.

The issue of American territorial expansion during this period became a matter of international relations since it impinged on the interests of various European powers. American policymakers who supported the building of a national economy generally favored a policy of expansion also. Alexander Hamilton favored expansion, not for purposes of settlement, which he feared would only increase the agrarian population and thus gain more support for agrarian interests, but for reasons of commerce and economic prosperity. In 1799 Hamilton proposed the conquest of Louisiana and Florida in order to round out the American empire. Conquest of these territories, Hamilton believed, would assure the United States of the free navigation of the Mississippi that was so vital for both internal and external trade.

Jefferson's writings also evidenced strong support for American expansion. The most significant single event in America's expansion, the Louisiana Purchase of 1803, which doubled the land size of the United States and assured it of free navigation of the Mississippi, occurred during Jefferson's presidency. In spite of his generally pro-French inclinations, Jefferson threatened war against France in 1803 were it to assert its control over New Orleans. Moreover the Republicans' constructionist views on the Constitution were set aside in order to clear the way for the Lousiana Purchase. Both Gallatin and Madison argued for the position of implied powers, their commitment to expansion overriding their consitutional principles.[102] While the doctrine of Manifest Destiny did not receive its official name until 1845, its aspirations go back much further to the latter part of the eighteenth century. Hamilton, Jefferson, John Quincy Adams and other national leaders all supported this idea, which linked American nationalism with the aspiration to spread American sovereignty over an entire continent.

The Priority of National Self-Reliance over Regional Cooperation

In their western policies American leaders of this period exhibited a kind of expansionist nationalism which was quite antithetical to the self-reliance of others, including native Americans, and also to the notion of regional and collective self-reliance as defined in chapter 1. As mentioned earlier, the War of 1812 had much wider support in the West than among maritime states. War hawks such as Henry Clay aspired to the removal of the British from North America and envisaged the American System as embracing the whole hemisphere.

Extent of territory, whether it be great or small, gives to a nation many of its characteristics. It marks the extent of its resources, of its population, of its physical force. It marks, in short, the difference between a great and a small power.[103]

President Monroe clearly continued his predecessors' commitment to expansion. The logical conclusion to this period of American expansion was the Monroe Doctrine, which in effect pointed toward the predominant power of the United States in the hemisphere after the collapse of Spain. The Monroe Doctrine declared that the United States would consider "any attempt on their part [European powers] to extend their system to any portion of this hemisphere as dangerous to our peace and safety."[104] In the same speech, Monroe went on to say that the "expansion of our population and accession of new States to our Union have had the happiest effect on all its highest interests. That it has eminently augmented our resources and added to our strength and respectability as a power is admitted by all."[105] American expansion was perceived as augmenting the United States' bid for increased autonomy and national power. While the Monroe Doctrine was framed, at least in terms of hemispheric solidarity, its aim was clearly to establish regional hegemony for the United States.

America's relations with the rest of the hemisphere during this period were designed to augment national power rather than to build regional cooperation. American interest in an independent Latin America was based primarily on the possibilities it opened up for commerce. American policy was aimed at capturing Latin American markets rather than letting the British do so. The first annual message of John Quincy Adams urged the conclusion of commercial treaties with Latin American states to be conducted under most-favored-nation principles.[106]

The tendency of all American presidents of this period to view South America in terms of markets for American exports suggests a policy dictated by commercial interests rather than a desire to build hemispheric solidarity. The possibility of a more cooperative partnership was initiated in 1822 by Simon Bolivar, who proposed a confederation of Latin American states which the United States might join; however, John Quincy Adams, then Secretary of State, declined. After the proclamation of the Monroe Doctrine the United States was invited to join a congress at Panama in 1825 to discuss the possibility of turning the Doctrine into a multilateral alliance. In spite of Adams' continued skepticism, Henry Clay as Secretary of State accepted on the grounds that it might provide a step toward putting the United States at the head of his American System.

Subsequent deliberations in Congress over the naming of American representatives revealed a strong resistance to pursuing political connections even with those states in the hemisphere that were struggling for liberty. While the decision to send representatives was finally approved, debate had revealed that any inter-American alliance formed in order to implement the Monroe Doctrine would not receive the necessary two-thirds vote of the Senate. Bolivar gave up the idea of a confederation when he realized that it would not receive the support of the United States; relations with Latin America were much weakened by this episode.[107]

It seems, therefore, that the policy of the United States in this period was more inclined toward hemispheric domination than regional self-reliance. A strong commitment to expansion and an interest in Latin American markets for American exports pointed toward a reproduction of the type of dependence against which the United States had recently fought in the War of Independence. An aspiration for national power in international relations took precedence over collective self-reliance, suggesting that the two may not be mutually compatible.

Conclusion

Contemporary self-reliance strategies try to prevent the import of foreign capital, technology, and all but necessary foreign goods, and attempt to build a balanced economy with an emphasis on the satisfaction of basic needs locally. By such a definition early American development cannot be considered self-reliant: the United States welcomed foreign capital and technology and only attempted to prevent the import of goods that competed directly with American industry. Neither can its development be considered a strategy in the modern sense, since government planning and direct government intervention in the economy was on a much smaller scale than is usually the case today.

Nevertheless the American case raises many issues of interest for contemporary self-reliance strategies by revealing common themes and concerns. It appears that American policy makers were crucially aware of the negative impact that an unregulated associationist relationship with the international system could have on political and economic development, and that, within the contextual constraints of the times, they supported policies to counter this impact. Moreover the policy discussion was framed in terms that parallel, to a surprising degree, contemporary self-reliance strategies. An investigation of these development debates challenges the assumption of the laissez-faire framework in which American development is often thought to have taken place.

Before 1815, American development was determined in large part by the international economy; we must assume therefore that the international system was an important influence on development possibilities, and federal policies suggest that it was not always benign. The vulnerable position of the United States as an ex-colonial raw materials producer was recognized; the fact that United States policy was not consistently dissociationist was probably due to its extremely favorable resource base, its large size, and its geographical isolation, which allowed for the building of a balanced national economy that could absorb foreign capital and products without impeding national development. The case of the South illustrates the dangers of association without the necessary management, infrastructure, and resource base.

The political, economic and social conditions of eighteenth-century America provided a context that was well suited to the practice of local self-reliance in its western liberal version. It was not, however, an environment that was propitious for national leaders trying to promote political and economic integration in order to achieve autonomy at the international level. While Hamilton's mercantilist strategy of tying creditors to the federal government was the direct antithesis of local self-reliance, Jefferson's early support for states' rights and decentralization also fell victim to the goal of national autonomy. The dispute between Federalists and Republicans provides a striking illustration of the contradictions between local and national self-reliance which, in the case of the United States, were resolved in favor of the latter, although an abundant resource base and a liberal political tradition mitigated the consequences of such a resolution for the individual in terms both of basic needs satisfaction and political participation. The choice of policies characteristic of a strategy of national self-reliance was also influenced by America's international relations during the period. The American experience provides a good illustration of the way in which external economic and military threats to the survival of the state impose their influence on development.

Jeffersonian agrarian local self-reliance was flawed in that it depended on free trade and expansion, both of which, in the international context of the time, threatened national autonomy. Free trade, which was necessary to preserve the agrarian economy, resulted in vulnerability and international tensions; expansion, through which sufficient resources for local basic needs satisfaction could be assured, caused sectional rivalries that contained possibilities for national disintegration. To solve both these dilemmas national leaders, including Republicans, chose to augment national power at the expense of local self-reliance. In the American case it seems therefore that both the ideological underpinnings and the economic conditions necessary for the practice of local self-reliance contained the seeds of its own destruction.

Both Republicans and Federalists realized that mercantilism, an eighteenth-century version of national self-reliance, with its emphasis on buildng the capability to be self-sufficient, was appropriate for a new nation that was weak both internally and externally. Federalist fiscal policies and later Republican support for internal improvements all contributed to the promotion of balanced growth through internal interdependence. Unlike most Third World cases today, however, the highly favorable economic conditions in early America meant that demands for government intervention in this task could be limited to the provision of an infrastructure to facilitate private enterprise.

From 1807 to 1814 the United States followed a policy of dissociation which, while detrimental to growth in the short run, resulted in the foundation of a nascent manufacturing industry, suggesting that such a policy may have had a positive effect on building national self-reliance in the long run. It also produced a generation of policy leaders committed to protection, expansion and hemispheric hegemony.

Such policy goals may not be consistent with the achievement of self-reliance of other states, however: this is a dilemma for any strategy that focuses on the achievement of national autonomy vis-à-vis the international system. The success of collective self-reliance and regional integration is particularly vulnerable to the policies of relatively large powers whose actions can reproduce dependency relations at the regional level. United States political and commercial interests in Latin America were motivated by a desire to dominate rather than to cooperate and they are suggestive of policies prescribed by List for both the United States and Germany. Evidence has suggested that the United States during this period put national autonomy as a high-priority developmental goal which took precedence over the promotion of either local or collective self-reliance. Local self-reliance was an early development stage which provided a desirable framework for basic needs satisfaction and was therefore a valuable basis upon which national autonomy could be built: in the American case it became anachronistic with the development of a national economy. Collective self-reliance, a policy that emphasizes regional cooperation, was sacrificed to aspirations for building regional hegemony.

PART FOUR
SELF-RELIANCE IN INDIA: GANDHIAN PRINCIPLES AND NATIONAL PRACTICE

The priority that Rousseau and the early Jefferson attached to the norms of local self-reliance, as a way of ensuring individuals' autonomy and political participation, is reproduced in an Asian context in the political and economic thought of Mohandas Gandhi, one of the leading self-reliance theorists of the twentieth century. In chapter 6, I shall outline Gandhi's vision for a self-reliant India and, in chapter 7, I will compare it with the development path that India has actually taken since independence. While Gandhi was the leader of an independence movement, he never occupied political office after independence and thus, unlike Jefferson, he was never faced with the problem of making compromises with his preferred development strategy. For Gandhi an independent India was to be not only economically self-reliant but also dedicated to the principles of nonviolence, a nation that would provide the moral leadership for a new and different world order.

While Gandhi's charismatic leadership provided an important symbol, the course that Indian political and economic development took after independence was far removed from that which Gandhi would have preferred. Although Indian policy leaders were strongly committed to self-reliance in 1947, the choice of a modernizing development strategy, based on the priority of industrialization, subsequently incurred a heavy reliance on the international system for technology and the shortfalls in production of a neglected agricultural sector. Just as List prescribed a strategy for Germany and the United States that was designed to "catch up" with the superior power of England, India's preference for a Western development model was based on a desire to play an important role in the existing international system rather than to build a new world order as Gandhi would have preferred.

CHAPTER SIX

DECENTRALIZED DEMOCRACY: THE POLITICAL AND ECONOMIC THOUGHT OF MOHANDAS GANDHI

G ANDHI'S WRITINGS show a remarkable perception of the development problems of an overpopulated, poor, rural society: grounded in the historical experience of early twentieth-century India, his insights into the causes of economic backwardness were quite prophetic and they show striking parallels with some contemporary approaches to development, particularly those of the communitarians discussed in chapter 1. Gandhi's belief in the centrality of the individual in shaping his or her own environment and in the principle of national autonomy make him one of the most significant self-reliance theorists of the twentieth century.

Gandhi was a proponent of a local basic needs development strategy as well as the architect of Indian independence. He believed that the way to achieve true national independence for India was through the creation of rural decentralized democracy designed to break the web of dependent relationships with England which had grown up under colonialism. For Gandhi, the attainment of this type of local self-reliance was critically dependent on every individual working for his or her own liberation. Personal liberation was to be attained through participation in mass movements such as satyagraha and swadeshi and through voluntary work in economic reconstruction, all of which were vital for the achievement of both national independence and national self-reliance. Thus the achievement of personal liberation would lead to political liberation as well: that the two were closely related is of crucial importance for the understanding of Gandhi's thinking.

Gandhi was not a political theorist like Rousseau but an activist

concerned with the tasks of removing the British from India and
building the kind of society in which the exploitation and repression that he associated with colonial rule could not be reproduced.
Since Gandhi was responding as a political practitioner to the im-
mediacy of particular events in the preindependence struggle,
placing his ideas into a consistent theoretical framework is difficult
and for this reason they have been subject to a wide variety of
interpretations. For Westerners, analyzing Gandhi's thought is particularly problematic because of the impossibility of separating ethical and political principles. Gandhi rejected the notion of a double
standard for personal and political life: he believed that spiritual
beliefs were at the core of all human actions whereas for Westerners
these spiritual beliefs tend to get in the way of an acceptance of
Gandhi as a serious political thinker.

While this study attempts to draw out common themes from the
writings of political thinkers from different cultures and time
frames, the development of any interpretive theory, particularly
one that deals with self-reliance, must be sensitive to the need to
place theorists in the context of their own cultural and epis-
temological traditions. This is an issue that is particularly pertinent
when comparing Gandhi with Western self-reliance theorists. Although Gandhi frequently acknowledged an intellectual debt to
certain Western authors, his political thought was firmly grounded
in Indian tradition and in the Indian experience as a colony of
England. Moreover, his attempt to develop theories and strategies
that grew out of the Indian context, rather than using Western
models, was as important for his conception of self-reliance as was
the end result of liberating India. Gandhi did not believe that there
could be an objective social science independent of the thinking of
social scientists themselves.[1] No theory, therefore, could be value
free nor could it claim universal validity across cultures and conditions.

In contrast to the Western pluralist tradition, which is primarily
concerned with the reconciliation of competing interests rather
than with postulating goals, Gandhi maintained that a society must
first establish its own normative goals and then devise theories with
which to obtain these goals.[2] Gandhi's goals for India were independence and autonomy, the eradication of poverty and the universal satisfaction of basic needs. Gandhi felt that Indian poverty could

never be eliminated through the market allocation mechanism of liberal economic theory nor could true political liberation be achieved were India to become part of the Western nation-state system. The divergence between the interests of individuals and those of society which, in the Western liberal tradition, are mediated by the state and the market, are presumed not to exist in Gandhian thought. In a just society Gandhi believed that personal and societal goals could be identical.

Personal self-reliance was to be furthered, therefore, through the individual's participation in social action. For Gandhi the ideal society was one in which political and economic institutions were built from the bottom, with the individual always at the center, thus eliminating the oppressive dependency relationships which he believed were the result of centralized institutional structures. For Gandhi the rejection of Western political ideas and institutions was as important for his conception of a self-reliant India as was economic self-reliance and nonparticipation in a Western-dominated world order. Consequently, Gandhi was not an institution builder in the Western sense. Any analysis of his thought must begin with the individual; for Gandhi, institutional structures were to be built only in so far as they were necessary for furthering the individual's role in building a just social order.

Self-Reliance for the Individual in Society

My humble occupation has been to show people how they solve their own difficulties. . . . My work will be finished if I succeed in carrying conviction to the human family, that every man or woman, however weak in body, is guardian of his or her self-respect and liberty.[3]

Gandhi's entire concept of self-reliance was built around the individual and his or her responsibility for building a just society. The role of the individual, as an autonomous being yet part of an integrated whole, is central to the understanding of Gandhi's political thought and action. Gandhi's strategy for achieving independence for India was based on the crucial assumption that each individual must be instilled with a large measure of self-respect, fearlessness and a capacity to be self-reliant before national independence could become a reality. Gandhi felt that India's subservience to England was due to a lack of such qualities in its people: he believed that England had many such individuals, however, and that this was one reason why England ruled over India (*CW* 5:45)[4]. The blame for India's plight, therefore, must rest with Indians themselves: "It is only a sinful people who have wicked rulers" (*CW* 7:456). "The country should learn to be self-reliant. It will be so when it has brave men and brave women"(*CW* 21:228).

The role of the individual, as the central focus in the regeneration of India, was based on Gandhi's interpretation of "dharma" or duty; defined in one of its great religious epics, the Bhagavadgita, dharma is a central concept in Hindu thought. The Gita taught that the individual had a moral duty to serve society rather than his own interests. According to the traditional dharmic model, which evolved from the Gita, duty came to be defined as working to preserve the existing social order embodied in the fourfold division of caste. Gandhi's interpretation of dharma was somewhat different, however: his strong belief in the potential of every individual to effect change, based on a personal search for what is true and right, implied a much more radical interpretation of the concept.[5] Nevertheless if, as Gandhi believed, in an ideal society the interests of the individual and the interests of society could be identical, duty would point the individual toward serving the needs of society. "Civilization is that mode of conduct which points out to man the path of duty" (*CW* 10:37). Dharma, the link between the individual and his or her social obligations, could hold society together harmoniously and act as a balance between individual freedom and social restraint.

Before Gandhi's ideal society could be realized, however, dharma must be linked with social action and political participation in effecting change: this shift in emphasis, from upholding a traditional order to working for social change, was quite revolutionary in early twentieth-century India and, given its primary goal of undermining the British raj, depended on a high degree of individual self-reliance. Gandhi believed that individual self-respect and self-reliance could be enhanced by participation in satyagraha, a technique of nonviolent protest which he employed on a mass scale at various times during the independence movement. Satyagraha, which means holding fast or firmness to truth, conveys much more than passive resistance. The concept of truth, a supreme value expressing the real or ultimate good, was central to Gandhi's thought and was something that he believed each individual must seek for him or herself. For Gandhi the search for truth was a highly personal quest which motivated all his thought and actions: since the meaning of truth could be subject to personal interpretation, Satyagraha undermined external authority and reaffirmed the moral autonomy and authority of the individual as an active performer in the arena of politics. "God alone is the strength for satyagrahi. He wants to walk on his own legs. He does not want a stick for support. He does not depend on any strength from outside" (CW 69:226).

Gandhi believed that satyagraha required more courage than violent resistance: it depended not on passivity but on self-suffering in a struggle for humanitarian goals and basic change.[6] Satyagraha could be practiced by the strong and weak alike if they had what Gandhi called "soul force," an indestructible commitment to the truth over which the force of arms would be powerless, a psychological state in which the individual would become fearless:

A satyagrahi enjoys a degree of freedom not possible for others, for he becomes a truly fearless person. Once his mind is rid of fear, he will never agree to be another's slave. Having achieved this state of mind, he will never submit to any arbitrary action. (CW 8:91)

As well as promoting individual self-reliance, nonviolent resistance appeared to be a rational strategy for a large, poor country with limited resources to achieve independence.[7] For Gandhi the goal of national independence was no more important than the means by which it was attained. Gandhi always emphasized that the means by which such goals were realized were as, if not more, important than the goal themselves. Only by employing just means could a truly just social order be built. While he realized that the majority of Indians could never achieve the kind of moral perfection necessary to become true satyagrahi, their commitment to fearlessness and individual self-reliance and the search for truth and justice was as important as the ultimate goal of removing the British from India.

Consistent with the idea behind satyagraha that every individual must discover truth for him or herself, Gandhi believed that individuals should not be required to obey unjust laws (*CW* 10:49):[8] it is the duty of the people to protest when the government is unjust, "that the Government is always in the right and the subjects are wrong: how can we tolerate this? The Government says that authority must be respected. Authority is blind and unjust" (*CW* 14:323). When state action was harmful to individuals they could withdraw support and employ nonviolent resistance. Gandhi's position on authority paralleled that of Thoreau, whom he greatly admired: for both men, sovereignty was located in the conscience of the individual rather than in the laws of the state. Even in democracies Gandhi had no particular respect for the will of majorities:

Democracy is not a state in which people act like sheep. Under democracy, individual liberty of opinion and action is jealously guarded. I, therefore, believe that the minority has a perfect right to act differently from the majority.[9]

Like Thoreau, and also consistent with the nineteenth-century Western political liberal tradition, Gandhi believed that, after independence, the best government for India would be the one that governed least: political power must reside with the people, who must be capable of thinking independently rather than following their leaders unquestioningly. Institutions, Gandhi maintained, accustomed people to rely on officials rather than think for themselves.

If national life becomes so perfect as to become self-regulated, no representation is necessary. There is then a state of enlightened anarchy. In such a state everyone is his own ruler. . . . In the ideal state therefore there is no political power because there is no State. But the ideal is never fully realized in life. Hence the classical statement of Thoreau that Government is best which governs the least. (*CW* 47:91; see also *CW* 62:92)

While Gandhi acknowledged that real-world compromises would have to be made with his utopian ideal, his optimism about the possibility of large-scale achievement of the level of disciplined self-regulation necessary for the eventual realization of this state of enlightened anarchy rested on his assumption that the human race was progressing morally toward an increasing commitment to "ahimsa," or nonviolence. In his earliest stages man had been a cannibal and then a hunter; when he began to practice agriculture, civilized life emerged and individuals became family members and ultimately formed communities and nations (*CW* 72:350). This last stage would presumably be a kind of world federation based on nonviolence and mutual toleration; Gandhi did advocate such a world order but was quite vague about its implementation.

Satyagraha was the road whereby this progression of the individual in society toward nonviolence might be realized. Gandhi maintained that, in his search for truth or nonviolence, the individual must not rely on a guru but follows ideas rather than men. In reality, however, Gandhi was one of the most charismatic leaders of the twentieth century and the independence movement relied heavily on his leadership for its success.[10] Gandhi's strong commitment to individual self-reliance rested on an intensely personal quest which, in theory at least, he wished others to follow for themselves but which, in practice, was somewhat eclipsed by the dominance of his forceful personality. Moreover, to follow Gandhi's search for truth is to experience the strivings of a saint for a perfection seemingly impossible for any human being.[11]

Gandhi made his own personal commitment to self-reliance in 1906, after he had taken the vow of Brahmacharya; he was determined that his new life-style would be emulated by others, but it is not clear whether this contributed to their own self-reliance. His voluminous personal correspondence to members of his family, friends, and coresidents of various ashrams, which he founded and lived in, was full of advice on matters both trivial and important.[12] In his *Autobiography* Gandhi describes how he dispensed with servants and taught his wife to do the laundry,[13] and how he was overcome by guilt after a momentary lapse when he succumbed to the purchase of life insurance; "I had robbed my wife and children of their self-reliance."[14]

In spite of this tendency to authoritarianism with his immediate coworkers, Gandhi was aware of the need to cure people of excessive dependence on himself (*CW* 50:26): his commitment to creating a decentralized participatory democracy was motivated in part by a desire to empower people and make them self-reliant rather than relying on a charismatic leader. Moreover, Gandhi believed that true democracy could never become a reality as long as there was discrimination against certain groups in Indian society. Two causes for which he worked unceasingly throughout his life were the equality of women and the eradication of untouchability. Individual self-reliance could not be universalized, nor could India become a truly self-reliant nation, as long as large groups of people were subject to discrimination.

Gandhi was truly outraged at the position of women, which he felt was due to their exploitation by men (*CW* 33:44–45). His view that a wife should not be a husband's slave but rather his companion, helpmate, and equal partner was quite a radical statement in early twentieth-century India.[15] Gandhi believed that India would remain a backward country as long as women were subservient; even with independence, progress could not be made as long as half the population remained "ignorant playthings of men."

"The women of India should have as much share in winning swaraj as men. Probably in this peaceful struggle woman can outdistance man by many a mile" (*CW* 22:22; see also 75:155). Gandhi felt that women were better suited to nonviolent resistance than men since they were inherently less aggressive. Satyagraha, therefore, was a technique that allowed women's equal participation with men. Gandhi was a great admirer of the British suffragettes and used them as an example to Indian women engaged in political struggle (*CW* 9:324–326). He made no secret of his belief in the superiority of the British people, which he felt was in part due to the fine qualities of British women. English women, Gandhi maintained, were superior to Indian women because of their greater self-confidence (*CW* 49:33–34; see also 6:336, 7:65, 8:188).

Gandhi's quest for the eradication of untouchability caused more antagonism than anything else he undertook. His practice of mingling with untouchables and staying in their homes during his travels throughout India was a violation of his caste and condemned him to ostracism by orthodox Hindus. Gandhi repeatedly emphasized that India could never become a self-respecting, independent nation until untouchability was eradicated, a goal which he included in his definition of home rule (*CW* 20:507–509).[16] Untouchability, he maintained, "has stunted the growth of nearly 40 million human beings" (*CW* 53:257).[17] With the solution of this issue, however, Gandhi believed, quite unrealistically, that all class conflict in India would cease (*CW* 56:300).

In spite of his views on untouchability, Gandhi supported the institution of caste as "the best possible adjustment of social stability and progress" (*CW* 19:175). He believed that it was the aberrations of caste, not the institution itself, which led to social hierarchy and connotations of superiority and inferiority: "If untouchability was a part of the Hindu creed, I should decline to call myself a Hindu and most decidedly embrace some other faith" (*CW* 23:485).

The true caste system for Gandhi denoted a fourfold division of labor: knowledge, represented by the Brahmins who were teachers or religious leaders; power, represented by the Kshatriya or warrior class; wealth, represented by the Vaishya or trading class; and service, represented by the Sudra or laboring class. Consistent with the dharmic tradition, Gandhi believed that every individual must perform his or her duty by following an occupation within the caste to which he or she was born, but he also maintained that all castes were equal in terms of social hierarchy.[18] This rigid assignment to various occupations by virtue of birth would seem to work strongly against social mobility and hence against individual self-reliance, although it could possibly be a useful nonviolent mediator of class conflict. Gandhi himself was not a Brahmin but a Vaishya; since he held manual labor in such high regard, believing it to be the only true form of labor, this might explain why he did not favor social mobility and thus could support a social system that was founded on such a seemingly hierarchical structure. Later in his life, however, Gandhi began to favor the elimination of caste altogether when he realized that his quest for the eradication of untouchability remained unfulfilled (*CW* 62:121–122).[19]

Just as Gandhi favored the eradication of social discrimination, he was strongly committed to religious tolerance and the right of individuals to follow their own religious practices. Gandhi was impressed with the New Testament, particularly the Sermon on the Mount, but felt that Christianity as a religion had been corrupted by Europeans, as evidenced by their frequent resort to violence (*CW* 13:220). Gandhi admired Hinduism for its tolerance and lack of proselytising, which allowed everyone to worship according to his or her own faith and thus live at peace with other religions (*CW* 21:250). His firm commitment to religious tolerance and his asser-

tion that Hinduism reflected this tolerance contributed to his belief
that Hindu-Muslim unity was possible in an independent India.
The outbreak of religious violence at independence was one of the
most disillusioning events of his political career.

Gandhi felt that religion, in the ethical rather than the doctrinal
sense, must be joined with politics, particularly for the success of
satyagraha, a quest which was constantly testing action in light of
moral principles (*CW* 10:248). Gandhi's personal search for truth
was deeply religious: its manifestation through social and political
action demonstrates a strong mixture of religion and politics and a
joining of political and social causes with a quest for personal salva-
tion.[20] Gandhi felt that his own shortcomings were due to his failure
to live up to the teachings of the Gita, just as he felt that natural
catastrophes, such as the Bihar earthquake of 1934, were God's
punishment for the existence of untouchability. If such attitudes
seem to denote both a certain loss of personal self-reliance and an
injection of doctrinaire views into politics, they are somewhat mitigated by Gandhi's characterization of God as a spirit defined by
each individual rather than as an external being defined through
religious dogma. It was therefore up to each individual to charac-
terize God for him or herself while at the same time respecting
others' concepts of a different religion.

This questioning of received knowledge was also evident in
Gandhi's views on education. Gandhi believed that a different type
of educational system could, along with the eradication of discrimination, eliminate class conflict and contribute to individual self-
reliance. He wrote a great deal on his plans for the reformation of
the Indian educational system, and hoped that they would result in
the economic leveling of the population through an emphasis on
manual skills and the provision by each individual for his or her
basic needs. Gandhi condemned the British educational system
with its required use of the English language which, he maintained,
widened the gulf between the educated few, who became tools of
the British raj, and the masses: "This excessive importance given to
English has cast upon the educated class a burden which has
maimed them mentally for life and made them strangers in their
own land" (*CW* 66:194).

Gandhi believed that Indians wasted many years in learning English and elite skills which were of little use for the development of

India's rural economy (*CW* 13:297–300). Although trained as a lawyer, he developed a particularly strong aversion to lawyers and doctors; Gandhi maintained that lawyers had tightened the grip of English rule through their support of a network of legal institutions based on British norms and practices, while doctors encouraged the practice of self-indulgence rather than the acquisition of mastery over oneself and one's body (*CW* 10:35). If one can penetrate through his somewhat quaint ideas about medicine, his basic principle of caring for oneself and learning to improve personal hygiene and sanitation is quite compatible with contemporary approaches, which advocate basic health schemes for poor rural societies as more appropriate than the provision of expensive and sophisticated health care facilities.

As early as 1920 Gandhi proposed a boycott of the existing educational system as a method of protest against Indian dependency on British rule.[21] Gandhi hoped thereby to make the youth of India less submissive to authority, a necessary prerequisite for the achievement of individual self-reliance and national independence alike. The kind of education Gandhi recommended be put in place of the British system was designed to achieve self-confidence and practical skills rather than book learning: "The real education of the people consists not in literacy but in building up character and in learning to use one's hands and feet" (*CW* 22:229; see also 8:215, 13:332).

Consistent with these ideas, in 1937, Gandhi outlined a self-supporting educational scheme that would provide universal education with minimal reliance on the state. After a primary education, which would include literacy in one's own language, the emphasis would be on manual work to allow the production of marketable items, thus ensuring a self-supporting system rather than one that relied on state funds (*CW* 66:118):[22] "The new system will fulfil the needs of the country as well as the individual and bring about self-reliance. Self-reliance is also a true test of the fulfilment of education" (*CW* 70:277).

Gandhi never endorsed full social equality, which would have gone against his position on the allocation of roles according to caste, but he strongly believed that every individual was entitled to a degree of respect and dignity and the right to the satisfaction of basic material needs. His commitment to women's rights, the erad-

ication of untouchability, freedom of religion, and universal education would ensure a social setting where such aspirations could be
realized, although clearly the ultimate achievement of self-reliance
rested with the individual alone. But, while the individual must
practice self-reliance, he or she must also be an interdependent
social being who learns the meaning of duty from participation in
political and social life and who in turn contributes his or her personal liberation to the good of society as a whole.

Individual Self-Reliance and Village Democracy

Like Rousseau and Jefferson, Gandhi believed that the political
and economic framework most likely to produce self-reliant individuals was a subsistence rural economy with decentralized political institutions. Gandhi came to this realization in South Africa in
1908 after he read John Ruskin's *Unto This Last,* which he said
transformed his life and instilled in him a determination to live in
accordance with the ideals of the book.[23] As did Rousseau and
Jefferson, Ruskin glorified the life of ordinary laborers, particularly farmers. To Gandhi, Ruskin seemed particularly appropriate
for India since he was strongly critical of the materialistic society of
the West.[24] After reading Ruskin Gandhi was to idealize agriculture
as being the pursuit most likely to increase morality. Like Rousseau
he believed that cities were iniquitous and that men and women
should live independently in small villages as farmers (*CW* 10:38).

Gandhi maintained that a decentralized political and economic
system, built around small villages which must become as self-
reliant as possible, was also the best way to achieve Indian independence and national development: "Till we enter the villages we
shall never know India" (27:178). The breaking of the web of interdependent political and economic networks, through the creation
of a self-reliant village economy and local self-government, was the
most effective way of undermining British rule and meeting the
basic needs of the people: "Every village has to be self-sustained
and capable of managing its affairs even to the extent of defending
itself against the whole world."[25]

Gandhi's writings on village democracy are quite similar to contemporary theories of local self-reliance and the basic needs ap-

proach to development. Gandhi maintained that the economy of India should be such that no one should suffer for want of food or clothing; in a situation of scarcity this could be achieved if no one had more than was necessary for his or her physical maintenance (*CW* 54:25, 37:411). Exploitation, which is often contained in hierarchical economic relationships, could be eliminated by a self-contained village structure: "When I say I want independence for the millions, I mean to say not only that millions may have something to eat and to cover themselves with, but that they will be free from the exploitation of people here and outside" (*CW* 58:400).

In 1934 Gandhi announced his retirement from the Indian Congress and set up the All-India Village Industries' Association to work for the rejuvenation of villages, a cause to which he gave considerable attention until the end of his life. The first priority was that villages should supply their own inhabitants' daily needs, particularly food and clothing, and consume what they produce rather than send supplies of raw materials out to cities and foreign trade: only if there were a surplus should they cater to the needs of city dwellers; this would in turn produce income for the villagers (*CW* 59:408–11, 60:17). Gandhi's ideal village would contain cottages built with materials available within a five-mile radius, vegetable gardens for domestic use, perfect sanitation, a dairy, and educational facilities; work would be conducted on a cooperative basis without government assistance (*CW* 64:217). Gandhi was extremely suspicious of government help, which he believed would sap individuals of their self-reliance:

[Each village must be] a complete republic, independent of its neighbours for its own vital wants, and yet interdependent for many others in which dependence is a necessity. Thus every village's first concern will be to grow its own food crops and cotton for its cloth.[26]

This village reconstruction was to be effected through Gandhi's Constructive Programme, a voluntary program based on egalitarian principles which would function independently of the state and begin to build a new social order while the old one was still in existence (*CW* 75:146–166).[27] The Constructive Programme called on all individuals to work for the achievement of an eighteen-point

program at the village level; it included the removal of untouchability, the equality of women, a new educational system, village
sanitation, and the promotion of village industries through khadi,
or the hand spinning of cloth. The significance of the khadi program, which was at the center of the Constructive Programme, was
its goal of decentralizing both production and distribution of the
necessities of life. It was also crucial for the alleviation of unemployment during the slack months of agricultural production.

The goals of the Constructive Programme were economic equality and village self-reliance. Gandhi believed that this kind of voluntary cooperation, at least among small groups, was entirely
possible; the mobilization of every individual through voluntary
participation would lead to the creation of a true democracy as well
as to the creation of self-reliant individuals. The most important
procedural aspect of the Constructive Programme was that it would
bring social and economic changes without the assistance of the
state; conflicts arising during its implementation would be resolved
through nonviolent protest.

Central to this type of village revival was the elimination of unemployment. "We must utilize all available human labour before we
entertain the idea of employing mechanical power."[28] Gandhi continually emphasized the importance of work, which he symbolized
through his personal commitment to khadi as a demonstration that
every person, including those in positions of power, should undertake physical labor of some sort, an idea that was never very popular with leaders of the Congress Party. Gandhi encouraged people
to glorify manual work for its contribution to the elimination of
poverty, but more importantly for its role in promoting self-reliance
and self-respect: "What else can an idle person become but a slave?
Idlers have never become, and never will become, self-reliant" (*CW*
28:135). Work is given a religious connotation based on Gandhi's
interpretation of the Gita, which he took to say that to eat without
producing one's own food is to steal, an idea that is paralleled in
Tolstoy's concept of bread labor:

Leisure is good and necessary up to a point only. God created man
to eat his bread in the sweat of his brow, and I dread the prospect of
our being able to produce all that we want, including our
foodstuffs, out of a conjurer's hat.[29]

Only physical work could be considered true work, and "if every-body lived by the sweat of his brow, the earth would become a paradise";[30] the mental work of poets, doctors and lawyers should be contributed free for the service of humanity.

Consistent with his idealizing of physical work and his belief that every individual should contribute some of his or her labor to the good of society, Gandhi was against charity as a method of alleviat-ing poverty, for "men who live on charity lose all sense of self-respect" (CW 21:238; see also 27:199). Gandhi deplored the grind-ing poverty of India, which drove more people into the ranks of beggars each year, but he criticized philanthropists for giving them alms rather than providing them with work.[31]

While Gandhi was rarely specific about the details of political organization, he did develop a plan for village democracy which, since it would be built around the concept of self-reliant villages, would be consistent with the Constructive Programme. In his Last Will and Testament, written after independence in 1948, Gandhi declared that the Congress Party had outlived its usefulness and he proposed that it should be converted into an Association for the Service of the People with the purpose of implementing the Con-structive Programme. All political and social action must be cen-tered in villages: each village would be a republic, with an assembly of five, elected by the villagers, whose function it would be to revive honesty and industry, settle disputes and teach people to live like brothers and sisters.[32] This political system, the panchayati raj, must be built from the bottom up:

In this structure composed of innumerable villages, there will be ever widening, never ascending circles. Life will not be a pyramid with the apex sustained by the bottom. But it will be an oceanic circle whose centre will be the individual always ready to perish for the village, the latter ready to perish for the circle of villages, till at last the whole world becomes one life composed of individuals, never aggressive in their arrogance but ever humble, sharing the majesty of the oceanic circle of which they are integral units.[33]

Under this system India would become a loose federation with representatives from village panchayats joining together at the dis-trict level and, above that, in some kind of a national council of panchayati representatives. All political authority would originate at the village level, however, and the center would only have authority in areas such as foreign policy, which were specifically delegated from below.[34] This extremely decentralized political system was important to Gandhi because he believed that only if power were broadly diffused could people be protected against exploitation. Such a participatory democracy would be possible only when the gap between the rich and the poor was reduced, since genuine power sharing could never come into existence in a situation of extreme economic inequality.

Gandhi's strategy for reducing economic inequality, through the eradication of unemployment and the elevation of the position of physical labor, was a strategy that made sense for a labor surplus economy such as India's with vast numbers of rural unemployed. By organizing production and political participation in such a way that everyone would be contributing to basic needs satisfaction at the local level, a strategy of local self-reliance could be devised. It was this concept of village independence, which was highly dependent on the contribution of each individual, combined with the eradication of social and political structures that denied people their self-respect, that constituted the core of Gandhi's program for the achievement of local self-reliance.

The Meaning of National Self-Reliance for Gandhi's India

If the core of political and economic action was to be at the village level, Gandhi's concept of nationhood was to be built on patriotism and a recognition of the cultural uniqueness of India and its differentiation from Western society. Gandhi also maintained that India must build a self-reliant national economy and a political system based on nonviolence, both of which would be capable of resisting outside penetration. For Gandhi a sense of national identity did not depend on centralizing political and economic institutions, as Hamilton proposed for early America, but on creating a different kind of nation-state which would be distinct from its Western counterpart and which would remain outside the Western nation-state system.

Gandhi was intensely nationalistic and patriotic; "Only if I die for

India shall I know that I was fit to live" (CW 14:43). One of Gandhi's greatest contributions to the achievement of national self-respect and self-reliance was his promotion of Indian culture, which he sharply distinguished from that of the West. He was extremely critical of Western civilization and lived his life as a demonstration against Western ideas and customs. Gandhi always maintained that he had no quarrel with the English people but rather with their civilization and institutions, particularly their form of parliamentary democracy, which he saw as a tool of an expansive capitalism that had created a gulf between rich and poor both within states and internationally. Gandhi's objection to modern civilization rested, therefore, on its materialism, which drove it to expansion and hence violence. He felt that the British people were obsessed by a commercial selfishness which had led them to the colonization and exploitation of India (CW 9:509).

Gandhi maintained that Indians had actually cooperated with England's colonization of India through their willingness to assist the East India Company in its search for markets and raw materials (CW 10:22).[35] Through its contact with English commerce and English rule, India was being drawn inexorably into modern civilization: if such a civilization were to continue after independence, India would be no better off than under colonial rule. Hence India must reject the trappings of modernity and return to its own cultural heritage:

The ancient civilization of India . . . represents the best that the world has ever seen. The British Government in India constitutes a struggle between the Modern Civilisation, which is the Kingdom of Satan, and the Ancient Civilisation, which is the Kingdom of God. The one is the God of War, the other is the God of Love. (CW 10:189; see also 9:479)

Postindependence India must therefore be distinctive. Gandhi's concept of independence, or "swaraj," was much broader than the usual definition of political sovereignty, being a combination of national independence and individual self-reliance. The root meaning of swaraj is self-rule (CW 20:506)[36] and, in accordance with his belief in the impossibility of separating individual and social action, Gandhi equated self-rule in the individual sense with home rule in the political sense. Indians must feel and be equal to the English (*CW* 18:270). Gandhi's concept of home rule for India, expressed in "Hind Swaraj," which he wrote in 1909, is a statement that interconnects the idea of a self-reliant nation-state, built on a superior civilization committed to the principles of nonviolence, with the idea that its success depended on the possession of such qualities by its individual citizens. "Real Home Rule is possible only where passive resistance is the guiding force of the people. Any other rule is foreign rule" (*CW* 10:51). "Swaraj will not drop from the clouds. It will be the fruit of patience, perseverance, ceaseless toil, courage and an intelligent appreciation of the environment" (*CW* 28:117).

The political and economic components of swaraj were broadly defined to include complete control over India's trade and political institutions, domestic satisfaction of basic needs, Hindu-Muslim unity, class unity and village democracy (*CW* 20:506–507). Gandhi always felt that responsibility for the achievement of the kind of independence he so desired lay more with the actions of Indians themselves than with the relinquishment of power by the British government. "We want to establish swaraj, not obtain it from others. . . . We would have to earn it for ourselves" (*CW* 20:133). When independence did come in 1947, shortly before Gandhi's death, he refused to participate in the celebrations: Hindu-Muslim emnity was already threatening Gandhi's principle of nonviolence and Congress policy was favoring a Western path to development. If independent India was to become a nation-state, built on the model of the West, Gandhi wanted no part of it.

Gandhi strongly believed that a nation's symbol of existence must be its people rather than its government; if political institutions were to be kept weak and limited as he wished, national independence must be built on a strong self-reliant economy, minimum contact with the outside, the meeting of basic needs through agricultural subsistence, and village-based production. Gandhi's plan for a self-reliant national economy was based on the concept "swadeshi," meaning "that spirit in us which restricts us to the use and service of our immediate surroundings to the exclusion of the more remote" (*CW* 13:219).[37] The swadeshi concept centered on the refusal to import foreign goods when similar domestic ones were available. Gandhi argued that the East India Company had ruined

India's cotton industry and that the importation of manufactured cotton contributed heavily to India's unemployment problems (*CW* 64:192). "Any country that exposes itself to unlimited foreign competition can be reduced to starvation and therefore subjection if the foreigners desire it. This is known as peaceful penetration" (*CW* 63:77).

Swadeshi economics emphasized the establishment of small-scale industry as a contributor to the alleviation of unemployment. As mentioned above, Gandhi felt that hand spinning of cloth was a particularly effective way to reduce unemployment and one which would lessen demand for English cloth and thus threaten England's dominant commercial relationship with India.

The argument that an economy that exports raw materials and imports manufactures is inherently weakened by the process parallels that made by many commodity exporters in the Third World today. Gandhi also argued that foreign imports were inappropriate for a subsistence economy that is short of capital and oversupplied with labor. Foreign goods were generally expensive and therefore unavailable to the subsistence sector, whose poverty and unemployment problems could only be alleviated by the local production of basic needs. Gandhi developed the concept of swadeshi economics because he felt that the compulsion to participate in the international economic system forced states into a development pattern designed for compatibility with the world market rather than one which was appropriate for solving the domestic problem of poverty.[38] Swadeshi therefore meant not just import substitution but implied a broader concept which centered on designing a domestic industry appropriate for economic reconstruction—in the case of India, import substitution with labor-intensive methods of production.

Swadeshi meant economic independence, but once again Gandhi broadened the concept to include a personal dimension, "the economic uplift of every individual, male and female, by his or her own conscious effort" (*CW* 64:192). As he traveled in rural areas Gandhi encouraged Indians to take personal responsibility for economic independence through the swadeshi vow, which committed them to the destruction of all foreign clothing and to spinning their own cloth on hand looms. The spinning wheel, "the charkha . . . a symbol of simplicity, self-reliance, self-control, voluntary cooperation among millions" (*CW* 25:20) became Gandhi's symbol of an economically independent India and, as when George Washington had urged Americans to abstain from wearing clothing made from foreign cloth, injected a note of patriotic self-reliance into the development process. "The charkha is the only device which makes us all feel that we are children of the same land" (*CW* 27:181). Gandhi himself spun every day in order to set an example and identify with the economic distress of the countryside.

The charkha was also a demonstration of a technology that Gandhi deemed appropriate for India. While Gandhi has often been described as a Luddite bent on destroying any possibility of modernizing India, a systematic examination of his attitude toward technology reveals a position that is actually quite close to contemporary thought on intermediate or appropriate technology[39] and one which was part of his strategy for alleviating unemployment and achieving economic self-reliance. Gandhi was against the type of technology that would lead to foreign dependence and exacerbate unemployment. Machinery had made India dependent upon England; if large indigenous factories were to supply all the needs of India, it would mean "the need of big capital and dependence for machinery and technical skill on foreign countries" (*CW* 56:146). In 1931, as a demonstration against this type of dependence, Gandhi suggested a boycott of all foreign and machine-made goods (*CW* 48:48). Gandhi also felt that centralized machine production tended to concentrate wealth in the hands of the few: "The big industries can never, they don't hope to, overtake the unemployed millions. Their aim is primarily to make money for the few owners" (*CW* 61:416; see also 28:189).

It was for such reasons that Gandhi urged Indians to use hand production. Another important dimension to his reservations about technology was the need to create employment in a labor-abundant economy:

Mechanization is good when the hands are too few for the work intended to be accomplished. It is an evil when there are more hands than required for the work, as is the case in India. (*CW* 59:356)[40]

Whatever the machine age may do, it will never give employment to the millions whom the wholesale introduction of power machinery must displace. (*CW* 60:55)

Gandhi favored technology, however, when it did not increase unemployment and when it could serve people by lightening their tasks; he also advocated machinery for manufacturing goods which could not be produced in villages (*CW* 68:258).[41] Gandhi was a great proponent of the Singer sewing machine because of its potential for adding to the efficiency of the worker while not causing him or her to become its slave (*CW* 61:187, 81:93); presumably a factory to make such machines would be acceptable and come within Gandhi's definition of manufacture that could not be carried out in the villages. Gandhi maintained that machines must work for people rather than the other way around (*CW* 59:225);[42] where traditional tools sufficed they should not be dispensed with:

Workers must not, without considerable experience, interfere with the old tools, old methods and old patterns. They will be safe if they think of improvements retaining intact the old existing background. They will find that it is true economy. (*CW* 60:354)[43]

Gandhi, however, strongly favored rural electrification to run village machinery such as the sewing machine: he felt that cottage industry with the help of cheap electricity could hold its own against mill production, and with much greater possibility for job creation.[44] Rather than condemning all machinery, it would be more accurate to say that Gandhi was against technologically dominant cultures where technology would induce consumerism and the creation of artificial needs.

While Gandhi's views on technology, economic self-sufficiency, and indigenous culture are evidence of a commitment to national self-reliance, it is less clear whether the type of institutions he advocated could ensure the kind of national autonomy that he sought. While Gandhi could never envisage the Indian nation as being geographically smaller than the area that now comprises India, Pakistan, and Bangladesh, he did not favor the kind of institution building that would seem necessary to hold such a large and diverse society together.

In the case of the United States the creation of a national political economy owed its success to the building of a national communications network. Gandhi was uncompromisingly against modern communications for India, in part because he was deeply suspicious both of the ability of large-scale distribution networks to satisfy basic needs and of the market as an allocator of goods to where they were most needed. He maintained that railways had impoverished India and increased the chance of famine because they encouraged the sale of grain where it would command the highest price, rather than its use for local food needs (*CW* 10:26). Gandhi also felt that India had been one nation before railways were introduced but that their introduction had heightened an awareness of local differences, thus serving as a potential for disintegration.[45]

It appears therefore, that for Gandhi as for Rousseau, the concept of nationhood would exist in people's minds rather than in concrete institutional structures: but it is hard to imagine, with the minimal tasks Gandhi assigned to the state, that his self-reliant independent nation could become a reality. While Gandhi was never very specific about what the functions of the central state would be in his decentralized village democracy, it is clear that they would be few and, as mentioned earlier, they would depend on authority delegated from below.

I look upon an increase in the power of the State with the greatest fear, because although while apparently doing good by minimizing exploitation, it does the greatest harm to mankind by destroying individuality, which lies at the root of all progress. (*CW* 59:319)

Gandhi was more specific about what the state should not look like, however; he could accept neither liberal capitalism, which was prone to exploitation by virtue of its tendency to expand and concentrate wealth, nor Soviet-style socialism which, he believed, destroyed the individual's self-reliance. British representative democracy, which ideally should express the will of the people, was not truly representative since it was subject to the pressure of special interests: "If the voters wake up only to register their votes every three years or more and then go off to sleep, their servants will become their masters" (*CW* 64:194).[46] Soviet communism was imposed from above (*CW* 64:312) and led to a kind of "armchair socialism" of which Gandhi so strongly disapproved: "My concept of socialism implies that people should be self-reliant. That is the only way they can be prevented from being exploited" (*CW* 59:225). For Gandhi, the Soviet example also demonstrated that violence would be the road to the creation of the socialist state, which would then rely on violence for its survival. His commitment to non-violence was central to his dislike of a strong state: "The State represents violence in a concentrated and organized form. . . . [It] is a soulless machine, it can never be weaned from violence to which it owes its very existence" (*CW* 59:318).

This viewpoint led Gandhi to the somewhat ambivalent position of favoring an extremely decentralized political system which, by virtue of its lack of a strong institutional structure, would avoid the oppressive tendencies of Western states. The state must never be an end in itself but "one of the means of enabling people to better their condition in every department of life."[47] Gandhi approved of certain state functions if they furthered the welfare of the people and were performed with a minimum of coercion. He suggested that the state should run large-scale industry, manufacturing the type of products that could not be produced in villages, and oversee necessary large-scale economic activities such as irrigation and power production. Gandhi also felt that the state should be responsible for education and the maintenance of order through a police force, provided that it be nonviolent. In short, the central state should contribute where possible to the attempts of peripheral institutions to further human welfare, an arrangement that would seem to reverse the usual relationship between center and periphery.[48]

The state would also assume a role in enforcing arrangements designed to enhance economic equality. Gandhi assumed, however, that this role would not be great due to his belief that, given the correct cultural setting and indoctrination, Indians could become a moral people who would be individually responsible for the alleviation of inequality. In line with this optimistic belief, Gandhi criticized socialists for their assumption of the necessary selfishness of human nature in capitalist, class-based societies; Gandhi believed that mutual antagonism between labor and capital was not inherent to societies based on private ownership and that this antagonism did not necessarily attain in India (*CW* 58:75).

Gandhi was not against private property rights, for "land and all property is his who will work it" (*CW* 64:192), but rather the inequality of distribution, which resulted in some individuals having more than they could work themselves. Gandhi's approach to land reform was consistent with his belief in individual responsibility and his preference for voluntarist solutions to social reform. He proposed that the landowners themselves must be reformed and persuaded to accept a system of trusteeship, which meant that those who had more wealth than necessary for their minimal requirements should use it to serve the needs of the less fortunate:[49]

Everything belonged to God and was from God. Therefore it was for His people as a whole, not for a particular individual. When an individual had more than his proportionate portion he became trustee of that portion for God's people.[50]

The capitalist class must realize "the signs of the times" and share with the poor; they must become trustees of wealth, not owners of it (*CW* 42:240, 45:328). The rich, Gandhi believed, had a right to earn and accumulate wealth but also a duty to spend it on the poor: "The rich should be taught the doctrine of stewardship and the poor that of self-help" (*CW* 72:136). Should the rich refuse to take on this role of guardian, the poor should retaliate and seize the land, using techniques of nonviolent protest and civil disobedience.[51] Gandhi also suggested that, if all these methods failed, the state should legally confiscate land, a move that was somewhat at odds with his minimalist state philosophy, but was consistent with his belief that political democracy could only be realized under conditions of relative economic equality.

True national independence could only be achieved if this unification of class interests were realized. While Gandhi believed such consensus to be entirely possible, he maintained that, as long as India remained under Western influence, class conflict would continue: in fact Gandhi's explanations for class divisions in colonial society closely parallel contemporary dependency analysis. Gandhi maintained that the Indian elite did not have any rapport with the masses nor did they represent them because they received their education in a foreign tongue. "If we take a handful of persons who have received English education to be the nation, it must be said that we do not understand the meaning of the word 'nation'" (*CW*

13:191). He believed that the alliance of the commercial classes with the British had allowed Indian wealth to be drained out of the country, a situation that would not change with independence with- out "the conversion of our own merchant princes and their depen- dents who are selling their country for their own interest" (*CW* 37:396).[52]

Gandhi shows an awareness of the vast gulf between rich and poor in a passage reminiscent of Rousseau: "Every palace that one sees in India is a demonstration not of her riches but of the inso- lence of power that riches give to the few, who owe them to the miserably requited labours of the millions of the paupers of India" (*CW* 33:272).[53]

"There is no room in the India of to-day and of to-morrow for a governing class," Gandhi declared in 1921 (*CW* 20:188): consistent with his minimalist state philosophy and his preference for volunta- rism, his solution for the eradication of such a class depended on moral suasion and the elimination of an English language educa- tion, neither of which would seem adequate for the task. "Class warfare is foreign to the essential genius of India which is capable of evolving a form of communism broad-based on the fundamental rights of all and equal justice to all" (*CW* 58:248). The achievement of Gandhian communism, since it must be nonviolent, depended ultimately on a change of heart by capitalists; Gandhi believed this to be entirely possible (*CW* 65:119).

Gandhi's notion of national self-reliance was a powerful vision which offered an insightful critique of the shortcomings of Western models of development and a strong commitment to a self-reliant ideology, but its extreme form of political and economic decentrali- zation was hardly a strong foundation on which to build a self-reliant state. Since Gandhi attached such importance to the centricity of the individual and the diffusion of power in the development process, he was unwilling to sacrifice these principles to the interests of building a nation-state capable of playing an active role in the exist- ing international system.

The Role of Gandhi's Nonviolent State in the International System

Gandhi's writings on India's international relations were not ex- tensive but certain themes emerge which are consistent with his

views on national self-reliance. As mentioned above, Gandhi believed that India should be as self-reliant as possible in international economic relations since its commercial ties with England
had placed it in a position of inferiority and given rise to a commercial class whose interests were well served by this detrimental connection:

Independence will not come for the asking. It will come only when
the interests, big or small, are prepared to forgo the crumbs that
fall to them from partnership with the British in the loot which
British rule takes from India. (*CW* 80:80)

Like Rousseau, Gandhi believed that the limitation of foreign
trade and the encouragement of self-sufficiency in basic needs
would contribute to India's invulnerability by removing India from
commercial rivalries which were themselves a cause of tension and
war. "We become prey to invasion if we excite the greed of foreign
nations by dealing with them under a feeling of dependence on
them" (*CW* 19:174)[54]. By becoming self-reliant in food and clothing,

[India would] not then be dragged into an imperialism which is
built upon exploitation of the weaker races of the earth, and the
acceptance of a giddy materialistic civilization protected by naval
and air forces that have made peaceful living almost impossible.
(*CW* 20:296)[55]

Gandhi felt that an agrarian nation was less likely to be drawn
into great power politics: if India were to become industrialized it
must pit itself against the military power of Britain, Japan, the
United States and Russia (*CW* 62:145). Gandhi's disillusionment
with Western democracy was in part due to its propensity for violence; the trauma of two world wars convinced him that Western
states were particularly prone to violence and that they could only
become real democracies when they abstained from war (*CW*
67:305). India must not become an armed country after independence, since this would Europeanize it (*CW* 10:41–42): instead it
must become a nonviolent state in order to be truly independent
rather than a replication of the British Raj. For Gandhi, consistency
between means and ends meant that this nonviolent state could

only come into existence through nonviolent means, which therefore posited a quite different development path from that taken by
the West and also a different relationship with the international
system.[56]

Gandhi believed that it would be entirely possible for such a nonviolent state to defend itself against the rest of the world: he maintained that, with a rural decentralized economy and devolved
political institutions, India was less likely to be captured by foreign
aggressors, a model that has proved plausible in other twentieth-
century colonial wars of liberation such as that in Vietnam. For
Gandhi, however, defense was to be based, not on military means,
but on civilian nonviolent resistance or war without violence.[57]
Gandhi never advocated neutrality in foreign affairs: he maintained that violence was better than cowardice but that violence as a
method would not be necessary when citizens were strong enough
to resist nonviolently.

For me there can be no preparation for violence. All preparation
must be for non-violence if courage of the highest type is to be developed. Violence can only be tolerated as being preferable always
to cowardice. . . . the real effective resistance lies in non-violence.[58]

Gandhi maintained that India was the least militaristic country in
the world. It was this belief that led him to advocate India's role as a
moral force in international relations and as an example of nonviolence, which he hoped would eventually lead to a peaceful, interdependent world order: "It is my unshakable belief that her
[India's] destiny is to deliver the message of non-violence to mankind. . . . No other country will precede her in the fulfillment of
that mission" (CW 62:28; see also 70:201).

Gandhi thought that the world would follow the example of nonviolence after India had adopted it. If the world became truly nonviolent, hierarchical relations between states would cease and every
nation could feel equal (CW 68:390): all nations must be fully independent and self-reliant before they could participate in building a
just world order. While India must be self-reliant it should not be
antiforeign, for Gandhi maintained that chauvinistic nationalism
led to imperialism (CW 25:369).

While Gandhi was a nationalist he believed that the particular kind of nonviolent nationalism he supported must work for the good of humanity at large (*CW* 27:255): when other nations came to adopt India's example of nonviolence, some kind of world federation of all nations could come into existence which, while it did not necessarily commit nations to open their borders to trade, would lead to greater international cooperation. Just as Gandhi believed in the combination of interdependence and self-reliance for the individual through the notion of dharma, this same interaction must be present at the international level in order that individuals might realize their oneness with the universe and so fulfill their duty to all of mankind.

Gandhi's views on international economic relations parallel quite closely those of contemporary proponents of national self-reliance, but his preference for weak state structures would seem to work against the successful implementation of such policies and leave open the possibility of outside penetration via unregulated commercial relationships. Like Rousseau, his foreign policy was constructed on the assumption that a renunciation of power politics, particularly in the military sense, would keep India out of an active role in international relations, a policy quite at odds with that chosen by Indian policy leaders since independence. Whether national self-reliance could be achieved and maintained when international relations were conducted from such a weak institutional base would seem to be extremely doubtful. The lack of institutional structure is compensated for by a reliance on morality and nonviolence, hardly an adequate basis on which to build a more just world order.

Conclusion

Gandhi's writings demonstrate a coherent strategy for self-reliance development, based on the crucial assumption that Western development models may not be appropriate or desirable in other cultural contexts or under different social and economic conditions. Although his belief in the possibility of joining ethical and political principles as a basis for a just society has often stood in the way of serious consideration of his ideas on development, Gandhi's insights into the causes of poverty and the appropriate strategies for dealing with it, in a labor-abundant, resource-scarce country such as India, actually parallel, to a considerable extent, contemporary development strategies, which emphasize basic needs and local self-reliance.

The tension, in Jefferson's thought and practice, between building national power and preserving individual and local self-reliance was resolved, philosophically at least, by Gandhi in favor of the latter. Like Rousseau, Gandhi built his version of national autonomy on a locally based agrarian economy and decentralized political institutions designed to avoid dependency and exploitation both within the state and externally from the international system. Although a staunch nationalist, Gandhi never advocated the kind of state-centered development evidenced in some strategies of national self-reliance such as List's and Hamilton's, which favored building national autonomy on economic power and strong centralized institutions. For Gandhi, political power was to be generated from below through widespread citizen participation in small-scale production and local political institutions.

Gandhi always looked at problems from the perspective of the ruled rather than the ruler: unlike Jefferson he was never a national policymaker, which in some sense absolved him from facing the contradictions between building a self-reliant nation-state and resisting the encroachments on local autonomy which such a strategy may involve. In so far as this tension between local and national self-reliance was addressed, Gandhi favored a kind of "bottom up" strategy which assumed that, with priority accorded to political and economic development at the local level, national institutions would act primarily to complement and support local development efforts.

While Gandhi accorded primacy to the individual in the development process, there were a number of problems that arose from his strategy for molding self-reliant individuals whose social and economic setting was supposed to ensure that they would be responsible for their own lives and welfare as well as for the well-being of others. Gandhi himself was a strong leader who relied on moral suasion and a high degree of voluntarism for the implementation of economic reforms, but his reluctance to enhance state power worked against the institutionalization of the kind of development strategy that he proposed. Gandhi was strongly committed to main-

taining a balance between state and society and he feared that any
strengthening of state institutions would result in a loss of individual self-reliance: this is a dilemma for any theory of self-reliance
but one for which Gandhi's voluntaristic solutions did not seem to
provide an entirely satisfactory answer.

The solution that Gandhi did present came out of his political
philosophy which, although its minimal reliance on the state has
some similarities with Western liberal political thought, rested
more immediately on the Hindu concept of dharma, or the assumption that the individual would use his or her freedom and self-
reliance to serve society. The emphasis on duties over rights, which
differentiates Gandhi from Western liberals, was based on Gandhi's
belief in the possibility of a moral and ethical basis for a just order
both nationally and globally and his assertion that the individual
must not rely on institutions for the implementation of such an
order. In some ways this resembles the Marxist assumption that the
behavior of the individual is shaped by his or her environment, a
position that allowed both Gandhi and Marx to envisage the ultimate withering away of the state in an ideal society. While it seems
extremely questionable whether such a moral basis for a just society
could ever obtain, for Gandhi it provided the resolution of the
contradiction between local self-reliance and state power.

Preference for a decentralized agrarian economy was common to
Rousseau, the early Jefferson and Gandhi: all of them shared the
view that rural life makes for more self-reliant people. For Rousseau and Jefferson small, culturally homogeneous groups ensured
that dominant and subordinate relationships could be controlled,
thus allowing everyone's self-reliance to be preserved. Gandhi was
not particularly concerned with the problem of homogeneity, since
he believed that different groups of people could learn to live together in mutual respect, but he did advocate widespread power
sharing in small groups as a way of minimizing exploitation and
dependence. Again, the lack of institutions to enforce policies designed to prevent social and economic inequalities would seem to
preclude success. Moreover, building political structures from the
bottom up was a unique way of ensuring local self-reliance, but was
not necessarily optimal for building national integration.

For Gandhi the achievement of national self-reliance depended
on instilling a sense of pride in Indian culture and society and

building a self-reliant national economy. Minimum needs would be assured for everyone by decentralizing production and ensuring full employment, both of which could be achieved through the use of small-scale technology. Gandhi was against free trade and territorial expansion, which had been crucial for the preservation of Jefferson's agrarian economy, since he believed that, at the material level he envisaged, India could satisfy most of its needs through economic production within its own borders. Gandhi's preference for withdrawal from the international system was not just for purposes of restructuration, as it had been for List, but was based on a more fundamental belief that participation in the existing world order would commit India to a development pattern similar to that of the West and to a foreign policy based on the threat or use of violence. He did envisage India's leadership in some kind of a reformed world order but was quite vague about strategies for achieving this.

Toward the end of his life, when the independence for which he had worked became a fact, Gandhi's ideas were increasingly diverging from the main trends in Indian development. His preoccupation with village reconstruction and village self-reliance, to be implemented through the Constructive Programme, and his increasing disagreement with the more conventional policies of the Congress party, reflected his personal reaction to the realities of an independent India that did not live up to his ideal of a moral society in which each individual's potential for self-realization and self-reliance could be fulfilled. Whereas Jefferson as a national leader sacrificed some of his earlier ideals to the realities of national power, Gandhi retreated from national policy making and reinforced his commitment to an idealized version of local self-reliance.

While Gandhi's nonviolent state has remained an important symbol of India's struggle for liberation, the path that Indian development has actually taken since independence has been far removed from Gandhi's ideas. The preference for Western models, implemented by a Western-educated elite, predetermined a quite different development strategy from that which Gandhi proposed. The divergence between Gandhi's preferences and the realities of Indian development is a striking illustration of the tension between local and national self-reliance.

CHAPTER SEVEN

INDIAN DEVELOPMENT, 1947–1980: GANDHI'S VISION COMPROMISED

GANDHI'S VISION of an Indian nation built upon democratic self-reliant communities was already threatened by the time India achieved its independence in 1947. His withdrawal from the Congress party and from the mainstream of national politics, as well as the preoccupation of his followers with the problems of Hindu-Muslim violence, considerably weakened his influence on framing the new Constitution. Gandhi's fear of state power and large bureaucracies, with their potential to inhibit local participation—a concern he shared with Rousseau—was largely ignored in the choice of subsequent development policies.

The development path taken by India since independence is actually closer to the Listian model, with its emphasis on building productive capacity and national power, than to Gandhi's version of self-reliance. The tensions found in the American case between achieving national self-reliance and building local community and international cooperation are present in the Indian case also; once again policies associated with the goals of national self-reliance prevail. While the Gandhian tradition provided a particularly strong model for a development strategy consistent with local self-reliance, this type of decentralized, basic needs-oriented development was discarded in favor of building industrial capacity and national power. And, in spite of India's early moralistic stance in international relations, collective self-reliance was not emphasized where it conflicted with India's goal of becoming a regional power.

Like the United States, India is a large country, which makes national self-sufficiency and self-reliance a realistic possibility. But, while India is fairly well endowed with natural resources such as coal, minerals and hydroelectric potential, the size of the population means that pressure on resources is much greater than it was in the early United States. Moreover there is no possibility for substantial territorial expansion, an important determining factor in the development pattern of the early United States.

India's political structure is closer than that of any other contemporary Third World country to a Western democratic political system. While the Indian parliamentary system follows the British model, Indian federalism is closer to that of the United States, where national development strategies were often constrained by federal and state conflicts of interest. In India, however, the central government has always been predominant in terms of constitutional powers, thus avoiding many of the conflicts characteristic of the early years of American independence; on the other hand, India's central government has relied on the states for implementation of development planning, and the tension between these two levels of government has at times been, in practice, a significant constraint on development. A further contribution to the relative strength of the center in Indian politics has been the predominance of the Congress party which, as the leader of the preindependence nationalist movement, achieved a kind of umbrella consensus with the result that it has been in power for all but three years since 1947. The Congress party has been an important contributor to the consensus among national elites for a strong nation-state, an issue that was not resolved in the United States until after the conclusion of the Federalist/Republican struggle.

Like the United States, India was a rural nation at independence and continues as such with 80 percent of the population still living in villages of less than one thousand inhabitants. In contrast to the early United States, however, any agricultural expansion must rely on increasing the yield per acre as there is little arable land not under cultivation. Growth rates in national income of as much as 4 percent per annum have been higher than those of the early United States but the combination of population growth, which has considerably reduced these rates in per capita terms, and the pressure on agricultural resources makes rural poverty an extreme problem in India; between forty and fifty percent of the population were still living below an acceptable, minimum calorie intake in the early 1970s.[1] It has been estimated that this poverty ratio has remained constant into the 1980s and it has been projected that the number of poor at the end of the century is likely to exceed the total population size at independence.[2] Moreover, unlike the United States, India does not have the benefit of an auspicious physical environment. An arid climate and other physical constraints make the task of raising agricultural productivity much more difficult.

In international affairs Indian policymakers, like those in eighteenth-century America, adopted a strongly moralistic tone at independence. Nehru's nonalignment policy emphasized India's desire to distance itself from the tradition of realpolitik and proclaimed the Indian nation to be a guiding force for a new and different type of world order. But, just as events leading to the War of 1812 forced the United States to confront the realities of international power politics, the Indo-Chinese War of 1962 moved India toward a more traditional security-oriented policy and a strong commitment to building military power. Indian foreign policy since 1962 has emphasized building regional hegemony rather than collective self-reliance, a priority that biases development in the direction of building national power rather than local self-reliance. As discussed earlier, United States policy in the American hemisphere exhibited similar characteristics in the early nineteenth century.

As colonies within the British Empire, the preindependence pattern of development of both the United States and India was determined to a large extent by their role as suppliers of raw materials to England and as markets for British manufactures. In both cases England did not interfere internally more than was necessary to maintain control. In the Indian case, British colonialism had been imposed upon an ancient culture with its own indigenous traditions; in the American case, however, colonialism had brought inhabitants from the mother country whose values and allegiances often coincided with those of England.

While it is possible to develop these analogies between the development patterns of the early United States and India, they must be strongly qualified particularly because of temporal and environmental differences. The degree of planning and government intervention in the economy in India is a phenomenon of the twentieth century which could hardly have been anticipated in eighteenth-century America. Nevertheless, despite important differences, the development choices made by these two nations are remarkably similar and seem often to have been made for similar reasons. Although the rural nature of the Indian economy, together with the Gandhian tradition, would seem to predispose India to a strategy that emphasized local agrarian self-reliance, I shall show that national self-reliance and industrial development have usually taken precedence when choosing development options. A considerable short-run dependence on foreign aid has been justified in the name of building self-reliance in the long run; but such a strategy has been necessitated in part by India's priority of building national power rather than local self-reliance.

The Failure of a Decentralized Development Model

A heterogeneous rural society and a liberal democratic political system, together with an avowed commitment to involving people in the political process, evidenced by leading Indian political figures such as Gandhi, Jawaharlal Nehru and Jayaprakash Narayan, would seem to point Indian development in the direction of local self-reliance defined in terms of widespread political participation and decentralized economic development. Yet such a strategy has had at best only partial success: the obstacles to widespread participation in a traditional rural society, together with a cumbersome bureaucracy and a national government committed to development goals that are not necessarily compatible with local self-reliance, have all contributed to a lack of local participation in the development process.

The Constitutional Foundation for Local Self-Reliance and its Limitations in Practice

In principle, the goals of broadening political participation and increasing social equality were embodied in the Indian Constitution of 1950. The Constitution guaranteed human rights, abolished untouchability and reserved seats in both the central and state legislatures for scheduled castes. Free compulsory education was mandated until age fourteen. The independence movement had built a consensus between rural and urban elites which was embodied in the initial strength of the national Congress party, thus ensuring that the distribution of power would favor the central government. The state governments did retain a large measure of control over the rural sector, however, through their power to tax agriculture and implement federal land reform schemes. And, in spite of the Congress party's predominance at the national level, the central government has continuously been required to counter local loyalties, which it sees as a threat to its own preeminence and to national integration in general: since independence such tendencies have resulted in a continual centralizing of power which reached a climax during the Emergency of 1975–77.

While the Indian Constitution did reflect an attempt to devolve power to the state level, provisions for any further devolution were weak. Article 14, which designated village panchayats as units of local self-government, was an addition that was not seriously intended or implemented.[3] Formulated at a time when Gandhians were not actively involved in the political process, the Constitution ignored the third level of government almost completely. Moreover, leading untouchables such as B. R. Ambedkar argued strongly against local self-government since they felt that untouchables could only achieve emancipation from their oppressed position in villages through recourse to external political authority.[4]

While the Congress Party, before and during the early years of independence, had developed a stronger and more widespread political organization than any other independence party in the Third World, increasing centralization of power and a neglect of institution building during Indira Gandhi's premiership contributed to the erosion of local participation in the development process. Moreover, certain features of Indian society together with developmental priorities have further reinforced these tendencies. First, the traditional values of village India, associated with the hierarchies of caste relationships and the overriding importance of dharma, act in opposition to the principles of liberal democracy with its emphasis on rights and individual political participation. Second, the lack of fundamental change in the social and economic structure has meant that existing elites, upon which the Congress party relies for political support, have been able to block many of the political, economic and social reforms embodied in the Constitution. Finally, the choice of an industrially led development model, which presumed that agriculture would be pulled up by a prosperous industrial sector, did not reflect the norms of local self-reliance. When this model failed, the result was an increasing reliance on imports both of food and the inputs such as machinery and fertilizers necessary for increasing domestic agricultural production, neither of which was compatible with the goals of local self-reliance.

In spite of the constitutional abolition of caste discrimination, caste is still the dominant mode of social organization in village India. Such an institution works strongly against individuals' determining their own fate in life, since it predetermines their occupational and social status at birth: a large measure of social control is exercised through dharma or the duty of performing one's prescribed role in society, which is reinforced by the rewards and punishments of reincarnation. While the Western concept of individual self-reliance is strongly associated with personal efficacy and the possibility of social mobility, the caste system sets the individual in a collectivist framework which constrains social mobility and emphasizes duty to caste over individual rights and rewards.[5]

At the national and state levels of government, particularly in the South, the rigidity of the caste structure has been broken; members of underprivileged castes have advanced through the political offices set aside for them under the Constitution, and in urban areas caste distinctions have become blurred. However, the use of legislation at the national level to eradicate the exploitative aspects of the caste system has not necessarily lessened local resistance to the abolition of an institution which remains fundamental to the structure of Indian society. An ambivalence to traditional institutions is manifest also in the views of national leaders: while Nehru supported the granting of special privileges to backward castes,[6] so that they might advance economically and culturally to a point where they could become self-reliant citizens,[7] he admired the collectivist orientation of Indian society, of which caste is one manifestation, as opposed to what he termed the excessive individualism of the West. In *The Discovery of India* Nehru suggested, as had Gandhi, that the disintegration of the traditional social structure of India might lead to complete social disorder.[8] However, Nehru realized that while this social order maintained stability it was not conducive to progress: as a solution to this problem he opted for what he called the "Third Way," a combination of Indian collectivism and Western progress through which a democratic pattern of socialism might be achieved.[9]

Nehru also strongly believed that underprivileged groups should rise through education rather than by relying on special privileges. While the constitutional guarantee of free primary education would seem to be a strain on the resources of a country such as India, by international standards educational spending has been high relative to national income.[10] However, India has allocated an abnormally large percentage of its education budget to higher learning,[11] a policy that produces an elitist and urban bias in educational philosophy and tends to reinforce colonial practices rather than increase social mobility. Attendance at primary schools is probably considerably lower than official estimates, particularly for females,[12] and while literacy has grown in percentage terms, the expansion of primary education has not kept pace with population growth, which has meant that the total number of illiterates has actually increased.[13] Moreover, agricultural education, which would increase personal efficacy in rural areas through the provision of relevant skills, is looked down upon even at the primary level.[14]

The position of lower castes in India has also been improved by universal suffrage; when a local subcaste is numerically dominant in a village, universal suffrage may make it possible for it to vie with a higher caste for political power. Measured in terms of percentage of eligible voters who vote, political participation is higher in India than in the United States:[15] the reaction against the Emergency of 1975–77, when the Congress party suffered its first major defeat at the polls, suggests that in spite of the traditional structure of village India, there is considerable support for the principle of political democracy.[16]

In spite of universal suffrage, the right to own private property, which was strongly reinforced in the Constitution and in subsequent land reform legislation, has been a severe brake on the achievement of relative social equality, an important condition for individual and local self-reliance. While, in the early United States, economic dependency was reduced by the widespread ownership of small landholdings and an expanding territorial base, in India, under conditions of land scarcity, the right to own property has strongly reinforced existing social and economic hierarchies at the village level. Local landowning elites, operating within a well-defined local hierarchy, are often able to block antidiscrimination policies of the national government.

The reluctance of the national government to alienate state and local elites is in part due to the need for their support for a development strategy that has generally favored industrially led economic growth over agricultural development. In spite of its attempts at local political reform in rural areas, the Congress party reflects an urban bias which is evident both in its approach to planning and in the system of economic rewards, political power, and education that it represents.[17] Since independence Congress has demonstrated a bias toward urban interests, one example of which is reflected in its commitment to keeping food prices low; at the same time it has attempted to develop a strategy to deal with rural problems without losing the support of entrenched rural power structures, upon which it depends for electoral success, and without changing the urban-rural terms of trade in favor of agricultural producers. Such a strategy involves compromises on issues of social reform and redistribution of resources, particularly in areas such as land reform.

A Weak Opposition to the Congress Consensus

Unlike the United States after independence, where Republicans and Federalists representing rural and urban interests respectively competed for political power, the Congress party in India has been in power almost continuously since 1947. In spite of the split in Congress, which developed in 1968, and the subsequent weakening of the party by Indira Gandhi's policies, no clear alternative has emerged at the national level. During 1977–80, the only time when Congress was voted out of office, India was ruled by the Janata coalition which included followers of Jayaprakash Narayan, the national political leader who most closely represented a Gandhian development strategy. While Narayan was a national figure of some importance who represented a program that strongly contrasted with that of Congress, he never managed to gain enough grass roots support to create a viable political alternative.

Narayan's political thought is quite compatible with Western theories of local self-reliance and contains elements that parallel both

Rousseau and the early Jefferson. He criticized representative democracy for not giving individuals enough scope in the management of their own affairs and advocated instead a communitarian or partyless democracy: "democracy requires that the people should depend as little as possible on the State."[18] Also, like Rousseau and Jefferson and closely following the ideas of Gandhi, Narayan believed that the setting in which individuals could best organize their lives on a self-reliance basis was in small communities: the self-governing village, which would engage in both agricultural and industrial production in a complementary manner, would be the key organization upon which some kind of federal structure could be built. While Narayan advocated the state ownership of any necessary large scale industry, he suggested that local manufacture should be cooperative or owned by workers, thus giving individuals a sense of personal efficacy in the management of their own lives.[19]

As has been the tendency in Indian politics, Narayan has been revered for his idealism but, apart from some of his ideas which were incorporated into the government's community development and panchayati schemes, his impact on policy issues was never very great. Narayan himself renounced party politics in 1957 after he had sought unsuccessfully to gain Nehru's commitment to radical structural reform: yet, with his voluntarist approach to institutional change, it is doubtful how successful he would have been in implementing his ideas. As discussed in chapter 6, the tension between the kind of social structure most suited to the development of individual self-reliance and the degree of state intervention necessary to implement it was problematic for Gandhi's approach also. Like Gandhi, Narayan assumed that national unity could be achieved through certain intangible factors which would obviate the need for a strong institutional framework:

National unity or strength does not depend upon the list of subjects that a central government deals with, but on such intangible factors as emotional integration, common experience and aspirations, national ethos, mutual goodwill and the spirit of accommodation.[20]

It is unlikely that, in a country as diverse as India, national unity

could be built on such "intangible factors": faced with the contradictory goals of building national power and satisfying basic needs,
the Congress party has increasingly opted for the former. Narayan
came out of his self-imposed political retirement in 1973 to protest
this increased centralization of power. While the Janata coalition
incorporated Narayan's ideas, its viability as a national political
party was impaired by ideological contradictions. Since it depended for support on both the urban middle class and prosperous
agriculturalists, its promises to the poor were more than it could
deliver: the electoral victory that Janata gained in 1977 was more a
protest against Congress than a vote of support for its own policies.

Narayan himself realized that the implementation of his political
program, given the existing political and social structure, was a
problem: "The question is can the picture be fundamentally altered
through the ordinary democratic process? Even if the opposition
[the Janata coalition] wins, will the picture change? I fear no."[21]
While Narayan's movement came closest to embodying the principles of decentralized democracy, built on the ethos of individual
and local self-reliance, its likelihood of success, without the strong
degree of enforced government intervention necessary for such
radical change, was not high.

Basic Needs and the Failure of Community Development

The attempt to meet basic needs through decentralized production is an important aspect of local self-reliance. As early as 1949
Nehru committed himself to a goal of self-reliance in food, predict-
ing that India would import food for no longer than two years.[22] In
actual fact Indian food production lagged behind domestic demand throughout the 1950s and 1960s: poor soil, a scarcity of arable land and adverse weather conditions, punctuated by severe
droughts, resulted in periodic emergencies which necessitated frequent importation of foreign grain. While poor physical conditions
certainly contributed to India's difficulties in achieving self-sufficiency in food, choice of policies and bureaucratic rigidity also had
their effect on productivity.

The attempt to increase agricultural productivity went through a
series of policy approaches: in the 1950s land reform and community development were emphasized, policies that are most compati-

ble with local self-reliance as previously defined. A more technocratic strategy, which was introduced in the mid 1960s in response to a series of crises, moved agricultural production closer to a more market-oriented approach.

In a situation of extreme inequality with respect to land tenure, land reform was declared to be a priority issue for the Congress party at independence. In 1949 a Report of the Congress Agrarian Reforms Committee proclaimed that a capitalist agrarian structure was not acceptable for India since it would result in the exploitation of one class by another.[23] In the early 1950s 13 percent of the rural population owned 64 percent of the land but, in spite of Gandhians' efforts to redistribute land and Nehru's strong initial commitment to land reform, this situation has not changed to any significant degree. Beyond the abolition of the zamindari, a class of landowners created by the British for revenue collection purposes, Congress has not implemented a great deal of land redistribution. Finding it necessary to rely on landowning elites for electoral support, its early stance on institutional reform has been considerably diluted: what reform it did propose was generally blocked at the state level by landowning elites who control state legislatures and by widespread evasion of land reform legislation.[24] This resistance to the implementation of land reform policies, along with states' refusal to increase agricultural taxation, has been a constant source of tension between national and state governments. Unlike in the early United States, the right to private property, which was written into the Constitution, has, under conditions of extreme inequality in a resource-scarce society, been a considerable stumbling block to the universal satisfaction of basic needs.

Most of the agricultural reforms that involved some degree of social change were made in the 1950s. The Community Development Programme, which was introduced in 1952, proposed to increase productivity through the social and political mobilization of peasants rather than through changes in production techniques. This program had a mixed record of success and community development has never been an area to which the national government has given priority in terms of attention or funds.[25] While involving government in rural development at the village level, the program has suffered from overbureaucratization and lack of sensitivity to local diversity. Implemented from above, it has frequently lacked a local leadership that understands local needs; often it has been local elites who have been able to capture the available resources. The panchayati raj, or system of local government, which was to be the political structure through which community development schemes would be implemented, has also suffered from lack of government support.

The Community Development Programme received the most attention during the years of the first Five Year Plan: its purpose was to delegate community organization, irrigation and other agricultural improvements, and the building of roads and schools to the local level with as little interference from government agencies as possible once the program was established.[26] An extensive review of the Community Development Programme during the 1950s, which was undertaken by the Balwantrai Mehta Committee in 1958, found that there had actually been little agricultural planning at the local level and that the program continued to rely heavily on government from above rather than on local initiative.[27] This Committee recommended further political decentralization centering on the revitalization of the panchayati raj, a three-tier system of local government at the village, block and district levels. Village panchayats, operating on an elective basis with reservations for women and scheduled castes, would raise resources through a property tax and be responsible for land management, water and roads: at the block level an elected panchayat samiti would oversee health, education and industry. The third tier, the district level, would be responsible for planning and coordination.

Although many districts did set up this system of local government on the recommendation of the Committee's report and were given full responsibility for implementing community development projects, its record of success has been disappointing. Conceived as an instrument whereby political power might be redistributed in favor of the peasant, in practice panchayats have been dominated by disproportionate numbers of the largest landowners and high caste members in any given village. The norms of traditional village government are often in tension with the practices of liberal democracy at the national level: administering the law under principles of legal equality is antithetical to caste privileges and customary village practices, a factor that reinforces the difficulties that arise with the implementation of nationally conceived development schemes.[28]

Moreover, village-sponsored development schemes have been rare, and plans conceived at the central and state levels have often been unresponsive to local demands. In spite of the advice of the Balwantrai Mehta team that "community development can be real only when the community understands its problems, realises its responsibilities, exercises the necessary powers . . . and maintains a constant and intelligent vigilance on local administration,"[29] the report's recommendations for democratic decentralization have generally not been taken seriously: in 1960 a majority of villages did not regard community development programs as their own and continued to rely on government for effecting the development of rural areas.[30]

Probably the most serious impediment to decentralized development, however, has been the bureaucracy. At all levels of government Indian development has been constrained by excessive controls and rigid bureaucratic structures which have strongly inhibited local initiative. The imposition of a British administrative model, which established a hierarchical system with little trust accorded to local officials, upon the tradition of dharma, where the individual performs tasks out of a sense of duty rather than concern for their results, produced a bureaucratic system more committed to order and rule than to initiative or social change.[31] Tension between the national and local levels of government and planning have reinforced the tendency of local officials to shun responsibility and look to superiors for guidance, with the result that manipulating the distribution of resources has taken priority over generating development plans. Attempts at local initiative, which are characteristic of the Gandhian tradition, have often been undermined by superiors trained in the traditional colonial approach to supervision. Bureaucratic control has tended to reinforce the belief among the population that government agents are performing their duties for the benefit of the government rather than for that of the villagers.

Bureaucratic rigidities and the lack of priority afforded to the Community Development Programme contributed to the failure of decentralized development. As Prime Minister, Nehru was unwilling to endanger the political consensus on which Congress relied by supporting the kind of radical reform that would have been necessary for effective decentralized development.[32] Moreover, Nehru never supported Gandhi's vision of the self-sufficient village, upon which the community development ideal was built, since he felt that such an economic arrangement would commit its population to an extremely low standard of living. In a passage reminiscent of List, Nehru advised that villages must "approximate more to the culture of the town";[33] basic needs could best be satisfied through a system of interdependence based on modern transportation.

During the second Five Year Plan, 1956–61, with its emphasis on industrial growth, Indian policy moved away from its initial priority of agrarian reform and the local satisfaction of basic needs: the share of plan resources allocated to agriculture dropped from forty-four to thirty percent.[34] A Ford Foundation report of 1959 suggested that agricultural production should be raised through technological changes and price incentives, a recommendation which initiated a shift in policy away from the initial emphasis on community development programs. A more market-oriented, technocratic approach to raising agricultural production offered a viable alternative to a government increasingly unwilling to implement institutional reform over the opposition of landed interests. After the death of Nehru in 1964, the Shastri government was even less receptive to land reform due to its weak political base: the increasing burden on the balance of payments, caused by necessary grain imports, as well as deteriorating relations with the United States, pushed it to find an alternative indigenous solution to the problem of agricultural productivity.

Given the problems that faced the Community Development Programme and the urgent need to increase productivity in the face of recurring agricultural crises, the choice of options appeared limited in the mid 1960s. The Green Revolution, which was the solution adopted, did succeed in increasing domestic agricultural production although it committed India to a program, recommended by the World Bank, that was based on Western values and techniques and was therefore quite antithetical to the ethic of local self-reliance or the Gandhian approach to development. The Green Revolution was a strategy based on the introduction of high-yielding seeds and chemical fertilizers to increase productivity on existing acreage. It was selectively targeted at certain crops, wheat in particular, and at certain geographical areas that were expected, because of favorable physical and social environments, to produce the highest yields.

With some setbacks, particularly in the early 1970s, this increase in agricultural production meant that, by 1980, India had become self-sufficient in food grains even to the extent of exporting some wheat. These gains in production have been extremely uneven, however, both in terms of crops and regions, the most dramatic gains having been registered in wheat in just three states, the Punjab, Haryana and western Uttar Pradesh:[35] with less than 2.5 percent of the total population, the Punjab accounted for 7.1 percent of the total output of food grains in the mid 1970s.[36]

The Green Revolution, by shifting agricultural production toward a more technological, market-oriented approach, highlighted the tension between supporters of community development and those who favored a capitalist agricultural sector. It stimulated an important debate among Indian policy makers which has continued into the 1980s.[37] The Green Revolution strategy reflects the norms of national self-reliance; it is quite compatible with the Listian model, which advocated modernizing agriculture and improving internal markets. But increasing food production by targeting certain areas and using techniques that may not be accessible to all raises the important question of whether inequality may actually have increased because of the uneven distribution of benefits and an increased reliance on the market.

The issue of whether the Green Revolution has caused an increase in inequality and a decline in the well-being of the poor is a subject of ongoing debate among scholars and policymakers.[38] While there is evidence that both small and large farmers are better off in Green Revolution areas, there is little to suggest that the gap between rich and poor in rural areas has narrowed. Even supporters of the Green Revolution acknowledge that India's improved performance in food production has not had much effect on the landless poor in growth areas nor on marginal rural populations outside these areas.[39] In spite of a food grains surplus in 1979, malnutrition levels remain high; any strategy that relies on internal markets for distribution is problematic in a society with a large subsistence population.

The Green Revolution also called for a high degree of support from an industrial sector that had committed itself to the priority of industrialization. The setback that Indian agriculture experienced in the early 1970s was not only due to adverse weather conditions but also to the failure of the industrial sector to provide adequate inputs for agricultural production. The growth rate in the provision of electricity to rural areas in the 1970s was less than that achieved in the 1960s; rural irrigation schemes and production of fertilizer also lagged behind what was needed to sustain initial gains made under the Green Revolution.

The Green Revolution was a strategy that attempted to raise agricultural production without the sweeping structural changes promised by the Congress party at independence. In spite of Indira Gandhi's assertion, after her massive victory in 1972, that she would be more aggressive in the promotion of land reform, the inability of Congress to organize support for reforms at the state level blocked implementation and was actually followed by a period of increased centralization of power. Centralization impedes local decision making in agricultural policy and works against designing policies that could narrow regional disparities.

As the debate between proponents of capitalist agriculture and those who favor community development has continued, a report of the Economic Advisory Council, set up by the prime minister in February 1983, advocated a renewed emphasis on decentralization.[40] Citing reasons such as high energy costs and climatic variations, it proposed planning more specifically for local needs, using alternate energy sources, and reviving the panchayati raj. While there appears to be renewed interest in development that is decentralized and closer to the Gandhi model,[41] established interests at the state and local level, upon which Congress depends for political support, as well as the continued problem of a rigid bureaucratic apparatus, raise the question of whether this approach can have more success in the future than it has in the past. While India has made important strides toward becoming self-sufficient in food at the national level, an agricultural strategy that is closer to the norms of local self-reliance, and that might relieve some of the problems caused by unequal growth, remains elusive.

The Commitment to Building a National Economy

Policy Priorities Since Independence

As was the case in colonial America, India's economy before independence was determined by its position in the British imperial system primarily as a supplier of raw materials to the mother country. Certain industries, such as sugar, cotton textiles, and iron and steel, had been encouraged, the latter for its contribution to the British war effort, although India was severely lacking in indigenous technology. In spite of its economic linkages with England, there was a greater consensus in India among urban and rural elites and national policymakers for building an economy free of foreign penetration than was the case in the United States at the time of independence, where elite loyalties were more closely tied to the mother country. In spite of the rural and extremely diverse nature of the economy, the British had left a transportation network which was impressive by Third World standards and which made an important contribution to the infrastructure necessary for building a national economy.[42]

There was, then, in India in 1947 a widely shared commitment among national leaders to the goal of building national self-reliance, which was to be achieved through a development strategy based on industrial growth and import substitution, particularly in industries that would generate further productive capacity. In spite of India's being a nation with one of the lowest per capita incomes in the world, the issue of poverty was not directly addressed by such a strategy, but it was assumed that the trickle-down from industrial growth would generate sufficient employment to raise per capita income.[43]

While both growth and social justice were stated to be among the goals of India's development strategy, the emphasis has generally been on growth of the kind that is consistent with building national power and autonomy. Policy leaders found it easier to identify with an industrial growth strategy that also promoted the political objectives of nation building that were so crucial in the early years of independence.[44] India's first priority has been building national power rather than social welfare issues, which might have been better addressed by a quite different development strategy. Consequently the Indian government has survived threats to national integrity with more success than it has solved the plight of the poor.[45]

The importance attached to nation building can be seen both in statements of leading policy makers and in the emphases and objectives of the planning process. While Jawaharlal Nehru had paid lip service to Gandhian policies before independence, it is clear from his speeches and writings that his goal for India was industrial modernization as the road to economic independence and national power:

Few of us, I think, accepted Gandhiji's old ideas about machinery and modern civilization. We thought that even he looked upon them as utopian and as largely inapplicable to modern conditions. Certainly most of us were not prepared to reject the achievements of modern civilization, although we may have felt that some variation to suit Indian conditions was possible. Personally, I have always felt attracted toward big machinery and fast traveling.[46]

In an overwhelmingly rural country, where agricultural productivity was to become the key to the success or failure of economic growth, Nehru was not an admirer of rural life:

A village, normally speaking, is backward intellectually and culturally and no progress can be made from a backward environment. Narrow-minded people are much more likely to be untruthful and violent.[47]

I have almost a horror of it [peasant life], and instead of submitting to it myself I want to drag out even the peasantry from it, not to urbanization, but to the spread of urban cultural facilities to rural areas.[48]

Consistent with this dislike of rural culture, Nehru did not believe in village self-reliance as did Gandhi: instead he proposed that the satisfaction of basic material needs should be achieved through a more market-oriented strategy based on improved transportation,[49] a solution compatible with the Green Revolution, which was implemented after his death. Nehru firmly believed that basic needs should be met within the national economy rather than by relying on foreign trade: like Gandhi, Nehru strongly supported limiting economic linkages with the international system.[50] As early as 1938 he was proposing national self-sufficiency in order "to avoid being drawn into the whirlpool of economic imperialism."[51]

While Nehru often referred to the advent of world socialism and the growing interdependence of nation-states, both of which would make isolation impossible, he strongly believed that India must meet its domestic needs for food, raw materials and manufactured goods internally: "to base our national economy on export markets might lead to conflicts with other nations and to sudden upsets when those markets were closed to us."[52] While such a statement would suggest a commitment to building a balanced economy, Nehru's personal preference for modernization and his desire to see India become a powerful nation in the international arena biased his development strategy toward industrialization and national integration over agriculture and decentralization.[53]

If commercial interdependence must be avoided because of its potential for exploitation, scientific and technological interdependence were the necessary building blocks of modernity. Nehru strongly supported sending Indian students to the West for scientific training: he believed that science was one of the most significant contributions made by the West and the only hope for solving problems of hunger and poverty. If the West had misused science for evil ends it was up to the East to see that its applications were for the benefit of mankind. Nehru believed that only societies that were willing to adopt modern scientific techniques could be dynamic, self-confident and hence self-reliant: "I do not think it is possible for India to be really independent unless she is a technically advanced country."[54]

Consistent with his admiration for Western science and technology, Nehru clearly favored giving priority to advanced technology in Indian development planning: although he often stated that he supported both large-scale and cottage industry,[55] it is clear that his preference was for the former: "The latest technique has to be followed, and to adhere to outworn and out-of-date methods of production, except as a temporary and stop-gap measure, is to arrest growth and development."[56] "An attempt to build up a country's economy largely on the basis of cottage and small-scale industries is doomed to failure." Nehru believed that such a country would end up as a "colonial appendage."[57] While the issue of technological dependence is not addressed directly, it must be assumed from Nehru's strong commitment to modernization that he felt that such dependence could be avoided through the economic power that comes from industrialization. Nehru often stated that political independence was meaningless without economic independence,[58] an issue that also confronted American policy makers after independence. "There is no such thing as freedom for a man who is starving or for a country which is poor."[59]

Before independence Nehru was strongly committed to socialism as the economic framework best suited to the satisfaction of the individual's basic needs and to the achievement of national power: after he became prime minister the latter goal clearly took precedence. In practice, socialism meant that industries that were producing capital equipment should be under government control:[60] Nehru as a politician was never willing to commit himself to the kind of socialist society that would include the structural reform necessary for a radical redistribution of income.

Although compromises necessary for the retention of political power forced Nehru to give up his earlier commitment to structural change and opt instead for what he called "pragmatic socialism," a policy of gradual social change necessitated by the constraints of pluralist democracy,[61] he was quite consistent in his support for industrialization. In an interview a few years before his death he reiterated: "We want to become an industrialized nation with greater production, greater income, more national and per capita income and independent and self-developing economy."[62]

While Nehru's political thought, particularly before independence, represented the left wing of the Congress party, there was a wide consensus among all shades of political thinking—excepting the Gandhian tradition which was a minor force in Congress politics in 1947—about the need to build a strong industrialized national economy. Representing economically conservative interests within Congress, Sardar Patel, deputy Prime Minister from 1947–50, also advocated a development strategy, built on industrialization and import substitution, to promote national self-reliance. In a speech given in 1949, Patel urged Indian industrialists "to try to manufacture the machines we now import and make our economy self-reliant."[63] Like Nehru, Patel linked industrialization to the achievement of national power: he believed that industrial growth was crucial in order that India might be strong militarily and self-reliant.[64]

Nehru as Prime Minister dominated Indian politics until his death in 1964: his views on the priority of national self-reliance in economic development were widely shared and to a large extent have continued to influence the planning process and the policy orientation of subsequent national policy leaders both within Congress and outside the party.

Although balance-of-payments crises in the mid to late 1960s forced greater attention to be paid to the agricultural sector, the commitment to economic independence through industrialization, based on a mixture of socialism and private enterprise designed to raise productivity rather than redistribute wealth, did not change. In spite of Indira Gandhi's rhetorical support for socialism, she never committed herself to any greater degree of social reform. Although in an important speech in 1972 Indira Gandhi suggested that maximization of the GNP should not be the only goal of economic development, she continued to emphasize the centrality of increased productivity. While trade deficits forced a stronger emphasis on export promotion in the 1970s, the priority goal of building national self-reliance through import substitution and the indigenous development of productive powers remained.

The stated objectives of India's Five Year Plans support the commitment to building national self-reliance found in the statements of policy leaders. The priority accorded to building productive powers is particularly noticeable in the dramatic shift in emphasis from the First Plan (1951–56) to the Second (1956–61), which was a much stronger statement of development objectives. The architect of the Second Plan, P. C. Mahalanobis, shared Nehru's desire to build a strong national economy, advocating that the planning process should give priority to the indigenous production of capital goods in order that India might be economically independent and militarily secure. Mahalanobis was extremely critical of liberal development strategies, which advocated development through comparative advantage and the international division of labor, since he felt that such strategies consigned countries like India to inevitable poverty due to their specialization in primary products.[65]

The result of this change in emphasis was a strong shift in resources from agriculture to heavy industry along with a drastic increase in the power of the Planning Commission. During the Second Plan period there was a large increase in aggregate investment in the public sector, which was primarily concerned with setting up and controlling heavy industries of "basic and strategic importance" such as arms, atomic energy, iron and steel, engineering, chemicals, and communications:[66] the goal of this policy was to increase capital stock and thus release India from its dependence on foreign trade in these areas, which were considered crucial for national power and security, thereby laying the foundations for a self-reliant national economy.[67] Import substitution was chosen over export promotion, since planners felt that such a policy would allow for more control by limiting planning to the domestic economy rather than being dependent on foreign considerations: import substitution was also considered to be a policy more consistent with the attainment of national power and prestige.

Such a strategy was not particularly useful, however, for other developmental goals such as reducing unemployment, decreasing inequality or satisfying consumer demands. Consumer industries were consigned to the small-scale private sector and, while it was hoped that unemployment would be reduced either by increased employment in cottage industries or by employment generated through increased savings and investment, its reduction was not a high priority issue nor was it to interfere with the industrial growth strategy of the Second Plan. Increasing the emphasis on small-scale, labor-intensive industry or agriculture, a strategy that presumably would have been more suitable for employment generation, was not perceived as meeting the domestic political needs of integrating a large divided country with aspirations for a major role in world affairs.[68]

The emphasis on industrial development was continued into the Third Five Year Plan period (1961–66). At various points in the Third Plan document, goals such as "self-reliant and self-generating" growth are referred to as a major objective of the planning process: for the first time self-reliance is mentioned specifically as a high priority goal, although it had been implicit in earlier documents.[69] Self-reliance, however, was used specifically in the sense of import substitution in heavy and machine-making industries.

The Draft Outline of the Fourth Plan (1966) was more explicit in its definition of self-reliance, which it described in terms of self-sustaining growth and freedom from foreign aid. While acknowledging that no country can aim at economic autarky, the Outline states:

What it [self-reliance] does mean is that the country's requirements will be met within to the maximum possible extent, and that what it must obtain from abroad will be limited to what it cannot produce within its borders or finds it uneconomic to do so it terms of comparative advantage, and even more important, that it is able to pay for these imports with its export earnings.[70]

Once again "overriding importance" was assigned to industrialization as the cornerstone of economic independence: in spite of the greater emphasis on food productivity, after the famines of the mid 1960s, the total share of the rural sector in proposed development outlay was only 21 percent during the Fourth Plan period.[71] By the time of the publication of the Fifth Plan in 1976, the problems of unemployment and the setbacks in food production had become sufficiently serious that some change was imperative. With the stated dual objectives of removing poverty and achieving self-reliance, the Fifth Plan reiterated the commitment to raising agicultural productivity through the technocratic strategy discussed earlier: although there was some shift in priorities to the agricultural sector, the emphasis on capital-intensive projects remained.

Indian National Development in Practice

In terms of actual performance the growth rate of the Indian economy after independence, approximately four percent per annum, was quite high by preindependence standards: but with the greater than expected population increases, per capita growth was a much lower 1.8 percent per annum. Moreover, the benefits from growth in the industrial sector have been quite unevenly distributed with the greatest gains being made in heavy industry where large-scale investment products have done considerably better than consumer items.[72] In the agricultural sector, gains have also been uneven, with disproportionate increases going to landowners in Green Revolution areas.

That state ownership has largely been confined to new heavy industries is proof of the importance that the government attaches to this sector of the economy. In spite of Nehru's stated commitment to socialism as a means to improve human welfare, nationalization has been tied to an attempt to increase productivity rather that to the attainment of social justice.[73] State ownership of "commanding heights" industries was also justifed in terms of national self-reliance since it was considered easier to protect publicly owned enterprises from the unwanted influence of foreign business and investment.

In spite of this desire to control crucial industries, the government has not attempted to compete with the private sector; while bureaucratic inefficiencies, as discussed earlier, have been very considerable at the national level also, thus generating a strong resistance to nationalization, this laissez-faire attitude toward the private sector can also be explained by the lack of political support for a radical transformation of society. The First Industrial Policy Resolution of 1948 sought to reassure the business community when it rejected a policy of nationalizing existing private enterprises; however, state monopolies were set up in the areas of defense and transportation, sectors of the economy that could be considered crucial for a nationalist economic policy. Where heavy industries such as steel, engineering and chemicals were already in private hands, the government sought to exercise a measure of control over them, but such intervention was generally limited to core industries that were considered essential for national self-reliance.

In the area of technological research India has pursued a policy consistent with this emphasis on the development of productive powers. With the highest scientific and technological capacity of any Third World country and the third largest pool of scientific manpower in the world, after the United States and the Soviet Union, India would seem to have the potential for leading the Third World away from its technological dependence on the North.[74] But with a large proportion of research and development, as in the West, going to high technology, particularly in areas such as defense, that build national prestige, the technological capacity has generally not been linked either to mass needs in India or to problem areas of particular relevance to other Third World countries.[75]

While national self-reliance has been the rationale for the attempt to build technological sophistication, rural areas in particular have suffered from this technological bias, and the record for promoting indigenous innovation and adaptation in areas such as health, food production, and alternative energy has not been impressive: these areas are crucial, however, if the goal of self-reliance in food and other basic needs is to be sustained. Moreover, the links between government and university-related scientific research and private industry have often been weak, with the result that industries have tended to buy into Western technology, which puts pressure on the balance of payments, increases technological dependence, and again weakens the potential for national self-reliance.[76]

This strong emphasis on government intervention in the economy in order to develop productive powers is quite consistent with the Listian strategy discussed chapter 3; but the resulting gain in heavy industry, relative to other sectors of the economy, has had a number of negative consequences for the achievement of self-reliance at all levels. The industrial growth strategy was not designed to promote income redistribution: heavy industry has remained quite capital intensive and has therefore failed to generate anywhere near adequate employment opportunities. The consequence of such a strategy has been the creation of a dual economy with an industrial sector, modeled on Western lines, where wages have remained relatively high: this has resulted in a concentration of income in industry and significant income gains for some sections of the middle class and some factory workers while, at the same time, unorganized labor has barely maintained its position.[77]

This intensification of the dual nature of the economy, along with the lack of priority given to the rural sector in the years after independence, were hardly consistent with the achievement of balanced growth or the universal satisfaction of basic needs, both of which are essential components of a successful self-reliance strategy. The industrialization model was designed with the intention of building a powerful national economy rather than as a direct attack on poverty. Such a policy increasingly failed to engender much popular support, with the result that the government was forced to abandon some of its emphasis on heavy industry and concentrate more on agriculture and consumer goods during the 1970s. But the erosion of popular support led to increased centralization and repression in the Indian political system, a trend that inhibits local self-reliance and may, in the face of the declining legitimacy of the government itself, undermine the planning process altogether.

An unintended consequence of India's industrialization strategy was an increased dependence on foreign aid. Import substitution, which was designed to promote national self-reliance, had the opposite effect of imposing a severe strain on the balance of payments, particularly in the 1960s, both because of the necessity to import needed technological inputs and because of the shortfall in agricultural production for which such a strategy was partially responsible.

While foreign aid to India has not been large in per capita terms, as a proportion of world aid flow it has been substantial[78] and has had a number of important consequences for Indian development. Ironically, foreign aid may have actually made India's capital-intensive, "self-reliance" development strategy possible both because it supplied a substantial proportion of the necessary capital and also because, until the mid 1960s at least, commodity assistance contributed to the relative neglect of the agricultural sector; moreover, such a strategy is one that is generally supported by aid donors and thus was strongly reinforced. Foreign aid may also have made development without structural reform possible since it lessened the burden on the extraction of domestic resources.

In spite of increased rhetoric about self-reliance, foreign aid to India rose dramatically during the 1960s, in part because of the conjunction of the war with Pakistan with a fall in agricultural production due to adverse weather conditions. But, in spite of some improvement in the balance of payments position during the 1970s, due to export promotion, remittances of emigrant labor, and increases in food production, India continued to receive substantial amounts of foreign aid.[79] Despite Indira Gandhi's justification of "aid to end aid," internal political failures did not help to increase the mobilization of domestic resources, in addition to which the Indian government, at the end of the decade, still remained basically committed to a development strategy that gave first priority to industrialization. With loan repayments in the late 1970s accounting for approximately one half of annual foreign aid receipts, India continued to be highly vulnerable to the international system.[80]

While the Fifth Five Year Plan (1974–79) included the goal of the

universal satisfaction of basic needs, industrialization and the enhancement of national power continued to demand high priority.
The dilemma for India has been the inability to satisfy both goals at
once. To delay industrialization would not have been consistent
with the vision Nehru and his successors had of a powerful self-
reliant India with aspirations to becoming a global power.

India's Quest for Regional Hegemony

Pursuing a Policy of Nonalignment

Like the United States at independence, India faced an international system dominated by great power rivalries which, due to their
global dimensions, impinged considerably on Indian development.
India's commitment to nonalignment was an attempt to remove
itself from cold war politics and implement a foreign policy that
would minimize dependence on either bloc. As was the case with
the early United States, India's policy was designed to achieve autonomy in spite of weakness and it is in the area of foreign policy
and national security affairs that India's quest for self-reliance has
been most evident. India's aspiration to move from this position of
weakness to becoming a great power has biased its economic development planning, with its heavy emphasis on industrialization, in
favor of a strategy that places a high priority on the achievement of
this goal. In the words of Indira Gandhi:

Eradication of poverty was an important ideal, but even more im-
porant was the preservation of India's freedom—the development
of a defense capability against external threats, the building up of
infrastructure to strengthen the economy and achieve self-reliance
and protect the nation's honor and self-respect.[81]

In part, Mohandas Gandhi's development schemes were unacceptable because their concern for mass welfare would act as a
brake on the type of development needed to build national power.
It is India's perception of the external environment and its determination to play an important role in international affairs which
have driven modernization: maximization of political sovereignty,
military security and economic independence have been sought in

order to ensure autonomy and self-reliance with respect to the international system.

The foundations for India's policy of nonalignment were laid by Jawaharlal Nehru and Krishna Menon who, in various diplomatic roles, was Nehru's principal aide in the formulation of foreign policy. The rationale for nonalignment contains striking parallels with American neutralism as anunciated in Washington's Farewell Address. In both cases it was perceived that the preservation of independence in the face of initial weakness could only be achieved by avoiding alliances with great powers: taking sides would also create internal divisions among peoples who needed unity and integration. The central task, in the opinion of both American and Indian foreign policy makers at independence, was to protect their countries' power potential until weaknesses could be overcome.

Nehru frequently expressed his aspirations for India's becoming the leader of the nonaligned world, a role that would considerably enhance its position in the international system, but which he felt was contingent on modernization: "I have little doubt that a free India on every plane will play a big part on the world stage, even on the narrowest plane of material power."[82] Nehru strongly believed that the emergence of India in world affairs would be "something of a major consequence in world history."[83] His vision of India, which "is bound to be a country that counts in world affairs,"[84] was to be achieved through nonalignment and the building of strong military capabilities. Siding with one of the great powers, "in the hope that some crumbs might fall from their table," would not be in India's best interests.[85] Reminiscent of Jefferson's early statements on foreign policy, Indian nonalignment rhetoric at independence carried strong moral overtones. It is clear, however, that it was perceived as the only possible policy for a newly independent weak nation with aspirations for a significant role in international politics:

The less we interfere in international conflicts the better, unless, of course, our own interest is involved, for the simple reason that it is not in consonance with our dignity just to interfere without producing any effect. We should either be strong enough to produce some effect or we should not interfere at all.[86]

It is evident then that nonalignment did not preclude a more active role in international politics after India had built up the capability to project its power more effectively. Already, in 1946, Nehru was describing India as the pivotal nation in Asia upon whom the defense of the Indian Ocean area would depend.[87]

This view of India's future role as a significant actor in the international system was shared by Krishna Menon: Menon described nonalignment as a policy of nondependence which would establish India as an "important quantity in world affairs" and give it self-confidence and inner strength.[88] He believed that India should never accept foreign assistance because this would compromise its nonaligned status and its bid for self-reliance. Clearly, Menon shared Nehru's belief that India would become a great power, and it was during the Menon era that the foundations were laid for the achievement of self-reliance in the production of armaments, including high technology weapons.

In spite of the attempt to build self-reliance in defense capabilities, the wars that India fought with China and Pakistan during the decade from 1962–71 placed a severe strain on its resources. Although Goa was seized from Portugal in 1961, the Chinese invasion of 1962 was a defeat and humiliation for India, and the 1965 Indo-Pakistan War, which followed the Pakistani invasion of Kashmir, was inconclusive in terms of gains for either side. These events had the effect of reducing India's role as a moral force in world politics and diminishing its status as a leader of the Afro-Asian world. After the subsequent victory over Pakistan in 1971, however, India reemerged as the undisputed power on the continent but in a somewhat different role, with a foreign policy more consistent with the principles of realpolitik than with the moral superiority that had been emphasized earlier.

India's extended role as a significant middle power with global aspirations and increased military capabilities coincided with the increased centralization of national power which was discussed earlier. As an emergent power India stressed self-reliance, particularly in terms of weapons production and the avoidance of external alliances: the Indo-Soviet friendship treaty of 1971 tainted this image of nonalignment somewhat, but India has always seen the West as the greater threat to nonalignment, due to international capital's potential for penetrating the economy and the extended role of the United States in Asia which began in the 1950s. Moreover, since the

Chinese invasion of 1962, China has been perceived as India's most immediate military threat, and an alliance with the Soviet Union could also provide an important counterweight to this threat. However, since the Soviet invasion of Afghanistan in 1979, Indo-Soviet relations have become more complicated: as the Soviet Union grows more interested in playing an active role in South Asia, India has shown signs of shifting back to a more neutral stance vis-à-vis the great powers.

International Trade and Investment Policies

The internal development strategy chosen by Indian policy makers after independence was quite consistent with this goal of building self-reliance and autonomy with respect to the international system. An international consequence of this strategy has been India's policy toward trade and investment, which has been quite rigid and protectionist in terms of the importation of both products and capital and also with respect to multinational corporations.

India has consistently followed a policy of import substitution since independence, the only modification being somewhat more emphasis on export promotion since 1966, when a severe crisis in foreign exchange necessitated such a change. The criteria for tariffs and other forms of protection have generally extended well beyond economic arguments alone; protection has been justified in terms of supporting the indigenous development of productive powers in order to achieve eventual autonomy in necessary investment and consumer goods. A 1945 government resolution stated that industries could be protected if it were in the national interest to do so, the result being that protection was often justified on grounds of "indigenous availability" regardless of cost.[89]

In order to implement its policy of import substitution, the government has been strongly interventionist in foreign trade, with controls on imports extending well beyond tariffs alone: a system of allocation of foreign exchange to industries has ensured a large measure of supervision over the quantity and type of imports allowed. Increasingly, foreign trade has been conducted through government agencies with more than half of Indian imports being channeled through the State Trading Corporation by 1973:[90] the two most important criteria for allowing imports have been necessity for the economy and domestic unavailability.

The result of this policy has been an almost complete ban on the importation of manufactured consumer products and a high level of importation of the type of capital goods necessary to build domestic productive capacity. It has been argued that such a policy has severely limited the economic efficiency of domestic industry.[91] The foreign trade sector in particular has suffered the consequences of rigid bureaucratic controls which, as discussed earlier, have impeded the development process at all levels; in this case cost, delays, and corruption have been particularly problematic. Clearly, however, this policy was dictated by the politicl considerations of building national power and prestige and national self-reliance.

Import substitution has also led to a number of unintended consequences with respect to foreign trade. As mentioned earlier, the heavy emphasis on industrial growth and the development of productive powers, along with the relative neglect of the agricultural sector, necessitated large grain imports in the mid 1960s: the subsequent high technology strategy chosen to increase food production, together with the substantial amounts of foreign capital needed to produce investment goods domestically, imposed a severe strain on the balance of payments and in this sense may actually have frustrated India's goal of national self-reliance.

India's shift to a policy of export promotion in the mid 1960s followed a period of relative stagnation in the export sector, in part due to the low priority it received in the early years of development planning.[92] Along with increased attention to exports, an attempt was made to diversify their composition. However, the heavy reliance on traditional exports such as jute and tea continued into the 1970s, although such commodities have experienced very little increase in terms of world demand; moreover, cotton textiles, which have been an area for Indian export promotion also, often face high tariffs in developed country markets.

The attempt to diversify the composition of exports was accompanied by the diversification of both markets and sources of supply and was aimed particularly at reducing trade with England.[93] The result of trade diversification has been a substantial shift to increased trade with the Soviet Union and the United States, India's two largest trading partners, and East Europe and Japan; however, there has been little progress toward increasing trade with other Third World countries, although promoting intra-Third World trade is a frequently cited goal of proponents of the New International Economic Order, of which India considers itself a strong supporter.

The economic difficulties of the 1960s led to a widely shared consensus among policy makers and scholars that increased agricultural productivity and export promotion must be undertaken in order to achieve India's goal of national self-reliance in light of the higher than anticipated volume of imports necessary for India's chosen development strategy. It has also been suggested that increasing exports of labor-intensive manufactures, an area in which India has a comparative advantage, would help solve the growing crisis in unemployment.[94] Increasing emphasis on labor-intensive exports is, however, quite at odds with the national power model of development that India has chosen, since it would direct internal development away from its priority on high technology industries, which feed into the military industrial complex. Moreover, in a large economy where the international trade sector accounts for only about five percent of the total GNP, it is doubtful whether any strategy of export-led growth would be successful in alleviating domestic development problems.[95]

India's attitude toward foreign investment has been both stringent and protectionist. At the time of independence India led the attack on foreign investment in various international organizations, and the Industrial Policy Resolution of 1948, which stated that all major industries should be in Indian hands, reinforced this rhetorical stance. While policy makers at independence believed that foreign direct investment would not be necessary for Indian development, foreign exchange difficulties and the need for sophisticated Western technology incurred by the type of development strategy India chose led to a more receptive attitude toward multinational corporations in the late 1950s.

Nevertheless, government policy toward direct foreign investment has always been cautious; the entrance of multinational corporations has generally been highly restricted and conditions placed on their operation have centered on issues of joint ownership and the sharing of technology.[96] Where foreign investment has been permitted, it has often been in high priority, high technology , import substitution industries, such as metals, chemicals, and petroleum, where indigenous technological capacity is insufficient.[97] While it has been argued that this cautious attitude toward foreign investment may have resulted in a number of missed opportunities in areas where such investment might be considered advantageous to India's development strategy,[98] such a policy has generally been consistent with the goal of maintaining national control over economic development.

Self-Reliance in National Defense and Security

Import substitution and the selective treatment of foreign investment were designed in part to aid the building of heavy industry, which was considered necessary for enhancing defense capabilities; it is in the area of building strategic capability that India has made the strongest bid for self-reliance. At the time of independence the Indian government declared that defense industries should be established and maintained whatever the cost.

In spite of Gandhi's commitment to pacifism, as early as 1938 Nehru was advocating the building up of Indian defense forces after independence. Nehru believed that defensive capability could only be built through industrial growth and modernization, with the state playing a large part in the management of defense industries:[99] "defence means industry and production, not all the soldiers in the world will be of any good to India otherwise."[100]

Immediately following the 1962 Indo-China war, in which India was defeated by a much more powerful Chinese military, defense spending increased from thirty to over forty percent of the government budget,[101] and has continued to be a high priority area of development planning ever since. By 1977 India had the third largest standing army in the world, the fifth largest air force, and the eighth largest navy:[102] "the main thrust of defence production is towards the twin objective of modernization of arms and equipment and achievement of progressive self-reliance and self-sufficiency."[103] The Indian domestic arms industry is the biggest among Third World non-communist states in terms of value, volume and diversity[104] and, in the late 1970s, defense production was the second largest sector of the Indian economy, with Indian arms beginning to enter the export market.[105] The military industrial research complex is also one of the largest in the Third World with one quarter of all research devoted to defense.

In spite of the high priority placed on self-reliance in arms production, the defense buildup after 1962 necessitated an importation of foreign armaments which has continued ever since. Until 1960, England was the major supplier of weapons to India but, after an attempt to diversify sources of supply in the 1960s, the Soviet Union replaced Britain as the major supplier in the 1970s, although its relative share declined somewhat toward the end of the decade.[106] In the 1960s India became the sixth largest importer of arms in the Third World: foreign purchases were made in highly complex systems, such as fighter aircraft, which India was not technologically capable of producing at home. At the same time, however, India attempted to contract with foreign companies to manufacture sophisticated weapons under coproduction agreements in India, and electronics has become an area of high priority in Indian industrial policy.

India's nuclear policy has also been consistent with its desire for self-reliance in the defense area. India was one of the first countries to become interested in nuclear power, having set up a laboratory for nuclear research as early as 1947. Nuclear research has been one of the most autarkic of India's scientific endeavors, and India is the only Third World country with a breeder reactor program. Although India is not far behind technically in weapons delivery systems, to date it has not opted for strategic nuclear capability. However, its refusal to sign the nonproliferation treaty and the detonation of a nuclear device in 1974 suggest that it is keeping the nuclear option open.[107] The capability to build nuclear weapons is thought to reinforce India's position of nonalignment and self-reliance in international politics,[108] and the "peaceful nuclear explosion" of 1974 has frequently been interpreted as an effort to gain respect and assert India's dominance in the subcontinent. Moreover India is almost unique in the lack of domestic criticism of the high priority placed on military production: there was such strong support for the nuclear option that it was felt that renouncing the nuclear explosion would have been politically unfeasible for Indira Gandhi.[109]

This strong emphasis on building indigenous strategic capability, which has to a large degree driven development options, is in part responsible for India's failure to meet the mass needs of the population: it is a demonstration of the problems that arise when Third World countries enter so heavily into the arms race that resources are diverted away from development. While it has been argued that economic resources used for military objectives may actually speed up economic growth,[110] the type of growth that has been generated in high technology industries has intensified the dual nature of the economy and has not been particularly effective in satisfying basic human needs. While the economy as a whole has grown at around three to four percent per annum since 1950, it has been estimated that heavy industry has grown at approximately ten to eleven percent per annum over the same period.[111] In the opinion of one analysis, "the poor in India, like those during the Western industrial revolution, are paying most of the price of rising national power."[112]

Regional Hegemony Versus Regional Cooperation

There should be an Eastern federation, not hostile to the West, but nevertheless standing on its own feet, self-reliant and joining with all others to work for world peace and world federation.[113]

Nehru's vision of Asia standing as a force for world peace was undoubtedly motivated by the Second World War: in 1939 he suggested such a federation, comprising India, Burma, Ceylon and Afghanistan. Just as Thomas Jefferson had envisioned the United States as a moral force remaining apart from Europe's quarrels during the Napoleonic Wars, Nehru, like Gandhi, frequently referred to Asia as providing an example for world peace, with India playing an important role in what he predicted would be a resurgence of Asia in world affairs.[114]

In reality, however, India has not focused its attention on Asia to any great extent except in the negative sense, over issues of security. In the early years of independence both Nehru and Krishna Menon appeared quite indifferent to regional issues and little attempt was made toward greater regional integration. The primary focus of attention was India's world role, the subcontinent being important only insofar as it was an arena for great power rivalries.

India's relations with Pakistan have been quite hostile since independence because of the legacy of partition, the unresolved dispute over Kashmir, and the tension caused by United States-Pakistani relations, which are based on the perception of Pakistan as part of the American security perimeter. The increased reliance on the Soviet Union in order to counter United States involvement with Pakistan, as well as to balance India's fear of a much larger China, works against India's desire to stay out of cold war issues and interferes with its policy of nonalignment.

While it is unlikely at this point that India would consider it feasible to try to reconquer Pakistan, India has followed a policy of retaining military dominance over Pakistan, which also furthers its claim to becoming a world power. After the 1965 Indo-Pakistani war, India's military buildup ensured its strong strategic superiority in 1971 when war broke out again:[115] currently India's military forces are more than twice the size of Pakistan's. India's explosion of a nuclear device in 1974 must also be considered part of this bid to establish superiority over Pakistan.

With a relationship dominated by strategic considerations, efforts to establish economic cooperation with Pakistan have been minimal; this is true also of interactions with other Southern Asian states where relations are less militarized. Again, strategic concerns have predominated and ties with states such as Nepal, Sri Lanka, Afghanistan, and Bangladesh have been conditioned by the goal of countering Chinese and Pakistani influence. Relations with these smaller Asian states have been quite paternalistic, similar to great power relationships with India; for example, India has provided Nepal with aid that is tied to India commodity exports, a form of aid to which India has been extremely opposed for itself. While India has made attempts to diversify trade with both Western and socialist countries, apart from Japan there has been little increase in trade with the rest of Asia since independence.

India's foreign policy within the region has been aimed therefore at maintaining superiority over its neighbors and countering any bid they might make to strengthen their positions. India's land armies on the Chinese and Pakistani borders are stronger than the forces they oppose and India is in the process of building two independent blue water navies in order to establish naval superiority in the region. By the late 1970s India's military power was probably more than adequate for maintaining its hegemony in Southern Asia.

Consistent with a policy designed for entry into global power politics, India's relationships with the rest of Southern Asia could be characterized as dominant rather than cooperative. In spite of rhetoric to the contrary, India's defense policy would suggest that it has been moving toward the role of a regional hegemon: such a policy is quite inconsistent with the principles of regional and collective self-reliance to which the Third World, including India, has committed itself in various world order debates. It would seem that India's foreign policy has contributed to the reproduction of realpolitik on a regional level; it has not been consistent with the more self-reliant strategy of renouncing power politics and pursuing a new kind of diplomacy, a strategy that was predominant among India's stated foreign policy objectives at independence.

Conclusion

The 1983 Mid-Term Appraisal of the Sixth Plan stated that, in 1980, fifty-one percent of the Indian population still lived below the poverty line. It proclaimed that the alleviation of rural poverty was to be, in the future, one of the primary objectives of the planning process. Its recommendations included a program of integrated rural development aimed directly at the rural poor through more cooperative production, land reform, minor irrigation schemes, and the revival of village industry, particularly the Khadi program, with renewed emphasis on the use of handlooms and a more important role for the village panchayats.[116] Such a program, which shares many common characteristics with the Gandhian development strategy discussed in chapter 6, is a dramatic shift from the priorities of the later 1950s, when development through industrialization was emphasized, and is an admission that trickle-down has not been successful in achieving the universal satisfaction of basic needs.

If the alleviation of poverty is taken to be the primary goal of development, then the Sixth Plan Appraisal is an admission of the failure to achieve this goal. While not denying that the eradication of poverty may be an overwhelming task under any type of strategy, this analysis has attempted to show that, in fact, goals other than the alleviation of poverty have taken precedence when policy choices for Indian development have been made.

Self-reliance, one such goal of India's development strategy, has been defined in terms of the priority of the development of indigenous productive powers and national self-sufficiency in food grains in order to build a modern industrial economy that could be politically, economically and strategically self-reliant with respect to the international system. Such a strategy, which emphasizes the goals and norms of national self-reliance, closely parallels the Listian model discussed in chapter 3. It is a mercantilist strategy which assigns an important role to the state in building national economic power in order to increase capability with respect to the international system. Consistent with Listian prescriptions, a strong attempt has been made to build national productive powers and to insulate the domestic economy from the detrimental effects of foreign trade and investment. The important role that India has assigned to planning has been at least partially justified by an attempt to resist foreign penetration and to build national political and economic autonomy.

By intent, therefore, Indian economic development policy was much more dissociationist than that of the early United States: in reality, however, it has been heavily influenced and heavily penetrated by the international system, which in turn is partially responsible for the type of development policies that have been pursued. The high priority placed on the achievement of self-reliance in industrial productive capacity and strategic capability forced India into a much greater reliance on foreign technology and capital than had been planned and resulted in severe foreign exchange problems during the 1960s, when this mercantilist strategy was at its height.

Even if it were to be successful, this type of strategy emphasizes only one aspect of self-reliance, that of building national power; other goals such as the satisfaction of basic human needs, widespread participation in the development process, and regional cooperation, were not promoted by such policies and progress toward their achievement may actually have been retarded. Local self-reliance of the type recommended by the Sixth Plan Appraisal carries with it implications for radical institutional reform which could be destabilizing for the existing social structure, and thus prospects for its successful implementation remain in doubt: moreover, an economic development strategy that emphasizes basic needs, intermediate technology, and labor-intensive methods of production does not build national power. Where there has been tension between welfare considerations, which might have been better served by such a strategy, and state building, the latter has taken precedence, a priority which was true during the era of state building in the West also.

Gandhi's vision of India as a nonviolent state that would lead the world in the establishment of a new order has been severely compromised. As the dominant nation-state in the region, the attention that India has paid to building national power has not been particularly conducive to furthering regional cooperation or collective self-reliance. The pursuit of national power results in the reproduction of dependency relationships on a regional level and severely inhibits the achievement of the multiple goals that should be part of a complete strategy of self-reliance. In both the American and Indian cases, regional hegemony took precedence over the achievement of these multiple goals.

PART FIVE
CONCLUSIONS

CHAPTER EIGHT

PROBLEMS AND PROSPECTS FOR SELF-RELIANCE DEVELOPMENT IN THE CONTEMPORARY THIRD WORLD

T HE MULTI-LEVEL self-reliance development strategy developed in part 1 aims at reducing dependency, both at the individual and national levels, and also at making possible more cooperative international relations among states. The Rousseau/List polarity, discussed in part 2, presents two strikingly different, even contradictory, interpretations of this multilevel strategy of self-reliance: Rousseau's concern for securing the self-reliance of the individual within his community was shown to contradict List's developmental emphasis on the independence of the nation-state. The case studies in parts 3 and 4 offered further evidence of this contradiction, raising the question of whether self-reliance as a multilevel, multiobjective strategy of development is realizable at all within the context of the contemporary nation-state system.

Although they advocated different resolutions of this dilemma, all the theorists under consideration recognized these potential conflicts between what I have called the communitarian and statist priorities of self-reliance development. Even though all of them, except Gandhi, were writing over one or even two hundred years ago, the debates in which they were engaged turn out to be very relevant for contemporary discussion of development in India and other Third World countries. After comparing and contrasting the views of these theorists and showing how their arguments continue to be part of the contemporary development debate, this chapter will assess the adequacy of their proposed resolutions to the conflicting priorities of self-reliance development, testing them against evidence from the American and Indian cases. I shall argue that, while the contradictions in development priorities are not inherent, they are highly likely due to the threatening nature of the international system of power politics and the penetrating effects of a dominant world economy. Finally, this chapter will conclude with some thoughts on the conditions necessary for a successful strategy of self-reliance development to be designed and implemented in the contemporary Third World.

Some Further Thoughts on the Rousseau/List Polarity

Table 8.1 summarizes schematically the central features of the Rousseau/List polarity. The components characteristic of a multi-level conception of self-reliance, listed in the first column, are taken from the outline in chapter 1. Components 1 through 5 are most often associated with a strategy of local self-reliance, 6 through 10 with the national level, and 11 and 12 with the collective or regional level. While table 8.1 shows no priority or emphasis on collective self-reliance by either of these theorists, their differences on components 1 through 10 are a strong demonstration of their preference for the characteristics typical of either local or national self-reliance.

The contradictions between them are significant: the only points of convergence in these areas are a shared concern for agricultural development and the necessity of minimizing international trade. Even on these topics there are important distinctions, however. List was arguing for a modernizing agricultural sector dependent for its efficient performance on its interdependence with a prosperous industrial sector, whereas Rousseau preferred a peasant subsistence agriculture far removed from urban influence. With respect to international trade, List's desire for delinkage was temporary and limited only to the industrializing stage, whereas Rousseau's anti-trade stance was a much more fundamental commitment to permanent isolation.

One of the major problems for the contemporary Third World is how to develop in a world dominated by more powerful states. Table 8.1 suggests some profound differences in orientation toward

Table 8.1 The Rousseau/List Polarity in Self-Reliance Development Strategies

Components	Rousseau	List
1. Priority of universal basic needs satisfaction	Strong	Not a priority
2. Emphasis on rural development	Strong	Yes, but linked to cities
3. Emphasis on decentralized political participation	Strong	No
4. Balanced economic growth at the subnational level	Yes, emphasize agriculture	No
5. Preference for small industry	Yes	No
6. Preference for large industry	No	Yes
7. Augment central state power	No	Yes
8. Balanced economic growth at the national level[a]	No	Yes, but food imports at later stage
9. Limit international trade	Yes	Yes, but only temporary
10. Build military capability	No	Yes
11. Build regional cooperation	No	No
12. Build horizontal international linkages	No	No

[a]Balanced economic growth at the subnational level means limiting markets even within the national economy. Balanced economic growth at the national level allows for internal distribution through market allocations.

this issue as well. While both Rousseau and List assumed, in their writings, a world that included more powerful developed states, Rousseau's strategy was community-oriented nation building: by positing a radical dissociation from an international system that was neither threatening nor tempting Rousseau focused inward on his most important level of dependency reversal, that of the individual and the local community. By not building up national wealth and power, he assumed that his preferred state could remove itself from the arena of power politics. List's desire for self-reliance was defined primarily at the level of the nation-state: by concerning himself with the relative power of foreign competitors, List focused outward, giving priority to more conventional state-strengthening and vulnerability-reducing measures.

Self-Reliance Development Within the Contemporary Debate

Is the appeal to self-reliance, so frequent in contemporary international order debates, mere rhetoric? My analysis has suggested that it need not be. A close examination of the writings of Rousseau, Jefferson, List, and Gandhi has demonstrated that they focus on many of the most central issues in the historical and contemporary development debates. These issues, which were salient to Rousseau over two hundred years ago in his quest to mold self-reliant citizens and states, are surprisingly similar to those that concern self-reliance theorists today. I shall now draw out these interconnections from a summary of the theorists and cases treated in this book.

The theorists whose views on development coincide most closely with the norms and goals of the contemporary communitarians discussed in chapter 1, are Rousseau, the early Jefferson and Gandhi. These three theorists were all reacting against economic growth characterized by industrialization, urbanization, and the larger, more complex social and economic structures associated with an increase in the division of labor. Such changes, they believed, would lead to inequality, alienation and a loss of individual self-reliance.[1] Nowadays this type of self-reliance is often criticized as economically reactionary and politically idealistic because so many of its proponents favor a return to simpler economic arrangements while, at the same time, they propose radically different political structures. While the same criticisms could be applied to Rousseau, the early Jefferson and Gandhi, a more fundamental debate on this issue would begin with the recognition that communitarians' recommendations for a simpler economics derive from their political preferences.

Rousseau, the early Jefferson and Gandhi all preferred quite different political structures, based on democratic institutions centered in local communities, that would allow as widespread political participation as possible in order to ensure that the interests of the state were closely connected with the interests and concerns of its individual citizens. Since political equality, participation and individual self-reliance were of overriding importance to these writers, their preferred economic arrangements were, to a large extent, predetermined by these normative objectives: each felt that the type of economy most likely to ensure the realization of these political goals would be a rural one composed of farmers with small land holdings. An agrarian economy based on a minimal division of labor and private ownership of property would also allow for the economic independence of the individual and encourage the satisfaction of basic material needs at the local level.

While each favored private ownership of property, provided that it was on a small scale and could be worked by the owner, both Rousseau and Gandhi were concerned with the tendency of private property ownership to foster inequality. Their ambivalence on this score can be explained by their fear of excessive state power under public ownership: yet both advocated state ownership as a last resort should equality not be realizable otherwise. Jefferson's neglect of this issue can probably be accounted for by the abundance of land in eighteenth-century America.

This defense of their political and economic priorities must acknowledge, however, a certain overidealization of rural life. For Rousseau, the early Jefferson and Gandhi the benefits of a rural existence went well beyond the satisfaction of material needs: the physical labor of a farmer was considered enobling since it contributed to self-respect and autonomy whereas urban life, with its inequalities and refined division of labor, created dependency and alienation. Even though these theorists felt that a decentralized agrarian economy was most likely to ensure widespread political participation, its potential for economic growth was limited. But neither Rousseau nor Gandhi favored growth beyond the level necessary for the universal satisfaction of basic needs, precisely because they could not resolve this dilemma of its potential to exacerbate inequality. The early writings of Jefferson resolved this problem by allowing for an increase in consumption and production through international trade, which would remove the dilemmas of inequality and dependence to the workshops of Europe, a solution that is hardly consistent with the principle of self-reliance.

Contemporary communitarians frequently display this same overidealization of rural life; it is evident in the debate over the type of agricultural strategy to be pursued in India today. Proponents of an efficient, capitalist agriculture seek to make India self-reliant in food grains with respect to the international system while

supporters of a community-based decentralized agriculture emphasize the satisfaction of basic needs without heavy reliance on the
internal market. Communitarians stress the sense of personal
efficacy and the lessening of market vulnerabilities associated with
rural subsistence agriculture and the local production of basic
needs. Statists counter that only with an efficient, modernizing
agricultural sector can production be increased sufficiently to meet
the needs of fast-growing urban and rural populations. They fault
communitarians' preference for small-scale agriculture as being
idealistic and impractical in heavily populated societies which must
generate considerable growth in order to eliminate poverty.[2] The
extent to which community-based strategies reduce economic
growth is a controversial issue in the contemporary development
literature.

A frequent criticism of the contemporary Third World, which
comes primarily from the First World, is that it is replete with new
nationalisms and radical ideologies. To many students of development from the First World, Third World leaders are seen as overly
preoccupied with national integration, economic planning and industrially based growth, to the detriment of social welfare and individual liberties. In this historical survey of self-reliance in its
European, American and Asian contexts, I have argued that there
are significant parallels between these contemporary priorities and
those that were important to policy leaders during an earlier period of nation-building in the West.

Policy leaders, both contemporary and historical, generally support strategies that are closer to the developmental priorities of
national self-reliance discussed in chapter 1. This statist or Listian
version of self-reliance, also evident to some extent in the writings
of Hamilton, Nehru, and Jefferson as president, rejects communitarians' preference for decentralized participatory agrarian communities and assigns primacy to the self-reliance of the nation-
state. The self-reliance of the individual is of secondary importance
to the well-being of the state which could best be assured through
greater political and economic integration. List's and Hamilton's
belief that the energies and passions of individuals should be har-
nessed to the building of a strong nation-state as well as their preference for an urban life-style, reenforced their support for
progress through industrialization. Jefferson's shift, after he be-

came president, to supporting a stronger central government and a manufacturing economy is also consistent with this priority. A similar shift can be seen when Nehru's early preference for democratic socialism gave way to support for a mixed economic system with government regulation of only the commanding heights of the economy, a policy designed primarily to increase productivity and build national economic power.

The tendency of industrialization and urbanization to economic duality, unequal development, and income and resource inequality, which was of such concern to Rousseau, the early Jefferson and Gandhi, was deemphasized by writers in the statist tradition: presumably they felt that the benefits of increased productivity through industrial growth, which would trickle down to all sectors of the economy, would outweigh the need for more radically egalitarian forms of economic organization. Gandhi and Nehru were the only theorists under consideration who lived in an era when industrial socialism was a practical economic possibility. While neither endorsed a socialist model, both used variants of socialist ideas when suggesting how to cope with the possibility of increased inequality and alienation that industrialization might bring. Although far from the statist tradition himself, Gandhi suggested that, in areas such as power generation and other necessary heavy industry where economies of scale seemed more practical, government ownership was preferable, but presumably his decentralized political system would ensure strong local control. Nehru also favored extensive government planning to implement a coherent strategy of development and to insulate the economy from the detrimental penetration of the international system.

An industrializing interdependent economy that would further the cause of national integration was as important to Hamilton and the Federalists as it was to Nehru and the Congress party. In supporting nationally based, industrially led development models, List, Hamilton and Nehru were all advocating catch-up strategies for late developers in the context of a world order dominated by more powerful states. Their emphasis on national development was autonomy seeking: it was intended as protection against the detrimental effects of the international system but, at the same time, it was also an attempt to create conditions whereby participation in that system might be undertaken on better terms.

Communitarians have different priorities when constructing national development strategies but, in an important sense, they too are talking about national autonomy. For Rousseau and Gandhi, building a nation did not necessarily involve national economic integration and, for Gandhi at least, strong centralized institutions were unnecessary since the function of the state was to complement and support local communities. Neither Rousseau nor Gandhi were willing to endow the state with the resources necessary to play an active role in international politics because they did not feel that the type of political and economic development necessary for this projection of national power coincided with the interests of the individual. Autonomy and national survival were to be assured by a nonexpansive, isolationist foreign policy defended, if necessary, by the mobilization of the entire population and the resilience of decentralized institutional structures.[3]

These communitarian and statist orientations toward international politics parallel an important distinction in postwar international relations scholarship between the idealist and realist approaches. Power-oriented, pragmatic, self-styled "realists" have criticized more radical, order-building communitarians for their "idealistic" attempts to envisage or construct a new world order.[4] Some of this same tension is evident between proponents of the statist and communitarian versions of self-reliance. Communitarians see the potential of self-reliance development for constructing a new world order, containing fundamentally restructured individual units, while statists envisage self-reliance as a strategy that would reproduce the old order with different states on top. Statists tend to dismiss the efforts of communitarians to construct a new set of international relations as unrealistic, given the structures of the contemporary nation-state and the existing world system. Their views blend easily with the realists' counsels to increase power nationally and balance it internationally.

As I have argued here and in chapter 1, the position of most contemporary Third World policymakers is closer to the statist version of self-reliance. The theorists who supported statist policies, Hamilton, Jefferson as president, Nehru as prime minister and List[5] were all national policy makers, while Rousseau and Gandhi were not. Table 8.2 depicts this transformative impact of national policy making. The closer the theorists got to national political power the more their theories changed in the Listian direction. Although none of the theorists showed much interest in policies associated with collective self-reliance, as we move across the table from theorists who were not involved in national policymaking to those closer to national office, a shift away from local self-reliance toward policies closer to national self-reliance emerges.

If communitarianism or local self-reliance provides the normative framework for human development, this shift is a significant demonstration of the tendency for national leaders to get caught up in structural patterns dictated by their desire for political survival in the face of threats from both domestic and international pressures: this process of mediation between a hostile international system and the need to retain the political support of existing domestic elites caused them to compromise their stated normative objectives. The shift in Jefferson's views, and Nehru's to some extent, offers strong evidence for the constraints imposed on policy leaders by the realities of both domestic and international political and economic arenas that predisposed them toward policies designed to ensure national integration over those that would promote local self-reliance. The imperatives of nation building may not, therefore, be in the best interests of the individual or of the autonomous locality: clearly the relationship between the stated preferences of the theorists and the contexts in which they were writing was a crucial determinant of their attitude toward self-reliance.

An important question that this raises for theories of self-reliance, and one over which there is considerable disagreement in the contemporary development debate, is the extent to which the international system constrains and determines national development and how much autonomy national policy makers have when making domestic policy choices. The debate ranges over positions that support a system-dominated deterministic approach, typical of the dependency perspective, to those that view the international environment as generally benign and nonconstraining, a view more characteristic of liberal approaches to national development.[6] The cases under consideration suggest that the answer to this question lies somewhere in between the system-determinist and the national-voluntarist positions. In the case of India, policy makers did exercise choices but these choices were constrained both by the

Table 8.2 From Theory to Practice: Changing Orientations Toward Self-Reliance Development

Components	Communitarian (Rousseau)	Early Jefferson	Gandhi	Early Nehru	Late Jefferson	Late Nehru	Hamilton	Statist (List)
1. Priority of universal basic needs satisfaction	Very important	Important	Very important	Important	Modified	Modified	Not priority	Not priority
2. Emphasis on rural development	Strong	Strong	Strong	No	No	No	No	Linked to cities
3. Emphasis on decentralized political participation	Strong	Strong	Strong	Yes	Modified	Modified	No	No
4. Balanced economic growth at the subnational level	Yes, emphasize agr.	Yes, emphasize agr.	Yes, emphasize agr.	?	No	No	No	No
5. Preference for small industry	Yes	Yes	Yes	No	Mixed	No	No	No
6. Preference for large industry	No	No	No	Yes	Mixed	Yes	Yes	Yes
7. Augment central state power	No	No	No	Yes?	Yes	Yes	Yes	Yes
8. Balanced economic growth at the national level	No	No	No	?	Yes	Yes	Yes	Yes
9. Limit international trade	Yes	No	Yes	Yes	Yes	Yes	Yes	Yes
10. Build military capability	No	No	No	No	Yes	Yes	Yes	Yes
11. Build regional cooperation	No	No	Ambivalent	Yes	No	No	No	No
12. Build horizontal international linkages	No	No	No	No	No	No	No	No

international and the domestic environments. However, both the United States and India are large countries, which presumably increases their capacity for autonomy; the margin of choice may be narrower for small states heavily penetrated by the international system.

The Limited Success of Self-Reliance in the American and Indian Cases

Now that I have shown how historical and theoretical discussions of self-reliance fit into contemporary Third World development debates, which, however, are not always conducted in self-reliance terms there still remains the issue of how successful various self-reliance strategies might be if tried today. The experience of my historical cases suggests some cautionary answers to this question.

Table 8.3 summarizes the variants of self-reliant development actually tried in the American and Indian cases and the degree to which these efforts were successful. Policies associated with goals of local self-reliance (components 1 through 5 in table 8.3) were not emphasized in either case; neither is there evidence of support for policies associated with collective self-reliance (components 11 and 12). Where self-reliant policies were followed, in both cases, they were pursued primarily at the national level (components 6 through 10).

India's policies with respect to limiting international trade were more dissociationist in intent than those of the United States, but not more successful. In spite of a more associationist relationship with the world economy, the achievement of one of the fundamental goals of national self-reliance, building a balanced economy, was more successful in the case of the United States. America's more favorable geographical position and resource endowment certainly made realization of this goal less problematic, but India's pursuit of an excessively statist version of national self-reliance, which included a heavy emphasis on industrialization and building military capability, may actually have impeded the achievement of this same goal given a more constrained set of circumstances. India's aspiration to become a regional power meant that some degree of accommodation between development objectives across levels which,

Table 8.3 The American and Indian Cases in Terms of Self-Reliance Development

Components	United States		India	
	Variant of self-reliance tried	*Degree of success*	*Variant of self-reliance tried*	*Degree of success*
1. Priority of universal basic needs satisfaction	Not conscious policy	Yes, except in South	No	
2. Emphasis on rural development	No		No	
3. Emphasis on decentralized political participation	Somewhat	Federal structure. National level predominates	Somewhat	Marginal
4. Balanced economic growth at the subnational level	No		No	
5. Preference for small industry	No		No	
6. Preference for large industry	Yes	Moves in this direction	Yes	Yes
7. Augment central state power	Yes	Yes	Yes	Yes
8. Balanced economic growth at the national level	Yes	Yes	Yes	
9. Limit international trade	Somewhat	Limited	Yes	Marginal
10. Build military capability	Somewhat	Yes	Yes	Limited
11. Build regional cooperation	No		No	Yes
12. Build horizontal international linkages	No		No	

given the relatively unfavorable population to resource ratio, might have produced a more successful strategy of self-reliance development, was not politically popular even though it might have been more feasible technically.

The United States and India, therefore, present a paradox which may be generalizable beyond these two cases. As large countries, which presumably gave them a realistic potential for self-reliance development, both aspired to play a dominant role in their respective hemispheres. At the time of independence, when the international positions of their nations were more precarious, both American and Indian policy makers voiced a strong commitment to a new, more cooperative world order and a determination to pursue a course of national development removed from the corrupting influence of the old. But, as the priorities of playing an important role in regional politics began to assume more importance, both became more preoccupied with building national economic power and less interested in a reformed national development or more cooperative international relations. Such aspirations can seriously undermine the achievement of self-reliance at all three levels, particularly when resource constraints are severe.

Could the Contradictions Be Resolved?

The American and Indian cases have demonstrated that there are serious contradictions associated with pursuing self-reliance at all three levels at once. Is this pessimism concerning past and present efforts to implement development strategies consistent with the goals and norms of multilevel self-reliance warranted? Could anything new be done to overcome the contradictions in self-reliance development possibilities that this chapter has emphasized? As a way of suggesting answers to these questions, I shall now return to the writings of the theorists under consideration to see how they attempted to resolve these contradictions. I shall argue that, while their resolutions may be plausible in theory, evidence from the cases suggests that they may not be realizable in practice given the constraints of the existing world order of nation-states. Prospects for their resolution may depend on the radical restructuring of both domestic and international environments.

For Rousseau, self-reliance for both the individual and the nation-state depended on a static economy which would avoid inequality and permit isolation from the international system. A no-growth economy, based on decentralized subsistence production, did not require the augmentation of state power either for purposes of redistribution or for the pursuit of an active role in international relations: thus it was also quite compatible with decentralized political institutions. Rousseau believed that, if production and consumption were balanced, states could avoid international penetration and conflict even if they were weak, provided that they had no aspirations for expansion.

Unlike Rousseau, Jefferson was unwilling to forego economic growth or America's expansion and participation in regional affairs: his proposals for a political structure comprised of various levels of government, with functions assigned to each according to their geographical jurisdiction, was an attempt to mediate between the egalitarian, participatory norms of decentralized democracy and the achievement of a level of national development and integration necessary for an independent role in international affairs. The tendency of growth to exacerbate inequality, which was a central concern for Rousseau, was not of such great importance to Jefferson given the favorable resource endowment of early America.

The Hamilton and List reconciliation between local and national self-reliance was based on a model that assumed that industrially led, growth-oriented *national* development would invigorate all sectors of the economy and thus lead to the satisfaction of basic needs at the local level. List, and Hamilton to some extent, supported a dissociative strategy during the industrialization stage of development only, although they were not against the assimilation of cultural values and scientific ideas from outside. List assumed also that political participation would increase and liberal political institutions would evolve once economic development was underway.

Gandhi, on the other hand, proposed that national development should take place through a kind of bottom up strategy which would originate at the local level: for Gandhi, both nation building and economic growth depended on building political and economic structures primarily at the village level. National institutions would facilitate local development efforts and undertake only those tasks that could not be performed at the local level. This decentralized political and economic system, together with the practice of non-violent resistance, would also protect against both economic and military threats from the international system.

Although critical of Gandhi's preference for village-based production, Nehru also raised the possibility of a uniquely Indian road to development when he proposed his "Third Way," a blend of Indian culture and Western progress. While Nehru admired the West for its science and technology, he was extremely critical of its individualism, which he saw as selfish and therefore containing a strong potential for social conflict. The Third Way was a form of socialism and collectivism that would integrate India's aspirations for a significant role in international affairs with a resolution of its problems of poverty. Before the Chinese invasion of 1962, Nehru was an admirer of Mao's policy of "walking on two legs," a synthesis of advanced technology with more traditional practices, and it is possible that the Third Way might have been somewhat similar had it ever been implemented.

Using evidence from the two cases under consideration, I shall now demonstrate why I believe that the resolutions of each of these theorists does not offer an adequate prescription for a successful multilevel strategy of development in the contemporary Third World and why their ideas must be extended further in order for them to have greater relevance for contemporary and future development problems. I shall suggest that any resolution of the contradictions between local and national self-reliance must consider a changed relationship with the international system that is more compatible with the norms of collective self-reliance, an issue with which none of the theorists under consideration were particularly concerned.

Rousseau's preference for a static economy to avoid dependence at both the individual and national levels is not realistic in the contemporary Third World, considering India's struggle to generate sufficient growth to at least keep pace with a rapidly expanding population. Neither does Rousseau's prescription for national isolation seem feasible for most states today. While there was some range of choice for Indian policy leaders at independence to prevent or overcome this dependence, India's chosen development options were also determined to a considerable extent by the international system. If this is true of large states, it would seem that small states would have even fewer options for independent actions, a consideration that is borne out by the fate of Rousseau's Poland.

On the other hand, Rousseau's fear of the tendency of private property to exacerbate inequality is supported by the Indian case where inegalitarian private property relations have contributed to the inability to reduce rural poverty. In many excolonial countries the absence of radical reform in property relations contributes to a continuation of detrimental external linkages since it is precisely the interests which block internal structural reform which often are most heavily linked to the international system also.

My analysis of early American development demonstrated that Federalist preferences for increasingly centralized political and economic institutions won out over Jefferson's multiple levels of government. Local government in the United States, and more particularly in India, was neglected due to the priorities of state building determined within the context of the international system. De Tocqueville observed, well over one hundred years ago, that decentralized democracy had a greater chance for success in the United States than in Europe because of America's isolated position with respect to world affairs. As the United States began to play a more significant role in the American hemisphere in the nineteenth century, so Federalist policies of political centralization began to erode the foundations of Jeffersonian democracy. In India development planning, centered at the national level, has inhibited local initiative and the possibility of genuine interdependence between levels of government. Gandhi's vision of village democracy and village-based production has been overwhelmed by the priorities of state building, industrialization, centralized bureaucratic planning and the pressure to adopt a market economy upon which such a strategy is built.

The inappropriateness of the Hamilton and List model has been demonstrated by many development cases in the contemporary Third World where industrially led development strategies in predominantly peasant-based agrarian societies had led to duality and the failure of the benefits of development to penetrate vast rural subsistence sectors. The American case is evidence that this type of model was built on assumptions growing out of Western experience where development took place under very different conditions, particularly with respect to factor endowments. List's model pre-supposed a capitalist agricultural sector, capable of surplus production, before industrialization was underway. Such conditions generally do not hold in contemporary Third World societies and, given very different labor to land ratios, it is questionable whether such a model is likely to succeed. The admission of the failure to solve the problems of poverty in India has led to a gradual reorientation of the planning process toward a more direct focus on agriculture, a trend that is evident more generally in Third World development strategies of the 1970s and 1980s.[7]

The inadequacy of an industrially led development strategy under conditions of scarcity is exacerbated by the inability of the type of liberal political institutions that List expected would evolve under his model of development to implement redistribution. India's failure to achieve social reform within the framework of a pluralist political system suggests that a much more radical change in property relations may be necessary for the achievement of a more genuinely egalitarian society. Political democracy is necessary but it may not always be a sufficient condition for the realization of the norms of local self-reliance.

The Listian version of self-reliance concentrates on strengthening the national economy so that international interdependence can be renegotiated on better terms. As demonstrated by the case of India, in the absence of fundamental structural reform this renegotiation process, which depends on the support of existing elites, tends to reproduce existing patterns of statist, realist international relations rather than moving toward relationships more compatible with the norms of collective self-reliance. An increase in nationalism in the contemporary Third World, which has undermined the success of regional integration schemes, suggests that the achievement of collective self-reliance may remain elusive for some time to come.[8] List postulated that more genuinely cooperative relations between states could only come about under conditions of relative equality, when the strong no longer threatened the weak.

That the Indian case provides stronger evidence than the American for the fragility of these resolutions is partially due to the abundant environment in which early American development took place, an environment that is not reproducible in the contemporary

Third World. Nevertheless, given their very different circumstances, the fact that the United States and India, as newly independent nations, behaved so similarly in terms of developmental priorities, as table 8.3 demonstrated, gives further support to the conclusion of this analysis that the imperatives of strengthening the nation-state predominated in determining developmental choices. While attempting to implement policies designed to mitigate the detrimental effects of the international system, both the United States and India were seeking, at the same time, to become a part of that system. A changed relationship with the international system, more typical of policies associated with the goals of collective self-reliance, was not seriously considered in either case.

The rhetoric of self-reliance, India's included, expresses dissatisfaction with liberal models of development and the penetration of a capitalist international system that constrains both domestic development choices and participation in the world economy. This analysis has suggested that conventional development practices and linkages with the world system are hard to discard, particularly in the absence of radical internal reform: state-centered policies tend to reinforce participation in the existing world system of nation-states rather than promote policies more compatible with a reordering of international relations away from a world where statist nation building is the expected developmental priority. In both the early United States and contemporary India, the priorities of local community building and enhanced international cooperation were discarded in favor of statist participation, on better terms, in the old order. Hence, self-reliance as a programmatic multilevel doctrine of development failed to gain acceptance as national policy in either case.

Could There Be a More Successful Multilevel Strategy of Self-Reliance Development?

A final question remains: could the contradictions so apparent within my two cases of self-reliance development be overcome so that self-reliance could become the truly transforming model its proponents have proposed? Any answer to this question must remain hypothetical since, at least in the capitalist world, there are as yet no existent models of self-reliance development simultaneously successful at all three levels.[9]

Self-reliance at any level is a weak developmental model in the contemporary world: this suggests that it is unlikely to succeed as a multilevel strategy without radical structural reform domestically and a reorientation of a state's relations with the international system. The extent to which self-reliance becomes embedded in the realist norms and practices of the nation-state reinforces the tendency of political practitioners to dismiss the views of proponents of its communitarian version as impractical and irrelevant. Yet communitarians who propose a new order with a different role for the nation-state may be correct in their assumption that this is the only way in which true self-reliance development can be achieved.

The Indian case raises the issue of whether the goals of local self-reliance can be realized without radical changes in property relations: often the state has been forced to compromise its policies in order to gain support of existing elites. Landed interests in particular have impeded the state's freedom to implement poverty-reducing developmental priorities. Property ownership that is more compatible with a strategy of local self-reliance might consist of small-scale private holdings or collective ownership: however, the latter can be problematic, as Gandhi realized, since it can result in a type of state control that is antithetical to the self-reliance of the individual. Yet clearly the liberal individualism of Jeffersonian democracy is not a possibility in the contemporary world: as evidenced by recent trends in post-Maoist China, some form of collectivism that includes small private property holdings might be a compromise. Worker-owned small-scale industry, employing labor-intensive methods with heavy industry owned by the state, would be compatible with these types of property relations.

Such a radical change in property relations and productive techniques would require implementation and protection from political institutions at the national level. Anti-Federalists in the United States, who were often subsistence farmers, feared increased governmental intrusion because they thought that the state favored the interests of large-scale capitalists. For decentralized, small-scale production to be realized, priorities at the national level must be reordered: reformed national institutions should complement and facilitate local political structures and protect local markets against the tendency of capitalist production and distribution relations at the national and international levels to overwhelm them. Only with this radical change in the balance between state and society could local interests also be protected from the oppressive features of state socialism: the success of self-reliance at the local level depends on democratic participatory development rather than national bureaucratic institutions that are unresponsive to local needs.

The conclusion of this analysis that, in the two cases under consideration, both local and collective self-reliance lost out to the priorities of state-centered nation building suggests a need for the reorientation of relations with the international system. I have argued that the desire to participate in the existing international system sets national priorities that are not in the interest of local or collective self-reliance. Moreover, the predisposition of policy leaders to adopt statist assumptions when analyzing their dilemmas reinforces the reproduction of the very system against which their rhetoric of self-reliance is directed. For local self-reliance to be successful, states may have to opt out of the existing world order or try to reconstruct their linkages with it toward policies more compatible with the norms of collective self-reliance. Either weaker or newer states must be sufficiently isolated to take independent action, or breakouts must be multiple, complementary and nearly simultaneous in order to prevent collective counterreactions by older states, the guardians of the traditional world order.[10]

Rousseau believed that, with genuine self-reliance at the local level, there would be less conflict in the international system as less expansionist states satisfied their basic needs locally. If the development dilemmas of such a transition could be overcome, this liberating potential of self-reliance development might indeed be possible. Local self-reliance, with its commitment to community building, and collective self-reliance, with its more cooperative approach to international relations, are both antistatist; therefore they are not necessarily in conflict.

The possible synthesis of the local and collective levels, both of which are reactions against what their proponents perceive as the nation-state's inability to solve the problems of human needs and international conflict, could provide the basis for an integrated strategy of self-reliance. Such a synthesis would meet its multiple goals and provide a genuine transformation in both internal and international relations which could be mutually reinforcing rather than contradictory.

These visions of a reformed world order may seem like an exercise in unrealizable utopianism. Rather, they are intended as an attempt to explore possible explanations for why self-reliance, which remains such a strong rhetorical force in the Third World today, may never be successful as a strategy for development without radical and widespread structural changes at both the domestic and international levels. The attempt to reproduce the Western state system in the contemporary Third World does not bode well for genuine self-reliance development. We have seen how two new nations with aspirations to lead in the creation of a different, reformed world order were instead caught up in reproducing the old order against which they had rebelled.

Gandhi doubted that the nation-state in its present form could be the best agent for the human development and international peace. If, negatively defined, the self-reliance ideal is a reaction against the historical legacies of a power-oriented, conflict-prone European state system, positively, it is a promising framework in which to devise new solutions for the human predicament. The self-reliance ideal should inspire us to think about the possibilities of transcending the contemporary order of statist nations. No case has been made here that movement toward a more self-reliant and less conflictual world is impossible; only that such movement is more difficult than its original advocates have maintained.

NOTES

INTRODUCTION

1. See, for example, G. D. H. Cole, *Social Theory* (New York: Stokes, 1920).

2. Such an analysis of the self-reliance ethic in contemporary America is provided in Paul M. Sniderman and Richard A. Brody, "Coping: The Ethic of Self-Reliance," *American Journal of Political Science* (August 1977), 21(3):501–521.

3. See, for example, Pierre Rosanvallon, *L'Age de l'Autogestion* (Paris: Editions du Seuil, 1976) and Carole Pateman, *Participation and Democratic Theory* (Cambridge: Cambridge University Press, 1970).

4. For a discussion of the meaning of collective self-reliance as it has evolved in various international fora associated with the New International Economic Order, see Karl P. Sauvant, "The Origins of the NIEO Discussions," in Karl P. Sauvant, ed., *Changing Priorities on the International Agenda: The New International Economic Order* (New York: Pergamon Press, 1981), ch. 1. See also Craig Murphy, *The Emergence of the NIEO Ideology* (Boulder, Colo.: Westview Press, 1984).

5. "The Cocoyoc Declaration," United Nations General Assembly document (A/C.2/292) of 1974 discusses self-reliance in this context. It is quoted and discussed in Johan Galtung, Peter O'Brien and Roy Preiswerk, eds., *Self-Reliance: A Strategy for Development* (London: Bogle-l'Ouverture, 1980), pp. 401–411.

6. There is a great deal more scholarly analysis of the concept of interdependence. See, for example, Robert O. Keohane and Joseph S. Nye, *Power and Interdependence: World Politics in Transition* (Boston: Little Brown, 1977). It has been suggested that self-reliance has received less attention than interdependence in the First World because it is not of direct relevance to relations between advanced countries.

7. Besides the People's Republic of China these include Tanzania, Burma, North Korea and Romania, which are all small countries with relatively little impact on the world economy. In spite of their policy of self-reliance, Tanzania and North Korea are both heavily in debt to the international system.

8. Early examples of the very extensive literature on political and eco-

nomic development include Gabriel Almond and G. Bingham Powell, *Comparative Politics: A Developmental Approach* (Boston: Little Brown, 1966), and Walt W. Rostow, *The Stages of Economic Growth: A Non-Communist Manifesto* (Cambridge: Cambridge University Press, 1960). For an important revisionist critique of this literature that focuses on the historical development of Western Europe, see Charles Tilly, ed., *The Formation of National States in Western Europe* (Princeton: Princeton University Press, 1975).

9. The chapters on the theorists will use the methodology of political theory which draws inferences from a close reading of texts, thus contributing to understanding through interpretation. For further elaboration of this idea of understanding through interpretation, which sets explanation within the framework of human intentionality and the cognitive orientation of society, rather than within more formal universal causal laws, a methodology characteristic of the natural sciences, see Donald Moon, "The Logic of Political Inquiry: A Synthesis of Opposed Perspectives," in Fred I. Greenstein and Nelson W. Polsby, eds., *Handbook of Political Science*, vol. 1 (Reading, Mass.: Addison-Wesley, 1975), pp. 131–228. See also Rom Harré and Paul F. Secord, *The Explanation of Social Behavior* (Oxford: Basil Blackwell, 1972), p. 132: "Since the giving and grasping of meanings is the mechanism of much of the patterns of social interaction, greater *precision* of the delineation of meanings is what corresponds in the social sciences to the development of greater *accuracy* of the *measurement* of parameters in the physical sciences."

1. SELF-RELIANCE IN THE CONTEMPORARY DEVELOPMENT DEBATE: DEVELOPING A FRAMEWORK FOR ANALYSIS

1. Such writers are clearly influenced by the trend in some recent development literature, which began in the 1970s, of assessing development in terms of standards such as meeting basic human needs, rather than GNP growth. See, for example, Dudley Seers, "The Meaning of Economic Development," in Charles Wilber, ed., *The Political Economy of Development and Underdevelopment* (New York: Random House, 1973), ch. 1.

2. Mahbub ul Haq, *The Poverty Curtain: Choices for the Third World* (New York: Columbia University Press, 1975), p. 71. Ul Haq himself would probably fit closer to the statist view on development. For other similar interpretations of self-reliance see various chapters in Heraldo Munoz, ed., *From Dependency to Development: Strategies to Overcome Underdevelopment and Inequality* (Boulder, Colo.: Westview Press, 1981).

3. The most famous statement of this viewpoint is E. F. Schumacher, *Small Is Beautiful: A Study of Economics as if People Mattered* (London: Blond and Briggs, 1973). See also George McRobie, *Small Is Possible* (New York: Harper and Row, 1981), and Guy Gran, *Development by People: Citizen Construction of a Just World* (New York: Praeger, 1983).

4. There are various international declarations that espouse such strategies. See, for example, the Arusha Declaration of 1967 and the Cocoyoc

Declaration of 1974, both quoted in Johan Galtung, Peter O'Brien, and Roy Preiswerk, eds., *Self-Reliance: A Strategy for Development* (London: Bogle-l'Ouverture, 1980), pp. 387–411. See also the Belmont Statement of 1974, quoted in Guy F. Erb and Valeriana Kallab, eds., *Beyond Dependency: The Developing World Speaks Out* (Washington, D.C.: Overseas Development Council, 1975), pp. 165–169.

5. See Rajni Kothari, *Environment and Alternative Development*, WOMP Paper 15 (New York: Institute for World Order, 1981); and Samuel L. Parmar, "Self-Reliance in an Interdependent World," in Erb and Kallab, *Beyond Dependency*.

6. See Johan Galtung, "The Politics of Self-Reliance," in Galtung, O'Brien, and Preiswerk, *Self-Reliance*, ch. 20.

7. See *North-South: A Programme for Survival: Report of the Independent Commission on International Development Issues*, Willy Brandt, Chairman (Cambridge: MIT Press, 1980), ch. 8. A model that emphasizes the primacy of the rural sector for self-reliance development is constructed by David Sylvan, "State-Based Accumulation and Economic Dependence: Toward an Optimal Policy," *Journal of Peace Research* (1983), 20(1):27–48.

8. This is stressed in the Arusha Declaration. For a further discussion of this reconceptualization of the meaning of work, see Mary Anderson, *Self-Reliant Development: A Comparison of the Economic Development Strategies of Mohandas Gandhi, Mao Tse Tung and Julius Nyerere*, Ph.D. dissertation, University of Colorado, 1978.

9. See Johan Galtung, "Self-Reliance: Concepts, Practice and Rationale," in Galtung, O'Brien, and Preiswerk, *Self-Reliance*, ch. 1.

10. Poona Wignaraja, "From the Village to the Global Order: Elements in a Conceptual Framework for 'Another Development,'" *Development Dialogue* (1977), 1:35–48.

11. See Roy Preiswerk, "Sources of Resistance to Self-Reliance," in Galtung, O'Brien and Preiswerk, *Self-Reliance*, ch. 19.

12. See Ivan Illich, *Deschooling Society* (New York: Harper and Row, 1971).

13. See Leopold Kohr, *Development Without Aid: The Translucent Society* (New York: Schocken Books, 1979); and Chadwick Alger, "The Role of People in the Future Global Order," *Alternatives* (October 1978), 4(2):233–262.

14. The most cited works in the world order literature are probably those of Richard Falk and Johan Galtung. See, for example, Johan Galtung, *The True Worlds: A Transnational Perspective* (New York: Free Press, 1980) and Richard Falk, *A Global Approach to National Policy* (Cambridge: Harvard University Press, 1975).

15. For a discussion of the historical development of Western mercantilist thought, see Witt Bowden, *An Economic History of Europe Since 1750* (New York: American Book Co., 1937). Besides the eighteenth- and nineteenth-century American and German mercantilist schools, there was an important school of protectionist writers in Romania in the 1920s which has recently undergone some reanalysis by writers interested in contemporary

self-reliance. An important example of this school is Mihail Manoilesco, *The Theory of Protection and International Trade* (London: P. S. King, 1931). For a contemporary reanalysis of this school, see Kenneth Jowitt, ed., *Social Change in Romania 1860–1940* (Berkeley: Institute of International Studies, University of California, 1978).

16. John Maynard Keynes, "National Self-Sufficiency," *The Yale Review* (June 1933), 22(4):755–769.

17. See Craig N. Murphy, "What the Third World Wants: An Interpretation of the Development and Meaning of the New International Economic Order Ideology," *International Studies Quarterly* (March 1983), 27(1):55–76.

18. Such views are shared by most Third World policymakers and proponents of the New International Economic Order. For a comprehensive analysis of the NIEO see Karl P. Sauvant, ed., *Changing Priorities on the International Agenda: The New International Economic Order* (New York: Pergamon Press, 1981). For a discussion of self-reliant industrialization, see Paul Streeten, *Development Perspectives* (New York: St. Martin's Press, 1981), ch. 10. As with several of the authors discussed, Streeten would also span the communitarian and statist positions. See also Manfred Bienefeld, summary paper on the deliberations of a conference on "Self-Reliance as a National and Collective Development Strategy," Institute of Development Studies, University of Sussex, November 11–13, 1979. This paper argues that, at present, the nation-state is the only political entity with the capacity to achieve successful delinking from the international system. It does, however, emphasize the importance of a multi-level definition of self-reliance. For a discussion of national autonomy with regard to technology, see Jairam Ramesh and Charles Weiss Jr., eds., *Mobilizing Technology for World Development* (New York: Praeger, 1979), p. 29.

19. See John Gerard Ruggie, "International Interdependence and National Welfare," in John Gerard Ruggie, ed., *The Antinomies of Interdependence: National Welfare and the International Division of Labor* (New York: Columbia University Press, 1983) ch. 1.

20. See Samir Amin, "Self-Reliance and the New Internationl Economic Order," *Monthly Review* (July/August 1977), 9(3):1–21. For an analysis of one such case see Thomas Biersteker, "Self-Reliance in Theory and Practice in Tanzanian Trade Relations," *International Organization* (Spring 1980), 34(2): 229–264.

21. See Faouez Mellah, "Self-Reliance and Self-Management," in Galtung, O'Brien and Preiswerk, *Self-Reliance* ch. 5.

22. Dieter Senghaas, "Dissociation and Autocentric Development: An Alternative Development Policy for the Third World," in Richard L. Merritt and Bruce M. Russett, eds., *From National Development to Global Community: Essays in Honor of Karl W. Deutsch* (London: Allen and Unwin, 1981), ch. 12. For an application of this kind of thinking to Latin America, see Dudley Seers, "The Stages of Economic Growth of a Primary Producer in the Middle of the Twentieth Century," in Robert I. Rhodes, ed., *Imperialism and Underdevelopment* (New York: Monthly Review Press, 1971), pp. 163–180.

23. This is an issue that is also fundamental to the concerns of writers in the Latin American dependency school. See, for example, Fernando H. Cardoso and Enzo Faletto, *Dependency and Development in Latin America* (Berkeley: University of California Press, 1979).

24. Some writers on self-reliance are quite critical of self-reliance as stage theory since they see such analyses as being reproductions of the same deterministic Western models against which self-reliance theory is reacting. For one such criticism, see Amin, "Self-Reliance and the New International Economic Order."

25. Some examples of possible strategies are discussed in Ali Mazrui, "Exit Visa from the World System: Dilemmas of Cultural and Economic Disengagement," *Third World Quarterly* (January 1981), 3(1):62–76; and Rehman Sobhan, "OPEC's Political Options: Case for Collective Self-Reliance Within the Third World," *Alternatives* (Summer 1981), 7(1):43–60. For a discussion of the rise of intra-Third World investment, see Louis T. Wells Jr., *Third World Multinationals: The Rise of Foreign Investment from Developing Countries* (Cambridge: MIT Press, 1983).

26. See Robert H. Johnson, "The New Populism and the Old: Demands for a NIEO and American Agrarian Protest," *International Organization* (Winter 1983), 37(1):41–72.

27. Craig Murphy, *The Emergence of the NIEO Ideology* (Boulder, Colo.: Westview Press, 1984), p. 94.

28. Belmont Statement of 1974, in Erb and Kallab, *Beyond Dependency,* p. 167.

29. See Galtung, "The Politics of Self-Reliance." Galtung is the only author who has adopted this multilevel framework in which to discuss self-reliance: his concept of self-reliance encompasses most of the characteristics given in the Outline but normatively he is closest to the values associated with individual and local self-reliance. Galtung admits, however, that for some time to come self-reliance in practice will tend to get stuck at the national level.

2. AGRARIAN DEMOCRACY: SELF-RELIANCE THEMES IN THE POLITICAL THOUGHT OF JEAN-JACQUES ROUSSEAU

1. Thomas Hobbes, *Leviathan* (New York: E. P. Dutton, 1950). See pp. 101–106 for Hobbes, description of the state of nature.

2. Jean-Jacques Rousseau, *The First and Second Discourses*, Roger D. Masters, ed. (New York: St. Martin's Press, 1964), p. 105.

3. *Ibid.,* p. 128

4. *Ibid.,* p. 139

5. *Ibid.,* p. 151

6. Jean-Jacques Rousseau, *Emile or On Education,* introduction, translation, and notes by Allan Bloom (New York: Basic Books, 1979), p. 185.

7. See Rousseau, *The First and Second Discourses,* p. 152, where Rousseau

states that it was the practice of agriculture that was partly responsible for man's giving up the state of nature.

8. *Ibid.*, p. 37. In *La Nouvelle Heloise* as well, Rousseau continually extols the virtues of country living. See, for example, p. 301 in Jean-Jacques Rousseau, *La Nouvelle Heloise, Julie, or the New Eloise,* translated and abridged by Judith H. McDowell (University Park and London: Pennsylvania State University Press, 1968).

9. Rousseau, *Emile*, p. 95.

10. *Ibid.*, p. 195.

11. *Ibid.*

12. Jean-Jacques Rousseau, "Discourse on Political Economy," in Rousseau, *On the Social Contract* with *Geneva Manuscript* and *Political Economy,* Roger D. Masters ed., Judith R. Masters, tr. (New York: St. Martin's Press, 1978), p. 224.

13. Jean-Jacques Rousseau, "Constitutional Project for Corsica," in Rousseau, *Political Writings,* Frederick Watkins, ed. and tr. (New York: Thomas Nelson, 1953), p. 283.

14. Rousseau, "Discourse on Political Economy," p. 225

15. Jean-Jacques Rousseau, *The Social Contract and Discourse on the Origin and Foundation of Inequality Among Mankind,* ed. with introduction by Lester G. Crocker (New York: Washington Square Press, 1976), p. 31. See also Rousseau, "Discourse on Political Economy," pp. 212–213. Here Rousseau maintains that a democratic state could not succeed if "the people is seduced by private interests that some wily men have been able to substitute for its own."

16. In *Emile,* Rousseau maintains that Europeans are more perfect people than others (p. 52). See also Rousseau, "Discourse on Political Economy," p. 219: "It seems that the sentiment of humanity evaporates and weakens as it is extended over the whole world, and that we can't be moved by calamities in Tartary or Japan as we are by those of a European people."

17. Rousseau, *The First and Second Discourses,* p. 147.

18. For a full discussion of Rousseau's views on women, see Susan Moller Okin, *Women in Western Political Thought* (Princeton: Princeton University Press, 1979), pp. 99–194. I have used the terms "man" and "he" throughout this chapter without any ambivalence, since whatever Rousseau said about men, he never intended to apply to women.

19. Rousseau, *Emile*, p. 365.

20. Stephen Ellenburg, *Rousseau's Political Philosophy* (Ithaca: Cornell University Press, 1976), p. 223. Ellenburg argues that Rousseau believed that property ownership was the most sacred right of citizens.

21. Rousseau, *The Social Contract,* p. 26.

22. *Ibid.*, p. 24. For similar ideas on labor as a mark of ownership of land, see Rousseau, *Emile,* p. 98.

23. Rousseau, "Discourse on Political Economy," pp. 230–236.

24. Rousseau, "Project for Corsica," p. 317.

25. See Isaiah Berlin, *Two Concepts of Liberty* (London: Oxford University

Press, 1958). The distinction made by Berlin between positive and negative freedom is relevant here. Berlin defines negative freedom as being consistent with liberal thought while positive freedom, with which he associates Rousseau, is concerned with self-mastery or the surrender of the will of the individual to the collective good of society. Clearly Berlin prefers the former and sees the possibility of a trend toward totalitarianism in the latter.

26. Rousseau, *Emile*, p. 39.

27. Jean-Jacques Rousseau, *The Government of Poland*, introduction, translation and notes by Willmoore Kendall (Indianapolis and New York: Bobbs-Merrill, 1972), p. 22. See also Rousseau, "Discourse on Political Economy," p. 223, where he says that education is the state's most important business and that citizens should be taught to perform their duties from birth.

28. Rousseau, *The First and Second Discourses*, p. 56.

29. After his marriage to Sophie ends in failure, Emile leaves his country to wander about the world, an unhappy man who seems to belong nowhere: "In breaking the bonds which attached me to my country, my dwelling place became the whole world and, in ceasing to be a citizen, I became more of a man." Rousseau, "Emile et Sophie ou les Solitaires," *Oeuvres Complètes de Jean-Jacques Rousseau*, 4 vols. (Paris: Librairie de Firmin-Didot, 1883), 2:739; my translation.

30. This tension between individuals and citizens is apparent also in Rousseau's views on religion. He disliked Christianity not only because it preached servitude and dependence, but also because it separated religion from the political system, thus leading to a perpetual conflict of jurisdiction in Christian states. Rousseau preferred that religion should serve the interests of the state by tying the individual to his country and encouraging patriotism: for this reason he particularly admired the religion of ancient Rome. For Rousseau's views on religion, see Rousseau, *The Social Contract*, pp. 136–147 and Rousseau, *The Government of Poland*, p. 8.

31. Rousseau, *The Social Contract*, p. 58.

32. *Ibid.*, p. 18.

33. *Ibid.*, p. 26.

34. Rousseau, "Discourse on Political Economy," p. 211.

35. Rousseau, *The Social Contract*, p. 54.

36. Rousseau, "Project for Corsica," p. 283.

37. Rousseau, *The Government of Poland*, p. 68.

38. Rousseau, *The Social Contract*, p. 24.

39. *Ibid.*, pp. 81–82.

40. *Ibid.*, p. 51.

41. *Ibid.*, p. 97. See also Rousseau, "Project for Corsica," p. 292: "The capital breathes forth a constant pestilence which finally saps and destroys the nation."

42. Rousseau, *The Social Contract*, p. 96.

43. Rousseau, "Project for Corsica," p. 293.

44. Rousseau, *The Social Contract*, p. 98: "In a country that is really free, the citizens do everything with their hands and nothing with money."

45. Rousseau, *The Government of Poland*, p. 76.

46. *Ibid.*, pp. 77–78.

47. Rousseau, "Project for Corsica," pp. 316, 318.

48. See Alfred Cobban, *Rousseau and the Modern State* (London: George Allen and Unwin, 1934).

49. Rousseau, "Project for Corsica," p. 293.

50. Rousseau, *The Social Contract*, p. 48.

51. Rousseau, *The Government of Poland*, p. 10.

52. *Ibid.*, p. 19.

53. *Ibid.*, pp. 11–12.

54. Rousseau, "Project for Corsica," p. 280.

55. Rousseau, *The Social Contract*, p. 109.

56. *Ibid.*, p. 49.

57. Rousseau, "Project for Corsica," p. 290.

58. Rousseau, *The Government of Poland*, p. 25.

59. For a contemporary discussion of the relationship between size and democracy see Robert Dahl and Edward Tufte, *Size and Democracy* (Stanford: Stanford University Press, 1973).

60. Rousseau, *The Social Contract*, p. 62.

61. Rousseau, *The Government of Poland*, p. 26.

62. *Ibid.*, p. 76.

63. *Ibid.*, p. 4.

64. Rousseau, *The Social Contract*, p. 23.

65. Ellenburg, *Rousseau's Political Philosophy*, p. 195.

66. Rousseau, *The Social Contract*, p. 98.

67. *Ibid.*, pp. 99–100. It must be remembered, however, that the economies of the Greek states and Rome depended on slavery for much of the labor associated with production, thus freeing citizens for political participation.

68. Rousseau, *The Government of Poland*, p. 31.

69. Rousseau, *The Social Contract*, p. 93.

70. *Ibid.*, p. 147.

71. See *ibid.*, p. 56, where Rousseau states that if a nation's borders are rocks that are inaccessible, "you will lead more peaceful, perhaps better, and certainly happier lives."

72. Rousseau, *The Social Contract*, p. 56.

73. Jean-Jacques Rousseau "Extrait de la Paix perpétuelle," *The Political Writings of Jean-Jacques Rousseau*, 2 vols., introduction and notes by C. E. Vaughan (New York: John Wiley, 1962), 1:373. Rousseau cites England as an example of such a country, an argument which is similar to that of List, to be discussed in chapter 3.

74. Rousseau, *The Government of Poland*, p. 69.

75. *Ibid.*, p. 74.

76. Rousseau, "Project for Corsica," p. 298: "Formerly an impoverished Switzerland laid down the law to France; now a rich Switzerland trembles at the frown of a French minister."

77. *Ibid.*, p. 283: "Commerce produces wealth, but agriculture ensures freedom."

78. See Jean-Jacques Rousseau, "L'état de guerre," Vaughan, *The Political Writings of Jean-Jacques Rousseau,* 1:293–307.

79. *Ibid.*, p. 301.

80. Rousseau, *The Government of Poland,* p. 81.

81. Rousseau, "Project for Corsica," p. 283.

82. Rousseau, *The Government of Poland,* p. 85.

83. *Ibid.*, pp. 10–11.

84. Rousseau, "Project for Corsica," p. 281.

85. Rousseau, "L'état de guerre," p. 299; my translation.

86. Rousseau, *The Social Contract,* p. 88.

87. *Ibid.*, p. 51.

88. *Ibid.*, pp. 53–54.

89. Rousseau, *The Government of Poland,* p. 111.

3. FROM AGRARIAN DEMOCRACY TO INDUSTRIAL POWER: THE SACRIFICE OF LOCAL SELF-RELIANCE IN FRIEDRICH LIST'S THOUGHT

1. The Romanian economist Mihail Manoilesco developed similar ideas in the 1930s and cites List as an important influence on his theory of productive forces. See Mihail Manoilesco, *The Theory of Protection and International Trade* (London: King, 1931).

2. Dieter Senghaas refers to List's theories of productive powers as analogous with the contemporary development strategies being pursued by North Korea and some members of the Soviet bloc countries' Council for Mutual Economic Assistance (COMECOM). See Dieter Senghaas, "Dissociation and Autocentric Development: An Alternative Development Policy for the Third World," in Richard L. Merritt and Bruce M. Russett, eds., *From National Development to Global Community: Essays in Honor of Karl W. Deutsch* (London: Allen and Unwin, 1981), ch. 12.

3. Friedrich List, *The National System of Political Economy* (London: Longman's Green, 1904). (Cited hereafter in text and notes as *NS.*)

4. See Louis Snyder, *The Roots of German Nationalism* (Bloomington: Indiana University Press, 1977), ch. 1.

5. Both W. A. Williams, *Contours of American History* (Cleveland: World Publishing Company, 1961), and Joseph Dorfman in the Introduction to Margaret Hirst, *Life of Friedrich List* (London: Smith, Elder, 1909), maintain that List was a free trader before going to the United States and that American conditions changed his mind. Later he believed that the Zollverein, an internal customs union, combined with external tariff barriers, was the best path to industrialization for Germany.

6. Hirst, *Life of Friedrich List,* p. 117, suggests that List was also influenced by the American protectionist Daniel Raymond. See Daniel Raymond, *The*

Elements of Political Economy, 3d ed., 1836, 2 vols. (New York: Kelley, 1964). This was first published in 1820 under the title *Thoughts on Political Economy.*

7. Friedrich List, "Speech to the Pennsylvania Society for the Encouragement of Manufactures," in Hirst, *Life of Friedrich List,* p. 277.

8. Joseph Schumpeter, *History of Economic Analysis* (London: Oxford University Press, 1966), p. 505 also notes List's emphasis on the national future, which modifies the welfare conditions of the present.

9. Friedrich List, "Outlines of American Political Economy," reprinted in Hirst, *Life of Friedrich List,* p. 203.

10. See *NS,* ch. 25.

11. Friedrich List, "Introduction to National System," which was omitted in the 1904 translation, but reprinted in Hirst, *Life of Friedrich List,* p. 301.

12. See List, "Outlines," pp. 245–253, and frequent references throughout *NS,* especially pp. 93, 294–295.

13. This is similar to the argument made by Karl Polanyi, *The Great Transformation: The Political and Economic Origins of Our Time* (New York: Farrar and Rinehart, 1944). Similar arguments have also been made for the United States during its period of hegemony in the post-1945 era.

14. See, for example, List, "Outlines," p. 152, and *NS,* p. 133 and all of ch. 31, pp. 277ff. List's criticism of Adam Smith on this score is not entirely justified. See particularly Adam Smith, *An Enquiry into the Nature and Causes of the Wealth of Nations* (New York: Random House, 1937), book 4, ch. 2, where Smith discusses exceptions to his pro-free trade stance, which he believed were necessary when dictated by the national interest. Smith frequently sounded like a mercantilist himself: for example, "defence is more important than opulence"; Smith, *Wealth of Nations,* p. 431. For further discussion of the parallels between Smith and List and their mercantilist approach to national power, see E. M. Earle, "Adam Smith, Alexander Hamilton and Friedrich List: The Economic Foundations of Military Power," in E. M. Earle, *Makers of Modern Strategy: Military Thought from Machiavelli to Hitler* (Princeton: Princeton University Press, 1943), pp. 117–154.

15. For a biographical sketch of List's years in the United States, see William Notz, "Frederick List in America," *American Economic Review* (June 1926), 16(2):249–265.

16. See Paul Bairoch, "Agriculture and the Industrial Revolution, 1700–1914," in Carlo M. Cipolla, ed., *The Fontana Economic History of Europe,* 6 vols. (London and Glasgow: Collins/Fontana Books, 1973), vol. 3, ch. 8.

17. "We find the powers of production, and consequently the wealth of individuals, growing in proportion to the liberties enjoyed . . . ," *NS,* p. 87. List believed in a stage theory of political development (*NS,* pp. 267–269), which paralleled his stages of economic development and moved from feudalism through absolutism to democracy, which was presumed to be the highest possible political form.

18. See for example, *NS,* pp. 153, 214.

19. See also List, "Outlines," p. 203.

20. List, "Outlines," pp. 216–217.

21. List, "Outlines," p. 212. All of Letter VI is devoted to this argument.

22. Although List is attacking English liberalism, in all his references to a well-integrated state he clearly had England in mind. This is typical of List's ambivalent attitude toward England, which is evident throughout his writings.

23. List, "Introduction to the National System," p. 303.

24. See *NS*, pp. 108–120 for a discussion of the development of productive powers.

25. "It may in general be assumed that where any technical industry cannot be established by means of an original protection of [40 to 60 percent] and cannot continue to maintain itself under a continued protection of [20 to 30 percent] the fundamental conditions of manufacturing power are lacking," *NS*, 251.

26. List, "Introduction to the National System," p. 306.

27. *Ibid.*, p. 309.

28. *Ibid.*, p. 312.

29. For further discussion of this important question, see Bert Hoselitz, "Theories of Stages of Economic Growth," in Bert Hoselitz et al., *Theories of Economic Growth* (Glencoe, Ill.: Free Press, 1961), pp. 193–238. Hoselitz compares List's stages with some contemporary growth theories and notes that there is no real explanation of the variables that are necessary for the movement from one stage to the next.

30. Thomas Jefferson also favored the importation of foreign skills and technology, but of course the conditions under which they were accepted, usually via immigration, were quite different from today's. This will be discussed further in chapter 4.

31. List, "Introduction to the National System," p. 301; see also *NS*, p. 101.

32. List's greatest business success while in the United States was the founding of the Schuylkill Railroad to connect the Schuylkill coal mines in Pennsylvania with the Schuylkill Canal. See Notz, *Frederick List in America*, pp. 258–259. As will be discussed in part 3, internal improvements were an important area for government intervention in the economy of the early United States, partly because of their potential for increasing national integration.

33. List, "Outlines," p. 164.

34. The analysis often parallels that of modern writers who deal with development in historical terms; see, for example, Barrington Moore, *Social Origins of Dictatorship and Democracy: Lord and Peasant in the Making of the Modern World* (Boston: Beacon Press, 1966).

35. The original terms of trade argument made by the Latin American dependency school as a counter to the liberal free trade position came from Raul Prebisch in 1964. See United Nations, *Towards a New Trade Policy for Development,* report by Raul Prebisch, Secretary-General of the United Nations Conference on Trade and Development (E/CONF.46/3, 1964).

36. This analysis of Anglo-Portuguese commercial relations is remarkably similar to a contemporary study of the same subject by S. Sideri, *Trade and Power: Informal Colonialism in Anglo-Portuguese Relations* (Rotterdam: Rotterdam University Press, 1970). This study is particularly interesting in that it reanalyzes Ricardo's famous example of comparative advantage over time.

37. List always maintained that the manufacturing sector was more productive than agriculture and I infer that this was one of his reasons for not advocating agricultural protection, i.e., not to keep capital and labor tied up in the less productive sector. It has also been argued (see Appendix C, Note by Translator, to *National System*) that one of List's main reasons for writing *National System* was to protest the English enactment of the Corn Laws. England was supplying manufactures to the German states but had blocked the export market for German agriculture by means of the Corn Laws. British commercial policy was not only ruining German agriculture but was also preventing the growth of a nascent German manufacturing industry which had been established under the Napoleonic blockade.

38. List uses the example of France and Germany, French soil being more suited to the cultivation of wine and German to the production of cattle and corn. This is just the kind of argument List would *not* have used in the case of trade between raw materials and manufactures.

39. This is similar to arguments made in the post World War II era for European cooperation as a counter to the superior economic power of the United States.

40. List, "Outlines," p. 271. List felt that American cotton exports, which were primarily directed at England, were subject to instabilities due to the likelihood of England's switching to cheaper sources of supply. See List, "Outlines," p. 263.

41. See *NS*, ch. 5 on the development of Spain and Portugal, which List felt was hindered by a false adherence to such principles. See also *NS*, p. 226.

42. This is the definition of mercantilism followed by Eli Heckscher, *Mercantilism*, 2 vols. (London: Allen and Unwin, 1935).

43. List, "Outlines," p. 162.

44. See Joseph Spengler, "Mercantilist and Physiocratic Growth Theory," in Hoselitz, *Theories of Economic Growth*.

45. List, "Introduction to the National System," p. 312.

4. BETWEEN THEORY AND PRACTICE:
THE TRANSFORMATION OF SELF-RELIANCE THEMES
IN THOMAS JEFFERSON'S THOUGHT

1. There is still an ongoing debate on the origins of Jefferson's political thought, but most of the literature emphasizes the importance of the influence of the English school of contract theorists, particularly John Locke, on

Jefferson's thought. Critics include Gary Wills, *Inventing America* (Garden City, N.Y.: Doubleday, 1978), who questions this assumption and suggests that the overriding influence on Jefferson came from Scottish writers of the Enlightenment such as Adam Smith, David Hume and Francis Hutcheson. The years that Jefferson spent in France during the 1780s and his admiration for the French people, if not for their institutions, have led some commentators to emphasize the French influence on his political philosophy. The leading proponent of this point of view is V. L. Parrington, *Main Currents in American Thought*, 3 vols. (New York: Harcourt Brace, 1927–30), 1:342–356.

2. Jefferson to John Jay, Paris, 1785, *The Writings of Thomas Jefferson*, Paul L. Ford, ed. 10 vols. (New York: Putnam, 1892–99), 4:88.

3. Thomas Jefferson, "Notes on Virginia," *Writings*, 3:268. Jefferson's only full-length piece of writing is famous for extolling the virtues of rural life.

4. *Ibid.*, p. 269.

5. Jefferson, "Proposed Constitution for Virginia," June, 1776, *Writings*, 2:7–30. Jefferson proposed that "every person of full age neither owning nor having owned (50) acres of land, shall be entitled to an appropriation of (50) acres or to so much as shall make up what he owns or has owned (50) acres in full and absolute dominion" (p. 25). Proposed property qualification for enfranchisement was a freehold estate of 1/4 acre in town and 25 acres in the country (p. 14). Jefferson's Constitution was not adopted nor were his subsequent proposals for changing the Virginia Constitution of 1776. For a later proposal to reform the Virginia Constitution see *Writings*, 3:320–333.

6. Jefferson, "Proposed Constitution for Virginia," *Writings*, 2:7–30.

7. This interpretation follows that of Joseph Dorfman, "The Economic Philosophy of Thomas Jefferson," *Political Science Quarterly* (1940), 55:98–121, and Joseph Spengler, "The Political Economy of Jefferson, Madison and Adams," in David K. Jackson, ed., *American Studies in Honor of William Kenneth Boyd* (Durham: Duke University Press, 1940), pp. 3–59. Dumas Malone, *Jefferson and His Time*, 6 vols. (Boston: Little Brown, 1948–), 2:430, suggests that Jefferson's preference for agriculture was based on moral and political grounds rather than on economics.

8. Jefferson, "First Inaugural Address," 1801, *Writings*, 8:4.

9. Jefferson to Edward Carrington, Paris, 1788, *Writings*, 5:20. Jefferson was commenting on proposals for the Constitution, here on the necessity for a rotating presidency.

10. Jefferson to John Taylor, Monticello, 1816, *Writings*, 10:29.

11. Jefferson, "Opinion on French Treaties," 1793, *Writings*, 6:220. Writing after the French Revolution, Jefferson is discussing what constitutes the legitimate government of France.

12. Jefferson to James Madison, 1789, *Writings*, 5:121. This is a famous statement in which Jefferson goes on to suggest that every constitution should be remade after nineteen years.

13. For further elaboration of this argument, see Spengler, "The Political Economy of Jefferson, Madison and Adams."

14. When discussing immigration, Jefferson frequently pleaded for cultural homogeneity and limited immigration to prevent alien peoples from corrupting American society. Since the American form of government was founded on consent and natural rights, Jefferson feared that immigrants from absolutist states would bring corrupting principles of government. The only exceptions were "useful artificers" who had something to teach. See Jefferson, "Notes on Virginia," *Writings*, 3:189–190. This raises an interesting issue about the desirability of cultural and social homogeneity for grass-roots participation, which could lead to the exacerbation of tensions on the national level, were the nation-state to be composed of various social or ethnic groups exercising widespread participation on the local level—an important feature of local self-reliance.

15. See Jefferson, "Notes on Virginia," *Writings*, 3:245–250. Jefferson's views on the inferiority of blacks are well known. An attempt to refute this is made by Wills, *Inventing America*, ch. 15, who argues that Jefferson regarded blacks as equal to whites at least in the moral sense. But this in no way refutes the point that Jefferson did not believe that blacks could become self-reliant individuals in American society.

16. Jefferson, "Notes on Virginia," *Writings*, 3:151ff.

17. "Confidential Message on Expedition to the Pacific," 1803, *Writings*, 8:192–202.

18. C.f. Johan Galtung, "A Structural Theory of Imperialism," *Journal of Peace Research* (1971), 2:81–117. Galtung's definition of cultural imperialism includes this dimension of teachers and learners.

19. Jefferson to Martha Jefferson, Aix-en-Provence, 1787, *Writings*, 4:373.

20. *Ibid.*

21. Jefferson did believe, however, that women had the right to inherit property along with men. See Jefferson, "Proposed Constitution for Virginia," *Writings*, 2:26.

22. Jefferson, "Notes on Religion," 1776, *Writings*, 2:92–103. These are materials and notes for Jefferson's speeches in the Virginia House of Delegates on petitions for the disestablishment of the Anglican church.

23. "A Bill for Establishing Religious Freedom" *Writings*, 2:237–239.

24. Jefferson's tomb commemorates him as the author of the Declaration of Independence and the Statute of Religious Freedom, and the founder of the University of Virginia. He did not wish his presidency or other political offices to be mentioned.

25. Jefferson, "Autobiography," *Writings*, 1:69.

26. Jefferson, "A Bill for the More General Diffusion of Knowledge" *Writings*, 2:220–229.

27. Jefferson's fear of "government excesses" was heightened by his stay in France before the Revolution. Correction of excesses comes from an educated citizenry: "were it left to me to decide whether we should have a

government without newspapers or newspapers without a government, I should not hesitate a moment to prefer the latter." Jefferson to Edward Carrington, Paris, 1787, *Writings*, 4:360.

28. Jefferson, "Notes on Virginia," *Writings*, 3:254. In 1782 Jefferson was still arguing for an amendment to the Virginia Constitution to establish public education. His proposals were never adopted.

29. Jefferson to James Madison, Paris, 1785, *Writings*, 4:37.

30. Jefferson did not think that domestic manufactures would succeed in the United States. He noted that American laborers were irresistibly drawn toward agriculture for reasons of higher productivity and also for reasons of personal preference. Jefferson to Thomas Digges, Paris, 1788, *Writings*, 5:27.

31. Jefferson to U.S. Minister in Portugal, Philadelphia, 1791, *Writings*, 5:344.

32. This strategy of balanced growth is not usually stressed in discussions of early American development. But Washington's Farewell Address of 1796, which will be discussed further in chapter 5, was actually an early statement of a balanced growth development strategy. The Address, along with its more familiar proposals for international isolation, advocates that each section of the United States should complement the others in terms of the development of industry, commerce and agriculture.

33. Jefferson to Thomas Leiper, Washington, 1809, *Writings*, 9:239.

34. Jefferson to John Melsh, Monticello, 1813, *Writings*, 9:373. Later, toward the end of his life, Jefferson's correspondence shows less enthusiasm for domestic manufactures. This appears to be due to the already declining position of the Virginia economy and the rising prosperity of other sections of the United States, particularly the Northeast, where manufacturing was prospering. Jefferson felt that this prosperity was due to federal government policies that favored manufactures over agriculture.

35. Jefferson to Lafayette, 1813, *Writings*, 9:434. War as a stimulus for domestic industry and consequent dependency reversal has been noted by modern dependency writers, particularly in reference to Latin American development during the two world wars.

36. For a discussion of American mercantilism see W. A. Williams, *Contours of American History* (Cleveland: World, 1961). While Williams does not believe that Jefferson was a mercantilist in principle, he admits that he employed mercantilist programs. This would be consistent with Jefferson's political and economic pragmatism.

37. Jefferson to Thomas Lomax, 1799, *Writings*, 7:374.

38. Jefferson to James Madison, Paris, 1786, *Writings*, 4:192.

39. Jefferson to George Wythe, Paris, 1787, *Writings*, 4:445.

40. As late as 1825, Jefferson was still expressing anxiety over federal encroachment on the rights of states. Areas such as internal taxation and internal improvements are cited as examples of this tendency. See Jefferson to William Giles, Monticello, 1825, *Writings*, 10:354. His dispute with Hamilton will be discussed more fully in chapter 5.

41. Jefferson to Samuel Kercheval, Monticello, 1816, *Writings*, 10:41.

42. *Ibid.*, p. 40. Such areas might include police, education, care of the poor, public roads, and choice of justices to serve in county courts. See also *Writings*, 9:427. Here Jefferson is advocating ward government for administering his public education scheme. Small units of government closer to the people would be less susceptible to corruption by inherited wealth and a hereditary aristocracy.

43. Jefferson to James Monroe, Paris, 1786, *Writings*, 4:247.

44. Jefferson to Gideon Granger, Monticello, 1800, *Writings*, 7:451.

45. Jefferson to John Taylor, Monticello, 1816, *Writings*, 10:29.

46. Jefferson to the Governor of the Mississippi Territory, Washington, 1807, *Writings*, 9:167.

47. Jefferson to James Madison, Monticello, 1815, *Writings*, 9:513.

48. Jefferson to Dr. Walter Jones, Monticello, 1810, *Writings*, 9:274: "Happily for us the mammoth cannot swim, nor the Leviathan move on dry land; and if we will keep out of their way, they cannot get at us." See also Jefferson to Baron von Humboldt, 1813, *Writings*, 9:431.

49. Jefferson to Elbridge Gerry, Philadelphia, 1797, *Writings*, 7:121.

50. For further elaboration of this argument, see Harvey Mansfield Jr., "Thomas Jefferson," in Morton Frisch and Richard Stevens, eds., *American Political Thought* (New York: Charles Scribners, 1970), pp. 23–50. This interpretation offers striking parallels with contemporary dependence and self-reliance themes. Mansfield also suggests that Jefferson's "Notes on Virginia" is a statement attesting to America's capacity for independence—that America had both the physical capability, through abundant natural resources, and the institutional capacity to prevent cultural dependence.

51. The argument is made in some detail in Jefferson's "Summary View of the Rights of British America," 1774, *Writings*, 1:421–447.

52. *Ibid.*

53. There are intimations in his writings that Jefferson supported the view, later espoused by nineteenth-century liberals, that trade promotes peace. See, for example, Jefferson to P. Fitzhugh, Philadelphia, 1798, *Writings*, 7:208.

54. For example, see Galtung, "A Structural Theory of Imperialism."

55. See Mansfield, "Thomas Jefferson," who suggests that Jefferson's republicanism was based on his confidence in the people as characterized by the independent farmer. When this base no longer existed, the theory must be rethought: "Men in remaking the environment remake themselves" (p. 41). Mansfield also notes the parallel with Rousseau in this aspect of Jefferson's thought.

56. The Embargo was in response to England's attempts to prevent neutrals from trading with its enemies. It declared that all exports from the United States would be stopped and that British manufactures would be refused entry. The Embargo was very unpopular with American commercial interests, particularly in New England: it was quite limited in its effectiveness and Jefferson was forced to repeal it in 1809.

57. Jefferson to John Adams, Monticello, 1812, *Writings*, 9:333. Jefferson noted with approbation that, by this time, household manufactures were well established in Virginia and that northern manufactories were already replacing England as the chief source of supply.

58. Jefferson to Colonel Humphreys, Washington, 1809, *Writings*, 9:226.

59. There is evidence that Jefferson supported a version of the theory of comparative advantage. See Jefferson, "Report of the Secretary of State on the Privileges and Restrictions of the United States in Foreign Countries," 1793, *Writings*, 6:479: "Could every country be employed in producing that which nature has best fitted it to produce, and each be free to exchange with others mutual surpluses for mutual wants, the greatest mass possible would then be produced of those things which contribute to human life and human happiness: the numbers of mankind would be increased, and their condition bettered."

60. Jefferson, "The Anas," 1791–1806, Notes of a conversation with Mr. Hammond, 1792, *Writings*, 1:198.

61. Jefferson to Elbridge Gerry, Philadelphia, 1799, *Writings*, 7:328.

62. Jefferson to James Madison, Paris, 1788, *Writings*, 5:47.

63. Jefferson to James Monroe, Paris, 1785, *Writings*, 4:32. Jefferson was determined to stay out of Europe's wars, at least until American strength could be built up. He noted, however, that war could have an extremely beneficial effect on American commerce. See Jefferson to Colonel John Harvie, New York, 1790, *Writings*, 5:213: "There will be war enough to give us high prices for wheat for years to come; and this single commodity will make us a great and happy nation." There are a number of other references to war as being advantageous for agricultural prices in international trade: see, e.g., Jefferson to Gouverneur Morris, Philadelphia, 1790, and to Francis Eppes, Philadelphia, 1793, *Writings*, 5:250 and 6:162.

64. Jefferson, "Eighth Annual Message to Congress," *Writings*, 9:223. This is the same Message as that in which Jefferson called for the domestic production of manufactures.

65. Jefferson to James Monroe, Washington, 1809, *Writings*, 9:243.

66. Jefferson to Lafayette, 1813, *Writings*, 9:434.

67. Jefferson to Philip Mazzei, Monticello, 1813, *Writings*, 9:442.

68. Jefferson to T. Leiper, Monticello, 1815, *Writings*, 9:520.

69. Jefferson to James Madison, 1784, *Writings*, 3:402.

70. Jefferson to James Madison, Paris, 1786, *Writings*, 4:334. See also Jefferson to James Madison, Paris, 1787, *Writings*, 4:363.

71. There are many references to the importance of free navigation of the Mississippi for American commerce. See, e.g., *Writings*, 5:17, 5:225, and 5:468.

72. Jefferson to James Madison, 1787, *Writings*, 4:479.

73. Contemporary dependency theory notes that the distortion of national economic growth is often due to an emphasis on external trading patterns rather than on internal communications, which developed during the colonial era between the colony and the mother country. Self-reliance

strategies advocate the breaking of these relationships and the development of better internal linkages between regions.

74. Jefferson to James Ross, Paris, 1786, *Writings,* 4:216.

75. Jefferson to George Ticknor, Monticello, 1817, *Writings,* 10:80.

76. Seymour Martin Lipset, *The First New Nation: The United States in Historical and Comparative Perspective* (New York: Basic Books, 1963), offers an interesting analysis of the states' role in the construction of internal improvements.

77. Jefferson to Dupont de Nemours, Monticello, 1811, *Writings,* 9:321.

78. Jefferson to James Monroe, Washington, 1801, *Writings,* 8:105.

79. In the same letter Jefferson suggested, as he did on many other occasions, that blacks should be sent to the West Indies. It was also at about this time (1803) that he proposed that Indians be encouraged to abandon hunting in favor of a more sedentary life in order to free more arable land for white ownership. See Jefferson, "Confidential Message on the Expedition to the Pacific," *Writings,* 8:197, regarding the Lewis and Clark expedition.

80. Jefferson to Secretary of State Madison, Monticello, 1807, *Writings,* 9:124.

81. Jefferson to James Monroe, Monticello, 1823, *Writings,* 10:261.

82. Jefferson to James Monroe, Monticello, 1823, *Writings,* 10:277.

83. Jefferson to James Monroe, Monticello, 1816, *Writings,* 10:20.

84. There is evidence that, in contemporary cases of self-reliance development, grass-roots participation and local self-reliance is practiced at the expense of national self-reliance. One example is the case of Tanzania's Ujamaa, which follows a strategy of local self-reliance: Tanzania, however, remains heavily in debt to the international system.

5. THE VICTORY OF NATIONAL AUTONOMY
OVER LOCAL SELF-RELIANCE IN THE EARLY UNITED STATES

1. Alexander Hamilton, "Report on Manufactures," in Henry Cabot Lodge, ed., *The Works of Alexander Hamilton,* 12 vols (New York: Putnam, 1904), 4:101–102.

2. See Robert Lively, "The American System: A Review Article," *The Business History Review* (1955), 29:81–96.

3. See Seymour Martin Lipset, *The First New Nation: The United States in Historical and Comparative Perspective* (New York: Basic Books, 1963) for a discussion of early United States development in terms of political development indicators such as integration and legitimation. Lipset compares the American case with that of contemporary underdeveloped countries.

4. For a description of the various economic interests in the mid eighteenth century see Frank Thistlethwaite, *The Great Experiment* (Cambridge: Cambridge University Press, 1955), ch. 1.

5. See Robert W. Fogel and Stanley L. Engerman, eds., *The Reinterpreta-*

tion of American Economic History (New York: Harper and Row, 1971), ch. 1 for a general discussion of this issue. Simon Kuznets, "Notes on the Pattern of United States Economic Growth," *ibid.*, ch. 2, analyzes data as far back as 1840; before that data are extremely scarce and for the period under consideration growth can only be estimated. The issue is further complicated by a high degree of local subsistence agriculture which does not enter into the estimates. See also Paul David, "The Growth of Real Product in the United States Before 1840: New Evidence, Controlled Conjectures," *Journal of Economic History* (1967), 27:151–197.

6. For a discussion of the tension between idealism and realism in the history of American politics see Samuel P. Huntington, *American Politics: The Promise of Disharmony* (Cambridge: Harvard University Press, 1981).

7. Carl N. Degler, *Out of Our Past: The Forces that Shaped Modern America*, rev. ed. (New York: Harper and Row, 1970), pp. 24–26.

8. See Alexis de Tocqueville, *Democracy in America*, trans. Henry Reeve (New York: George Dearborn, 1838), pp. 36–47.

9. *Ibid.*, pp. 210ff.

10. *Ibid.*, p. 75.

11. For an analysis of this phenomenon see Eugene P. Link, *Democratic-Republican Societies 1790–1800* (New York: Columbia University Press, 1942).

12. Nathan Rosenberg, *Technology and American Economic Growth* (White Plains, N.Y.: Sharpe, 1972), p. 38.

13. Thistlethwaite, *The Great Experiment*, p. 2.

14. Curtis P. Nettels, *The Emergence of a National Economy, 1775–1815*, vol. 2 of *The Economic History of the United States* (New York: Holt, Rinehart and Winston, 1962), p. 130. Twenty years later, the percentage had only increased to 4.9.

15. See H. C. Allen, "F. J. Turner and the Frontier," in H. C. Allen and C. P. Hill, eds., *British Essays in American History* (London: Arnold, 1957), pp. 145–166.

16. Gerald Gunderson, *A New Economic History of America* (New York: McGraw Hill, 1976), p. 53. Such a favorable land/labor ratio does not usually obtain in contemporary less developed countries.

17. See Jackson Turner Main, *The Antifederalists: Critics of the Constitution 1781–88* (Chapel Hill: University of North Carolina Press, 1961), ch. 1.

18. See *ibid.*, ch. 11.

19. This analysis follows Daniel J. Boorstin, *The Lost World of Thomas Jefferson* (New York: Holt, 1948), which analyzes the political thought of members of the American Philosophical Society, a group of Jeffersonians including Thomas Paine, Benjamin Franklin and Joseph Priestley. Boorstin sets this specifically American philosophy in contrast to Federalist thought which, he maintains, was more grounded in the European aristocratic tradition.

20. Hans Kohn, *Nationalism: Its Meaning and History* (Princeton, N.J.: Van Nostrand, 1955), pp. 16–20.

21. James MacGregor Burns, *The Vineyard of Liberty* (New York: Knopf, 1982), p. 34.

22. Howard Fast, *The Selected Work of Tom Paine and Citizen Tom Paine,* (New York: Modern Library, 1945), pp. 6–8.

23. See Nettels, *The Emergence of a National Economy,* ch. 3.

24. John Miller, *Alexander Hamilton: Portrait in Paradox* (New York: Harper and Row, 1959), p. 252.

25. The Alien and Sedition Acts ordered the removal of dangerous aliens from the United States, raised the probationary period of naturalization and imposed restrictions on the freedom of the press and speech. The Kentucky Resolutions, drafted by Thomas Jefferson, stated that, in the event that the Federal Congress transcended its stated powers, each state had the right of redress; powers not specifically delegated were to remain with the states. See *The Writings of Thomas Jefferson,* ed. Paul L. Ford, 10 vols. (New York: Putnam, 1892–99), 7:289–309. James Madison formulated a similar set of resolutions for Virginia.

26. Hamilton's Report on Manufactures was resurrected in 1816 as part of the argument for the tariff bill of that year. In the same year, the Second Bank of the United States received its charter.

27. For a discussion of collectivization as a component of local self-reliance in the cases of China and Tanzania see Mary Anderson, *Self-Reliant Development: A Comparison of the Economic Development Strategies of Mohandas Gandhi, Mao Tse Tung and Julius Nyerere,* Ph.D. dissertation, University of Colorado, 1978.

28. See August O. Spain, *The Political Theory of John C. Calhoun* (New York: Bookman, 1951).

29. Charles M. Wiltse, *The Jeffersonian Tradition in American Democracy* (Chapel Hill: University of North Carolina, Press, 1935), p. 224.

30. See W. A. Williams, *Contours of American History* (Cleveland: World, 1961), for a discussion of the rebirth of European mercantilism in eighteenth-century America.

31. See chapter 3. A Listian development model is an example of mercantilism as a "catch-up" strategy.

32. See Arthur Schlesinger, Jr., "Ideas and the Economic Process," in Seymour E. Harris, ed., *American Economic History* (New York: McGraw Hill, 1961), pp. 3–25.

33. This is corroborated by the work of revisionist economic historians: see, for example, Fogel and Engerman *The Reinterpretation of American Economic History*; Lively, "The American System"; Harry Scheiber, ed., *United States Economic History: Selected Readings* (New York: Knopf, 1964), ch. 5; and George Rogers Taylor, *The Transportation Revolution 1815–1860,* vol. 3 of *The Economic History of the United States* (New York: Holt, Rinehart and Winston, 1951). See also Lipset, *The First New Nation,* pp. 48ff.

34. See Nettels, *The Emergence of a National Economy,* chs. 5 and 6. Nettels emphasizes that the whole Federalist program was designed to achieve balanced independent growth.

35. Alexander Hamilton, James Madison, John Jay, *The Federalist,* Paul L. Ford, ed. (New York: Holt, 1898), No. 4, by John Jay, p. 21.

36. *Ibid.,* No. 15, by Alexander Hamilton, pp. 87–96.

37. "Import and Tonnage Duties," speech in Congress, April 9, 1789, in *Papers of James Madison,* vol. 12, Charles Hobson and Robert A. Rutland, eds. (Charlottesville: University Press of Virginia, 1979), p. 99.

38. United States Congress, *Abridgement of the Debates of Congress from 1789–1856: From Gales and Seaton's Annals of Congress,* 16 vols. (New York: Appleton, 1857–61), 1:465.

39. See Curtis P. Nettels, *George Washington and American Independence* (Boston: Little Brown, 1951), pp. 70–72.

40. George Washington, January 8, 1790, in James D. Richardson, ed., *A Compilation of Messages and Papers of the Presidents,* 20 vols. (New York: Bureau of National Literature, 1897), 1:57.

41. Similar ideas about national economic self-sufficiency appear in Washington's correspondence. For example, see Washington to Lafayette, January 29, 1789 and Washington to Jefferson, February 13, 1789, *Writings of George Washington,* ed. John C. Fitzpatrick, 39 vols. (Washington, D.C.: GPO, 1931–1944), 30:186, 199.

42. George Washington, "Farewell Address," in *Old South Leaflets,* 5 vols. (Boston: Old South Meeting House, n.d.), 1:12.

43. For example, a standard textbook on American history mentions only this aspect of the Farewell Address. See Samuel Eliot Morison and Henry Steele Commager, *The Growth of the American Republic,* 2 vols. (New York: Oxford University Press, 1950), 1:368.

44. Washington, "Farewell Address," p. 5.

45. The type of interregional balanced economy favored by Washington can of course become the *source* of sectionalism as is evidenced by the experience of the South which climaxed in the Civil War. Strategies of balanced growth that rely on regional specialization can reproduce dependencies internally, similar to those with respect to the international system. This is a contributing factor in the development of subnational movements, which are evident in some developed states today, such as Britain, Canada and Spain.

46. Economic historians generally place American *economic* independence after 1815 and the development of a national economy during the period 1815–1830.

47. See W. R. Brock, "The Ideas and Influence of Alexander Hamilton," in Allen and Hill, eds., *British Essays in American History,* pp. 40–60. See especially pp. 57ff. Even before independence, Hamilton saw the importance of developing colonial manufactures and commerce linked by the intercolonial trade, i.e. America as an economic whole to promote unity, much as List had envisaged the Zollverein would do for Germany. See Miller, *Alexander Hamilton,* p. 12.

48. Clinton Rossiter, *Alexander Hamilton and the Constitution* (New York: Harcourt, Brace and World, 1964), p. 135. See also Cecilia Kenyon, "Alexan-

der Hamilton: Rousseau of the Right," *Political Science Quarterly* (June 1958), 73(2):161–178, and Miller, *Alexander Hamilton*, p. 47.

49. Alexander Hamilton, "The Continentalist," July 4, 1782, quoted in Richard B. Morris, ed., *Alexander Hamilton and the Founding of the Nation* (New York: Dial Press, 1957), p. 73.

50. Alexander Hamilton, "Report on Manufactures," December 5, 1791, Lodge, ed., *The Works of Alexander Hamilton*, 4:70. The Report contains many parallels with the writings of Friedrich List: for a comparison of Hamilton and List see E. M. Earle, "Adam Smith, Alexander Hamilton and Friedrich List: The Economic Foundations of Military Power," E. M. Earle, ed., *Makers of Modern Strategy: Military Thought from Machiavelli to Hitler* (Princeton: Princeton University Press, 1943), pp. 117–154.

51. Hamilton, "Report on Manufactures," pp. 131–132.

52. *Ibid.*, p. 96.

53. *Ibid.*, p. 102.

54. *Ibid.*, pp. 133–134.

55. The United States was also short of capital. Hamilton encouraged foreign capital to fill this gap, in contrast to contemporary self-reliance strategies which try to exclude foreign capital, which they fear will create dependencies.

56. The following discussion of Gallatin is based on E. James Ferguson's Introduction to his edition of *Selected Writings of Albert Gallatin* (New York: Bobbs Merrill, 1967).

57. Albert Gallatin, "Report on Roads and Canals," 1808, *Selected Writings*, p. 232.

58. Albert Gallatin, "Report on Manufactures," 1810, *Selected Writings*, pp. 240–264.

59. James Monroe, "Message to Congress on the Subject of Internal Improvements," May 4, 1822, in Richardson, *Messages and Papers of the Presidents*, 2:713.

60. According to Williams, *Contours of American History*, p. 209, Monroe's plea for a constitutional amendment was to save the whole idea of a mutually responsible system: Monroe believed that expansion without such an amendment would lead to sectional strife.

61. James Monroe, "7th Annual Message to Congress," December 2, 1823, in Richardson, *Messages and Papers of the Presidents*, 2:785.

62. John Quincy Adams, "First Annual Message to Congress," December 6, 1825, in Richardson, *Messages and Papers of the Presidents*, 2:877.

63. For an analysis of the constitutional thought of John Marshall, see Samuel J. Konefsky, *John Marshall and Alexander Hamilton: Architects of the American Constitution* (New York: Macmillan, 1964), and Robert K. Faulkner, *The Jurisprudence of John Marshall* (Princeton: Princeton University Press, 1968).

64. For a detailed discussion of Marbury vs. Madison see Konefsky, *John Marshall and Alexander Hamilton*, pp. 81–91.

65. McCulloch vs. Maryland, 1817, was the most significant decision regarding implied powers.

66. For example, the case of Dartmouth College vs. Woodward of 1819 stated that the New Hampshire legislature had no right to rescind the prerevolutionary charter of Dartmouth College.

67. Stanley Lebergott, "Labor Force and Employment, 1800–1960," in Conference on Research in Income and Wealth, *Output, Employment, and Productivity in the United States after 1800*, pp. 117–204 (New York: National Bureau of Economic Research, 1966), Studies in Income and Wealth, vol. 30.

68. See Louis Hacker, *The Course of American Economic Growth and Development* (New York: Wiley, 1970), ch. 7.

69. See Fogel and Engerman, *The Reinterpretation of American Economic History*, ch. 1. According to the estimates of Robert Zevin, which they cite, production in the cotton textile industry experienced an annual growth rate of 15.4 percent from 1816–1860, half of which is attributed to increase in demand and only one third to improvements in machinery.

70. Lance Davis and Douglass North, *Institutional Change and American Economic Growth* (Cambridge: Cambridge University Press, 1971), see government involvement in transportation as an important exception to an otherwise rather low level of direct government intervention.

71. Lipset, *The First New Nation*, p. 48, maintains that, where national planning failed, it was due to states' rights issues rather than laissez-faire economic policy; government played a major role in economic development on the state level.

72. Williams, *Contours of American History*, p. 211.

73. See Taylor, *The Transportation Revolution*, ch. 16, for an extended discussion of the role of government in economic development during this period.

74. See Douglass North, *Economic Growth of the United States 1790–1860* (New York: Norton, 1966). North's general thesis is that the pace of economic development was determined primarily by the export sector, particularly the export of cotton. Revisionists have criticized North for not giving enough weight to internal determinants of growth, such as public policy. See David, "The Growth of Real Product in the United States before 1840."

75. See North, *Economic Growth of the United States*, ch. 2.

76. See Nettels, *The Economic History of the United States*, ch. 3 for a discussion of postwar trade and depression.

77. See United States Congress, *Abridgement of the Debates of Congress*, pp. 465ff., January, 1794.

78. Nettels, *The Economic History of the United States*, pp. 109–110. The Act levied duties on 65 types of articles, 55 of which were manufactures made in the U.S. Rates ranged from 5 percent to 15 percent; only six kinds of noncompetitive imports were taxed.

79. *Ibid.*, p. 111. A duty of fifty cents per ton on foreign-owned vessels entering U.S. ports and six cents on American vessels.

80. In his Report on the Commerce of the United States of 1793, Jefferson estimated that $9.4 million worth of exports went to Britain, the next largest market being France, which took $4.7 million. His estimates on the

source of imports are $15 million, the highest figure, from Britain; the next highest figure is $2 million, from France. See *The Writings of Thomas Jefferson*, 6:472.

81. See James Madison, 1794, in United States Congress, *Abridgement of the Debates of Congress*, 1:467. Madison thought that if the U.S. stopped importing British luxuries, it would deal a blow to British commerce. Paul A. Varg, *Foreign Policies of the Founding Fathers* (East Lansing: Michigan State University Press, 1963), ch. 5, agrees that this was the Republican attitude toward retaliation against British commerce but suggests that Republicans were somewhat unrealistic in assuming that it would have any effect on British policy.

82. Nettels, *The Economic History of the United States*, p. 236.

83. For Jefferson's justification of the Embargo see his Eighth Annual Message to Congress, November 8, 1808, in *Writings of Thomas Jefferson*, 9:213–225. Although designed to punish both Britain and France, the immediate provocation for the Embargo, which stated that no ships were to leave American ports, was the firing on the U.S. Chesapeake by a British frigate.

84. Nettels, *The Economic History of the United States*, p. 328. In Charleston the price of cotton sank from twenty-one cents per pound in December 1807 to thirteen cents in February 1808.

85. The Embargo, which was extremely unpopular with American commercial interests, was abandoned in 1809 and replaced by the Non-Intercourse Act which reopened all trade except with England and France. In 1810 the Macon Bill provided for the reopening of trade with either belligerent were they to repeal orders against neutral shipping. Britain refused to yield and this became one of the immediate causes of the War of 1812.

86. Fred A. Shannon, *America's Economic Growth*, 3d ed. (New York: Macmillan, 1951), p. 177. Essentially, the status quo was restored. The United States lost nothing but its fishing rights in British waters (these were restored in 1818), and gained nothing but the validation of its claim to West Florida.

87. F. W. Taussig, *The Tariff History of the United States*, revised 8th ed. (New York: Capricorn Books, 1964), pp. 10–11. Taussig sees the period up to 1808 as a continuation of the colonial period: an absence of development promoted by the peculiar conditions of foreign trade.

88. This could be compared with the more rapid development of various Latin American countries during the two World Wars, which has been noted by "dependencia" writers. For example, see F. H. Cardoso and E. Faletto, *Dependency and Development in Latin America* (Berkeley: University of California Press, 1979).

89. The position of the South, which became antitariff after 1816, was somewhat different and will be discussed separately.

90. Taylor, *The Transportation Revolution*, p. 192.

91. There is some evidence that List knew about Raymond's work. See

Margaret Hirst, *Life of Friedrich List* (London: Smith, Elder 1909) and my chapter 3 for further discussion of this issue.

92. See Tench Coxe, *A View of the United States of America in a Series of Papers Written at Various Times, in the Years between 1787 and 1794* (New York: Kelley, 1965).

93. The Pennsylvania Society for the Promotion of Manufactures printed many of List's writings on protection. Matthew Carey, secretary of the Philadelphia Society for the Encouragement of American Manufactures, based his support for protection on the necessity of balanced growth in order to catch up with England. Carey was an Irishman who, like List, both hated and admired England. See Kenneth Rowe, *Matthew Carey: A Study in American Economic Development* (Baltimore: Johns Hopkins University Press, 1933).

94. For a discussion of Clay's political thought see Glyndon Van Deusen, *The Life of Henry Clay* (Westport, Conn: Greenwood Press, 1979).

95. See Paul David, "Learning by Doing and Tariff Protection: A Reconsideration of the Case of the Ante-Bellum U.S. Cotton Textile Industry," *Journal of Economic History* (1970), 30:521–601.

96. See Taussig, *Tariff History of the United States,* pp. 25–45. In the case of the iron industry, Taussig maintains that it did not prosper until the 1830s even with protection, due to inferior technology. *Ibid.*, pp. 46–59.

97. See Fogel and Engerman, *The Reinterpretation of American Economic History,* p. 5. North, *Economic Growth of the United States,* agrees that the tariff had little effect on domestic manufactures.

98. The nullification doctrine was approved by the legislature of South Carolina in 1828. It stated that, since the Federal Constitution was established by the sovereign states, these states had the right to judge when the federal government exceeded its powers. If it had done so, the state could prevent enforcement of the legislation within state limits.

99. See Fogel and Engerman, *The Reinterpretation of American Economic History,* ch. 1.

100. In 1800 the South still exported 75 percent of its cotton crop. Eugene Genovese, "The Significance of the Slave Plantation for Southern Economic Development," in Scheiber, *United States Economic History,* p. 151.

101. For a similar argument, see Robert O. Keohane, "Associationist American Development, 1776–1860: Economic Growth and Political Disintegration," in John Gerard Ruggie, ed., *The Antinomies of Interdependence: National Welfare and the International Division of Labor* (New York: Columbia University Press, 1983), ch. 2.

102. Nettels, *The Economic History of the United States,* ch. 15, maintains that Republican principles did not stand in the way of projects to which Republicans were committed. The Lousiana Purchase was the outstanding example of this: it considerably stretched a narrow interpretation of the Constitution, which said nothing about the powers of the federal government to acquire new lands.

103. James Monroe, "Message to Congress on the Subject of Internal Improvements," May 4, 1822, in Richardson, *Messages and Papers of the Presidents*, 2:747.

104. James Monroe, "Seventh Annual Message," December 2, 1823, in Richardson, *Messages and Papers of the Presidents*, 2:787.

105. *Ibid.*, p. 788.

106. John Quincy Adams, "First Annual Message," December 6, 1825, in Richardson, *Messages and Papers of the Presidents*, 2:868.

107. See Samuel Flagg Bemis, *John Quincy Adams and the Foundations of American Foreign Policy* (New York: Knopf, 1956).

6. DECENTRALIZED DEMOCRACY:
THE POLITICAL AND ECONOMIC THOUGHT OF MOHANDAS GANDHI

1. See Ashis Nandy, "From Outside the Imperium: Gandhi's Cultural Criticism of the West," *Alternatives* (Fall 1981), 7(2):171–194. Gandhi's rejection of Western economic theory is particularly interesting in light of the contemporary criticism of Western development models for their lack of success in solving development problems in different economic contexts.

2. See Mary Anderson, "Self-Reliant Development: A Comparison of the Economic Development Strategies of Mohandas Gandhi, Mao Tse Tung, and Julius Nyerere," Ph.D. dissertation, University of Colorado, 1978, for a detailed discussion of this point.

3. Gandhi, quoted in Raghavan N. Iyer, *The Moral and Political Thought of Mahatma Gandhi* (New York: Oxford University Press, 1973), p. 373.

4. Mohandas K. Gandhi, *Collected Works*, 90 vols. (Delhi: Ministry of Information and Broadcasting, Government of India, 1958–). Cited hereafter in text and notes as *CW*, with volume and page numbers. Gandhi often wrote sketches of Westerners he particularly admired for newspaper articles; some examples were Elizabeth Fry, Abraham Lincoln, Florence Nightingale, and George Washington.

5. Stanley J. Heginbotham, *Cultures in Conflict: The Four Faces of Indian Bureaucracy* (New York: Columbia University Press, 1975), p. 222.

6. Gene Sharp, *Gandhi as a Political Strategist* (Boston: Porter Sargent, 1979), p. 62.

7. Gunnar Myrdal, *Against the Stream: Critical Essays on Economics* (New York: Pantheon Books, 1972), p. 235.

8. Martin Luther King's views on this subject were clearly influenced by Gandhi.

9. Gandhi, quoted in O. P. Goyal, *Studies in Modern Indian Political Thought: Gandhi, An Interpretation* (Allahabad: Kitab Mahal, 1964), p. 55.

10. Jawaharlal Nehru, *Nehru on Gandhi* (New York: John Day, 1948), p. 64. Nehru reveals that, while the Congress leadership did not accept many of Gandhi's ideas, they felt that they could reach the masses through Gandhi's charisma.

11. For example, Gandhi's vow of Brahmacharya or abstinence from sex, which he took in 1906 along with a commitment to a minimal diet and the renunciation of worldly goods, are standards that are quite unrealistic for most people. See Mohandas K. Gandhi, *Autobiography: The Story of My Experiments with Truth*, Mahadev Desai, tr. (Boston: Beacon Press, 1957), pp. 204–211.

12. An example is a 1945 letter to M. Shah: "A discussion was going on between Shakaribehn and you when I was in the bathroom. Both of you were talking at the top of your voices. Why? The discussion was between you two only, and was not meant for anybody else to hear. How can this be tolerated? You should try and somehow learn to exercise control over your voice. It is a matter of common sense how loudly one should talk on what occasion" (*CW*, 79:121).

13. Gandhi, *Autobiography*, p. 214.

14. *Ibid.*, p. 263.

15. *Ibid.*, p. 25.

16. Gandhi's assasination was at the hands of an orthodox Hindu protesting, among other things, Gandhi's position on untouchability.

17. Gandhi believed that Indians were not fitted for independence unless this issue was solved.

18. *The Selected Works of Mahatma Gandhi*, 6 vols., Shriman Narayan, ed. (Ahmedabad: Navajivan, 1968), 6:473–478. Gandhi observed, probably incorrectly, that in England there was social stratification but not hostility between classes. He noted the affection between noblemen and their servants and approved of such a society where everyone knew his place. He suggested that the biggest vices of the English lay not with their institution of class but rather with their addiction to horse racing and alcohol! (*CW*, 56:290).

19. By 1945 Gandhi was advocating intercaste marriages as a way of breaking down the system; see *CW* 80:77.

20. This idea of the unity of religion and politics appears throughout Gandhi's *Autobiography*; see, in particular, p. 504.

21. A Congress resolution of 1920 pledged the withdrawal of children from government schools (*CW* 19:208).

22. Gandhi was particularly upset by state-funded education, since it was financed by a tax on liquor.

23. Gandhi, *Autobiography*, pp. 298–299.

24. Gandhi translated "Unto This Last" into Gujarati in 1908 under the title of "Sarvodaya," which means "The Advancement of All." It was serialized in *Indian Opinion* and appears at intervals in *CW*, vol. 8, between pp. 239 and 375. Ruskin's social utopia countered the utilitarian principle of the greatest good of the greatest number, with a concern for the good of every individual, even the lowest. "Sarvodaya" was written in the form of a Socratic dialogue; Gandhi was a great admirer of Socrates because of his commitment to civil disobedience.

25. Gandhi, *Selected Works*, 6:351.

26. *Ibid.*, 6:345.

27. For further discussion of the Constructive Programme, see Sharp, *Gandhi as a Political Strategist*, ch. 5.

28. Gandhi, *Selected Works*, 6:323.

29. *Ibid.*, 6:331.

30. *Ibid.*, 6:330.

31. Gandhi, *Autobiography*, p. 434.

32. Gandhi, *Selected Works*, 6:452.

33. *Ibid.*, 6:449.

34. This would be the opposite of the way power is delegated by the American Constitution, which has generally been interpreted as saying that functions not specifically delegated to the states reside with the federal government.

35. This argument is similar to that of today's dependency theorists.

36. For a further discussion of swaraj as self-rule see Erik Erikson, *Gandhi's Truth* (New York: Norton, 1969), p. 397.

37. Swadeshi has some similarities with the dissociative and restructuring stages of some contemporary theories of self-reliance.

38. See Amritananda Das, *Foundations of Gandhian Economics* (New York: St. Martin's Press, 1979), pp. 63–65.

39. See, for example, E. F. Schumacher, *Small Is Beautiful: A Study of Economics as if People Mattered* (London: Blond and Briggs, 1973).

40. See also *CW* 59:435, where Gandhi states that he has no quarrel with the use of heavy machinery except when it replaces human labor which would otherwise be unemployed.

41. Gandhi did not say that he was against large-scale production but rather that he was against it when villagers could produce the goods for themselves.

42. In answer to the question whether Westerners should come to India, Gandhi said that he would welcome their scientific talent to help make the kind of tools useful for villages (*CW* 64:99). This is very close to the view of contemporary supporters of appropriate technologies.

43. Consistent with his concern with small detail, Gandhi urged the use of a babul twig rather than a factory-made toothbrush. He maintained that it was more hygienic and that the opposite end could be used as a tongue scraper (*CW* 60:109).

44. D. G. Tendulkar, *Mahatma: Life of Mohandas Karamchand Gandhi*, 8 vols. (Delhi: Ministry of Information and Broadcasting, Government of India, 1953), 7:186. Cottage industry would also prevent village disruption, which would create dependency. See also Anderson, "Self-Reliant Development," p. 183.

45. This somewhat peculiar point is in opposition to the nationalism literature, which talks about the need for social mobilization for the achievement of national unity. See, for example, Karl Deutsch, *Nationlism and Social Communication: An Enquiry into the Foundations of Nationality* (Cambridge: MIT Press, 1953). Gandhi also had a personal dislike of modern machinery

and transportation: "The modern rage for variety, for flying through the air, for multiplicity of wants, etc., have no fascination for me" (*CW* 70:242).

46. This is similar to Rousseau's attitude toward representative democracy. Rousseau maintained that the English were only free on election day. See Jean-Jacques Rousseau, *The Social Contract and Discourse on the Origin of Inequality*, Lester G. Crocker, ed. and tr. (New York: Washington Square Press, 1976), p. 99.

47. Gandhi, quoted in Gopinath Dhawan, *The Political Philosophy of Mahatma Gandhi* (Ahmedabad: Navajivan, 1951), p. 330.

48. Das, *Foundations of Gandhian Economics*, p. 43.

49. See *CW* 69:218–219, where Gandhi describes trusteeship. Besides its obvious impracticality in terms of implementation, it is not clear how this wealth could be used for social services without raising the possibility of charity, which Gandhi so strongly deplored. See also *CW* 58:275.

50. Gandhi, *Selected Works*, 6:365.

51. *Ibid.*, 6:367.

52. See also *CW* 38:14 and 64:193, where Gandhi argues that the middle class had bartered away the economic independence of India.

53. For a similar statement made by Rousseau, see Rousseau, *Social Contract*, p. 97.

54. This is similar to Rousseau's views on trade. See chapter 2.

55. This was written soon after the conclusion of World War I, which contributed to Gandhi's disillusionment with the West.

56. Charles Tilly, *The Formation of National States in Western Europe* (Princeton: Princeton University Press, 1975) emphasizes the important contribution war made to the formation of the Western state system. It is interesting to note Gandhi's awareness of this relationship and his determination that India's international relations must be different in order for its internal development to be different also.

57. For a discussion of Gandhi's concept of national defense based on nonviolent resistance, see Sharp, *Gandhi as a Political Strategist*, chs. 8 and 9.

58. Gandhi, quoted in *Sharp*, p. 150.

7. INDIAN DEVELOPMENT, 1947–1980:
GANDHI'S VISION COMPROMISED

1. Francine R. Frankel, *India's Political Economy, 1947–1977* (Princeton: Princeton University Press, 1978), p. 4. Population growth of around 2.1 percent per annum resulted in a per capita growth rate of about 1.8 percent per annum between 1951 and 1960. The estimation of poverty levels in India continue to be a subject of considerable debate; however, estimates up to the present day, rarely go below 40 percent.

2. See Raj Krishna, "Growth, Investment and Poverty in Mid-Term Appraisal of Sixth Plan," *Economic and Political Weekly*, (November 1983), vol.

INDIAN DEVELOPMENT, 1947–1980

18, no. 47. This is because of the high population growth rate: the percentage of the population below the poverty line may be slowly decreasing.

3. L. C. Jain, "Power to the People: Decentralization is a Necessity" (Hyderabad: Academy of Gandhian Studies, n.d.), p. 10.

4. Reinhard Bendix, *Nation-Building and Citizenship*, 2d ed. (Berkeley: University of California Press 1977), p. 294. This view is corroborated by Gilbert Etienne, *India's Changing Rural Scene 1963–1979* (Delhi: Oxford University Press, 1982), p. 154.

5. See George Rosen, *Democracy and Economic Change in India* (Berkeley: University of California Press for the Rand Corporation, 1966), ch. 2. Particularly when discussing self-reliance, one must exercise caution in imposing Western categories on definitions.

6. Dorothy Norman, ed., *Nehru: The First Sixty Years*, 2 vols. (New York: John Day, 1965), 2:109.

7. Jawaharlal Nehru, *Independence and After: A Collection of Speeches, 1946–1949*, (New York: John Day, 1950), p. 51.

8. Jawaharlal Nehru, *The Discovery of India*, edited, with a foreword and comments, by Robert I. Crane (Garden City, N.Y.: Anchor Books, 1959), p. 149.

9. Jawaharlal Nehru, *The Mind of Mr. Nehru: An Interview by R. K. Karanjia* (London: George Allen and Unwin, 1960), p. 100.

10. John W. Mellor, *The New Economics of Growth: A Strategy for India and the Developing World* (Ithaca: Cornell University Press, 1976), p. 255. Between 1950 and 1965, the share of GNP allotted to education rose from .8 percent to 2.6 percent.

11. *Ibid.* In 1966 universities received 24 percent of the total educational budget compared with 12 percent in Thailand in 1968, 11 percent in Japan in 1965, and 12 percent in the Soviet Union in 1965. India's share of educational resources allotted to higher education is comparable to that of the United States, the United Kingdom and other high income countries.

12. *Ibid.*, p. 254. Mellor cites a village study which reveals that in villages where the research was conducted, 32 percent of children between the ages of six and twenty-one were in school, with the participation rate for girls being half that of boys.

13. Lawrence A. Veit, *India's Second Revolution* (New York: McGraw-Hill, 1976), p. 58.

14. See Michael Lipton, "Strategy for Agriculture: Urban Bias and Rural Planning," in Paul Streeten and Michael Lipton, eds., *The Crisis of Indian Planning* (London: Oxford University Press, 1968), ch. 4. For the country as a whole, research and development in agriculture is small relative to total expenditure. The author notes that research in village studies is disparagingly referred to as "cow-dung economics" (p. 132).

15. See Robert L. Hardgrave Jr., *India: Government and Politics in a Developing Nation*, 3d ed. (New York: Harcourt, Brace and Jovanovich, 1980), ch. 7. Hardgrave estimates that, in the 1977 election, voter turnout was 60.4 percent of eligible voters.

16. For an analysis that emphasizes the relatively high level of political

participation in India see John O. Field, *Consolidating Democracy* (New Delhi: Manohar, 1980).

17. Lipton, "Strategy for Agriculture," p. 135. The author concludes that rural policy has been made by towns for towns.

18. Bimla Prasad, ed., *Socialism, Sarvodaya, and Democracy: Selected Works of Jayaprakash Narayan* (London: Asia Publishing House, 1964), p. 61.

19. *Ibid.*, p. 262. Here Narayan is addressing the issue of personal motivation of individuals working in state enterprises. His solution, some private enterprise at the local level, is one the Chinese are beginning to adopt by allowing the peasants to farm private lots and sell their produce in "free markets." This issue is crucial for any strategy of local self-reliance.

20. *Ibid.*, p. 246.

21. Jayaprakash Narayan, March 27, 1977, quoted in Frankel, *India's Political Economy*, p. 574.

22. Nehru, *Independence and After*, p. 145.

23. Frankel, *India's Political Economy*, pp. 68–69.

24. In the opinion of one analyst more land was redistributed under Gandhi's Bhoodan movement than under government legislation. Bhoodan failed because there was no follow-up to legalize voluntary transfers that had already taken place. Conversation with L. C. Jain, Harvard Divinity School, April 30, 1984.

25. Bendix, *Nation-Building and Citizenship*, p. 297. While three fourths of the work force contributed 48 percent of the national income working in agriculture, only a quarter of government expenditure went to this sector under the first two plans.

26. For a detailed analysis of the history of the Community Development Programme see L. C. Jain, *Grass Without Roots: Rural Development Under Government Auspices* (New Delhi: Institute of Social Studies Trust, 1983).

27. *Ibid.*, p. 22. For details of the recommendations of the Balwantrai Mehta Committee see Sugan Chand Jain, *Community Development and Panchayati Raj in India* (Bombay: Allied Publishers, 1967).

28. Bendix, *Nation-Building and Citizenship*, p. 340.

29. Jain, *Grass Without Roots*, p. 22.

30. *Ibid.*, p. 31.

31. For an important analysis of the cultural contradictions of Indian bureaucracy see Stanley J. Heginbotham, *Cultures in Conflict: The Four Faces of Indian Bureaucracy* (New York: Columbia University Press, 1975).

32. India came closest to large-scale land reform during the Nehru era with the Nagpur Resolutions of 1959, which imposed ceilings on land holdings. In the face of strong protest from the landed class, however, Nehru was forced to back down. After the Chinese invasion of 1961, Nehru also began to backtrack on agricultural cooperatives.

33. *Nehru: The First Sixty Years*, 2:180.

34. Veit, *India's Second Revolution*, p. 217.

35. Etienne, *India's Changing Rural Scene*, p. 149.

36. Veit, *India's Second Revolution*, p. 226.

37. This is the subject of an unpublished manuscript by Myron Weiner,

"Capitalist Agriculture, Peasant Farming and Well Being in Rural India," 1983.

38. Among the supporters of this proposition are Frankel, *India's Political Economy,* ch. 7 and Wolf Ladejinsky, "Ironies of India's Green Revolution," *Foreign Affairs* (July 1970), 48(4):758–768. Those who argue the opposite include Etienne, *India's Changing Rural Scene* and Weiner, "Capitalist Agriculture."

39. See Etienne, *India's Changing Rural Scene,* particularly chs. 13 and 14.

40. See "Decentralisation of Development Planning and Implementation Systems in the States," Second Report of Economic Advisory Council, *Mainstream,* (January 1984).

41. For examples of renewed interest in Gandhian development see M. L. Dantwala, "Two-Way Planning Process: Scope and Limitations," *Indian Journal of Agricultural Economics* (April–June 1983), 38(2), and various articles under the heading "Gandhism Today," *The Economic Times,* (October 2, 1983).

42. In 1947 there were 300,000 miles of roads and 41,000 miles of railroads. See Jagdish N. Bhagwati and Padma Desai, *India: Planning for Industrialization: Industrialization and Trade Policies Since 1951* (London: Oxford University Press, 1970), ch. 3, for a description of the Indian economy at independence.

43. A reevaluation of the goals of this strategy and its adequacy for alleviating poverty is the subject of an ongoing debate in India today. See Jagdish N. Bhagwati, "Growth and Poverty," unpublished manuscript, May 1985.

44. Mellor, *The New Economics of Growth,* p. 271.

45. Veit, *India's Second Revolution,* p. 372.

46. *Nehru: The First Sixty Years,* 1:76.

47. *Ibid.,* 2:179.

48. *Ibid.,* 1:373.

49. *Ibid.,* 2:179.

50. For a comparison of Gandhi's and Nehru's economic policies see Raj Krishna, "Nehru-Gandhi Polarity and Economic Policy," *Mainstream,* (August 5, 1978).

51. *Nehru: The First Sixty Years,* 1:691.

52. *Ibid.,* 1:692. In Nehru, *The Discovery of India.* p. 214, Nehru maintained, like List, that the development of agriculture and industry must be dealt with simultaneously.

53. One of Nehru's reasons for resisting Indian partition was his assertion, also reminiscent of List, that small states have no future in the international system. *Nehru: The First Sixty Years,* 2:171.

54. *Ibid.,* 2:179. The problem with the use of advanced technology, which presumably must come from the North, is technological dependence, which was one reason for Gandhi's rejection of such technology. Beyond a vague allusion to the possibility of adapting technology to Indian conditions, Nehru does not address this issue.

55. *Ibid.*, 1:623 and 2:113. See also, Nehru, *The Discovery of India*, p. 328.

56. Nehru, *The Discovery of India*, p. 329.

57. *Ibid.*, p. 328.

58. *Nehru: The First Sixty Years*, 2:146. Nehru goes on to acknowledge that if the economy has both kinds of machines, the large will dominate, but he feels that this cannot be helped given the imperatives of national power. Nehru's commitment to heavy industry as part of a strategy designed to achieve national power and independence is corroborated by Baldev Raj Nayar, *The Modernization Imperative and Indian Planning* (Delhi: Vikas Publications, 1972), pp. 113–140.

59. Nehru, *Independence and After*, p. 160.

60. *Ibid.*, p. 190.

61. Nehru, *The Mind of Mr. Nehru*, pp. 56–57.

62. *Ibid.*, p. 56.

63. Sardar Patel in a Delhi speech, October 31, 1949, quoted in Nayar, *The Modernization Imperative*, p. 142.

64. After partition he remarked: "Now that we have been able to salvage a major part of India and have been able to build it up into an extensive single unit, let us make it powerful"; "Speeches of Sardar Patel," in Nayar, *The Modernization Imperative*, p. 143.

65. See Nayar, *The Modernization Imperative*, pp. 107–112.

66. Expenditures on social services declined from 25 percent in the First Plan to 18 percent in the Second, whereas organized industry and minerals grew rapidly from 7 percent in the First Plan to 20 percent in the Second. Bhagwati and Desai, *India: Planning for Industrialization*, p. 115.

67. Frankel, *India's Political Economy*, p. 117.

68. See Mellor, *The New Economics of Growth*, ch. 11. See also Nayar, *The Modernization Imperative*, the main thesis of which is that Indian development was driven by the necessity to modernize in order to achieve national power. Nayar argues that this was also the motivation for Western development and that considerations for mass welfare are actually an obstacle to this type of development. Nayar also maintains that the Indian fascination with Chinese planning is due to China's achievement of self-reliance and political autonomy vis-à-vis the international system, rather than to its economic performance.

69. Nayar, *The Modernization Imperative*, p. 104.

70. "Fourth Five Year Plan: A Draft Outline, 1966," quoted in Nayar, *The Modernization Imperative*, p. 107. Implementation of the Fourth Plan was delayed until 1969 because of various economic crises.

71. Frankel, *India's Political Economy*, p. 302.

72. Between 1951 and 1965 the basic metals industries grew over thirty-fold, while textile and food manufactures suffered losses in relative position. Mellor, *The New Economics of Growth*, p. 119.

73. Michael Kidron, *Foreign Investments in India* (London: Oxford University Press, 1965), p. 85.

74. William K. Stevens, "India, Once a Giant in Science, Tries to Rekindle the Creative Fire," *New York Times,* November 9, 1982, sec. C, p. 1.

75. See Helge Hveem, "Selective Dissociation in the Technology Sector," in John Gerard Ruggie, ed., *The Antinomies of Interdependence: National Welfare and the International Division of Labor* (New York: Columbia University Press, 1983), ch. 7.

76. See F. A. Long, "Science and Technology in India: Their Role in National Development," in John W. Mellor, *India: A Rising Middle Power* (Boulder, Colo.: Westview Press, 1979), ch. 8.

77. See Rosen, *Democracy and Economic Change,* ch. 9.

78. Between 1951–52 and 1961–62 India received a total of $13 billion in foreign aid. See Myron Weiner, "Assessing the Political Impact of Foreign Assistance," in Mellor, *India: A Rising Middle Power,* p. 58. Weiner, p. 58, estimates that between 1950 and 1970 foreign assistance averaged 16 percent per annum as a proportion of capital formation. Between 1947 and 1975 the major aid donors were: United States 45 percent; World Bank 15.8 percent; Great Britain 9.1 percent; West Germany 8.1 percent; Soviet Union 5.4 percent; and Japan 3.3 percent. Hardgrave, *India.,* p. 255.

79. India's reliance on external assistance reached 15 percent of total plan outlay during the Fifth Plan period. Frankel, *India's Political Economy,* p. 561.

80. Hardgrave, *India,* p. 255.

81. Indira Gandhi in a 1972 speech, quoted in Hardgrave, *India,* p. 237.

82. *Nehru: The First Sixty Years,* 2:302.

83. *Ibid.,* 2:455.

84. *Ibid.,* 2:468.

85. Nehru, *Independence and After,* p. 213. For Nehru's definition of non-alignment see also *Nehru: The First Sixty Years,* 2:249, 353, 382, and Nehru, *Independence and After,* pp. 202, 239.

86. Nehru, *Independence and After,* p. 215.

87. *Nehru: the First Sixty Years,* 2:217, 250.

88. Michael Brecher, *India and World Politics: Krishna Menon's View of the World* (New York: Praeger, 1968), pp. 12, 13.

89. Padma Desai, *Tariff Protection and Industrialization* (Delhi: Hindustan Publishing Corporation, 1970), p. 24.

90. Veit, *India's Second Revolution,* p. 285.

91. See, for example, Desai, *Tariff Protection and Industrialization,* and Bhagwati and Desai, *India: Planning for Industrialization,* ch. 16.

92. In 1951 India's share of world exports was 2 percent: by 1973–74 it had declined to .55 percent. Weiner, "Assessing the Political Impact of Foreign Assistance," p. 61.

93. Before World War I England was supplying three fifths of Indian imports and taking one quarter of exports. Kidron, *Tariff Protection and Industrialization,* p. 34. By 1973–74 England was supplying only 8.4 percent total imports and taking 10.4 percent total exports. Mellor, *The New Economics of Growth,* pp. 320–324.

94. This is a major thesis of Mellor, *The New Economics of Growth*. See especially ch. 1.

95. Frankel, *India's Political Economy*, p. 558.

96. Long, "Science and Technology in India," p. 243. Collaborative arrangements by the government reached a high of 403 in 1961 and 1964. Veit, *India's Second Revolution*, p. 296.

97. In 1961 the percentage of foreign investment was 25.6 percent in petroleum and 37.8 percent in manufacturing. See Bhagwati and Desai, *India: Planning for Industrialization*, p. 221, table 11.1.

98. For example, in the negotiations of 1965 with Bechtel for the construction of a fertilizer plant, Bechtel agreed to 51 percent Indian ownership but insisted that Bechtel retain technological and managerial control. For this reason the agreement was vetoed by the Indian government. Frankel, *India's Political Economy*, pp. 267–268.

99. *Nehru: The First Sixty Years*, 1:502, 692.

100. Nehru, *Independence and After*, p. 152.

101. Rosen, *Democracy and Economic Change in India*, p. 237.

102. John Mellor and Philip Oldenburg, "India and the United States," in Mellor, *India: A Rising Middle Power*, p. 3.

103. Maharaj K. Chopra, Indian Ministry of Defense, quoted in Helena Tuomi and Raimo Vayrynen, *Transnational Corporations, Armaments and Development* (Aldershot, Hants.: Gower Publ., 1982), p. 198.

104. Onkar Marwah, "India's Military Power and Policy," in Onkar Marwah and Jonathan D. Pollack, eds., *Military Power and Policy in Asian States: China, India, Japan* (Boulder, Colo.: Westview Press, 1980), ch. 4, p. 101.

105. Stephen P. Cohen and Richard L. Park, *India: Emergent Power?* (New York: Crane, Russak, 1978), p. 19.

106. Tuomi and Vayrynen, *Transnational Corporations*, pp. 194–196.

107. This viewpoint was strongly corroborated by Girilal Jain, Editor in Chief, *Times of India*, in a seminar given at the Center for International Studies, MIT, on November 22, 1982.

108. Sampooran Singh, *India and the Nuclear Bomb* (New Delhi: S. Chand, 1971), pp. 130–132. Singh goes on to state: "Any nation state that does not develop national power commensurate with its size and population is not likely to be permitted to continue that way for long. It will be reduced in size and population commensurate with its power" (p. 132).

109. See George H. Quester, "Enlisting Post-1974 India to the Cause of Nonproliferation," in Mellor, *India: A Rising Middle Power*, ch. 7.

110. Cohen and Park, *India: Emergent Power?*, p. 12. This thesis is disputed by Riccardo Faini, Patricia Annez, and Lance Taylor, "Defense Spending, Economic Structure and Growth: Evidence Among Countries and Over Time," MIT, Cambridge, Mass. More generally, the Faini manuscript is a refutation of Emile Benoit, *Defense and Economic Growth in Developing Countries* (Lexington, Mass.: Lexington Books, 1973), a widely cited source on the positive correlation between economic growth and defense

spending. Faini et al. use time series estimates for India as their major example.

111. Marwah, *Military Power and Policy in Asian States,* pp. 118–119.

112. John Mellor and Philip Oldenburg, "India and the United States," in Mellor, *India: A Rising Middle Power,* ch. 1. (Quote on p. 7)

113. *Nehru: the First Sixty Years,* 2:51.

114. *Ibid.,* 2:98. See also Nehru, *Independence and After,* pp. 231, 248, 298.

115. In 1971 the ratio of Indian to Pakistani forces was 8–1 in aircraft, 4–1 in troops and 5–1 in naval vessels.

116. Planning Commission, *Sixth Five Year Plan 1980–1985: Mid-Term Appraisal* (New Delhi: Government of India, August 1983), pp. 90ff.

8. PROBLEMS AND PROSPECTS FOR SELF-RELIANCE DEVELOPMENT IN THE CONTEMPORARY THIRD WORLD

1. Jefferson, even in his earlier years, was more committed to economic growth than was Rousseau or Gandhi, however. As is well known, Jefferson was not antiscientific; he was responsible for a number of scientific inventions of his own. He was, however, against social and economic arrangements, such as urbanization, that are a result of industrialization.

2. See Gilbert Etienne, *India's Changing Rural Scene 1963–1979* (Delhi: Oxford University Press, 1982), ch. 16. This chapter is a critique of development theorists whose views generally coincide with the communitarian position.

3. Although for Gandhi it must be nonviolent, this type of defensive strategy contains parallels with wars such as the Vietnam and Afghanistan wars where great powers, in spite of overwhelming military superiority, have had difficulty overcoming this type of resistance.

4. This debate is summarized and analyzed in Hayward R. Alker Jr. and Thomas J. Biersteker, "The Dialectics of World Order: Notes for a Future Archeologist of International Savoir Faire," *International Studies Quarterly* (June 1984), 28(2):121–142.

5. I am aware that List never held a major political office either in Germany or the United States. His minor political offices in Würtemburg and his term as an American consul would seem to place him in this category, however. His political work suggests that he had ambitions for higher political offices also, had he not been banished from Würtemburg.

6. This issue is discussed in Peter Gourevitch, "The Second Image Reversed: The International Sources of Domestic Politics," *International Organization* (Autumn 1978), 32(4):881–911. For further discussion of this issue see Peter B. Evans, Dietrich Rueschemeyer, and Theda Skocpol, eds., *Bringing the State Back In* (New York: Cambridge University Press, 1985); and Immanuel Wallerstein, *The Politics of the World Economy* (Cambridge: Cambridge University Press, 1984).

7. This shift in emphasis is evident in a textbook of this period. See Michael P. Todaro, *Economic Development in the Third World,* 2d. ed. (New York: Longman, 1981).

8. For an analysis of the failure of regional integration schemes in the Third World see Andrew W. Axline, "Underdevelopment, Dependence and Integration: The Politics of Regionalism in the Third World," *International Organization* (Winter 1977), 31(1):83–105.

9. In my Introduction I stated that this investigation would limit itself to the capitalist world. The case of China is usually cited as one of the more successful models of self-reliance development. But whether China has achieved self-reliance at all three levels is doubtful.

10. For a discussion of the security problems that may arise as a result of dissociation see Barry Buzan, "Security Strategies for Dissociation," in John Gerard Ruggie, ed., *The Antinomies of Interdependence* (New York: Columbia University Press, 1983).

INDEX

DATE DUE

DEC 15 '88	
MAY 24 '89	
JUN 14 '89	
Ref 6/21	
OCT 2 0 '93	
MAY 15 1999	
APR 2 5 2000	
BRODART, INC.	Cat. No. 23-221